# the ultimate
# paris
## survival guide
### (for travelers)

D1523086

THE CELINE CONCIERGE GUIDE

SELENE FLORES

# THE ULTIMATE PARIS SURVIVAL GUIDE
## (for travelers)

## The Céline Concierge Guide

If you dream of exploring the City of Light like you already live here, this is your ultimate guide! This is more than a travel guide; it's a Paris handbook blended with a collection of carefully curated stories from travelers and expats.

After 8 years of living in this heavenly place, I want to share it with you in a fun and comprehensive way to experience and live out Paris for yourself— stress free!

I only wish this guide existed when I first came to Paris.

Céline Concierge

THE ULTIMATE PARIS SURVIVAL GUIDE (for travelers)
The Céline Concierge Guide

For permission requests, write to the publisher "Céline Concierge" at the address below.
9 Rue des Potiers
92260, Fontenay-aux-Roses, France
www.celineconcierge.com

ISBN: 978-2-9580619-0-6 (ebook)
ISBN: 978-1-8046-7151-1 (print book)

Written by: Selene Flores
Book cover design: Aleyna Moeller
Book layout design: Davor Nikolić
Developmental Editor: Claire Staley
Proofreading Editor: Megan Sanders

Please note that this book has been written to the best of my knowledge, taking into consideration my experience of living in Paris, as well as external research. However, I do not guarantee that the places, shops, and cafes mentioned hereafter will remain open due to the pending COVID pandemic and its effects.

DISCLAIMER: This book contains affiliate links which will reward me monetarily or otherwise when you use them to make qualifying purchases. For more information, please read my privacy policy and disclaimer.

# EXCLUSIVE OFFER
## WITH YOUR PURCHASE

With the purchase of this book, I want to offer you an exclusive offer of **10%** off all future services with Céline Concierge. When you **contact me**, mention that you purchased this book, and I would be happy to apply this discount toward your services.

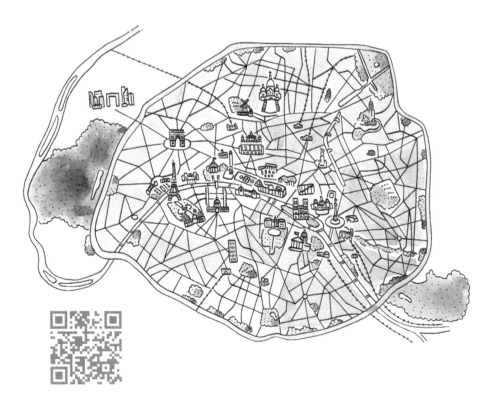

*to citizens of the world*
*but mostly to Mila*

# WHAT'S IN THIS GUIDE?

**11**   **INTRODUCTION**

Bienvenue ! Welcome!................................................. 12

Where My Paris Story Begins: Céline à Paris........................ 17

Why Paris? What is Paris All About?........................ 22

What was Your First Impression of Paris? Quotes
from Other Travelers & Expats................................. 25

**29**   **PLANNING YOUR TRIP**

Planning to Visit Paris (or anywhere else you wanderlust) .. 30

How To Plan a Trip The Smart Way + Travel Hacks
For Finding Great Airline Tickets............................. 32

How Long Should You Visit Paris?............................. 38

When Should You Visit Paris: Broken Down By Season.....40

Travel Resources — Airlines, Travel Websites, etc............. 50

**53**   **YOUR ARRIVAL**

Airport Info and How to Get From the Airports
to Paris City Center............................................ 54

The Paris Train Stations ......................................60

Late Night Spots to Check Out When You're Jet Lagged..... 65

Interview: John Arndt, Musician and France Newcomer ... 69

**75**   **YOUR STAY**

Key Facts You Should Know About Paris and France......... 76

A Quick Guide on the Arrondissements of Paris................. 81

Accommodation in Paris: Luxury Hotels, Boutique
Hotels, Home Stays and Apartments .....................90

Where to Stay in Paris: My Top Neighborhoods to
Stay in Paris................................................... 93

How to Find Homestays & Luxury Apartments ............... 100

Favorite Luxury Palace Hotels.................................. 105

Favorite Boutique Hotels....................................... 115

Transportation and How to Get Around Paris.................. 119

Interview: Jim Le, Seasoned Expat Turned French
National ........................................................................126

## 133 WHAT TO DO IN PARIS

The Must-See Monuments and Landmarks ...........................135
Museum Guide ...............................................................144
Noteworthy, Lesser-known Museums....................................150
Parks and Jardins ...........................................................157
Must-Visit Streets in Paris................................................163
The Most Instagrammable Spots in Paris.............................173
Paris Passages ...............................................................180
Secret, Underground Paris Spots & Adventures................189
Live Like a Local: The Best Things the Locals Do ..............194
Spas in Paris  ................................................................ 202
Best Day Trips from Paris................................................ 206
Must-See Regions .......................................................... 214
Interview: Hope Curran, American Studying
Abroad in France ...........................................................219

## 227 FOOD PARADISE

An Introduction to French Gastronomy.............................228
Where to Eat & Drink: Tried and True Best
French Restaurants ....................................................... 234
Traditional French Restaurants & Bistros to
Take You Back in Time...................................................238
Contemporary French Restaurants & Neo-Bistros
to Try...........................................................................243
All Things French Wine  ................................................248
Caves à Vin .................................................................. 254
Tapas in Paris................................................................259
Hip Bars & Restaurants to See and Be Seen in...................265
Michelin-Star Restaurants.............................................. 269
Best Food in Paris that Isn't French.................................. 281
Best Burgers in Paris......................................................292
Best Brunch Restaurants in Paris.....................................297
Best Coffee Shops on Both Sides of the River ................... 302
Best Tea Houses.............................................................. 314

Best French Bakeries & Patisserie Shops.............................. 320
French Cheese Shops.............................................326
Best Outdoor Markets ...........................................335
Interview: Eric Davis, Architect who Moved
to Paris with Visitor's Visa ............................................ 341

## 349 PARIS NIGHTLIFE

Cheap Bars & Good Happy Hours ...............................351
Favorite Craft Beer Bars........................................355
Favorite Speakeasies & Cocktail Bars........................363
Ritzy Hotel Bars ...............................................368
Rooftop Bars & Restaurants .....................................374
Jazz Bars and Live Music Venues..............................380
Clubbing & Table Service.......................................388
Lounge Bars ....................................................394
Cabarets........................................................398
Interview: Hannah S., Digital Nomad and
Seasonal Visitor to Paris (without a vias) .......................... 403

## 409 SHOPPING

Shopping in Paris...............................................410
Best Shopping Streets for Luxury and Designer ............... 413
Vintage Shopping in Paris .......................................417
*Grands Magasins* de Paris ...................................... 421
Specialty Home Good Stores.................................... 426
Favorite Food & Beverage Stores and What You
Can Get at Them ............................................... 431
French Beauty Stores............................................ 435
Antiques, Brocantes, Flea Markets and Shops.................. 438
Best Flower Shops .............................................443
Best Bookstores & English-Speaking Bookstores.............449
Interview: Eliza Sweeny, Art and Drama Therapist
from Melbourne, Australia ........................................ 454

## 461 LIFESTYLE

10 Secret French Lifestyle Rules Revealed ...........................463
Recommended French Cooking Books ..........................470

Favorite French Products............................................ 472
Recommended Reading List Before You Go France......... 476
French Songs for Inspiration & Music to Get You
in the French Mindset.................................................. 479
Recommended Films to Watch Before You Go
to France.................................................................... 486
Instagram Accounts to Follow For Your Daily
Dose of Paris.............................................................. 490

## 497 LES PETITES CHOSES (THE LITTLE THINGS)

Safety and Emergency Numbers................................. 498
Non-Emergency Doctors Consultation........................ 499
Hospitals In Paris ..................................................... 501
Useful Apps to Download When in France.................. 503
Simple Paris Travel Tips / *Les Petites Astuces*...................... 508
Savoir Faire: Quirks About Paris You Must Know
Before Visiting........................................................... 512
An Abridged History of France and French Culture........ 518
Helpful Words and Phrases to Know When Visiting
France ....................................................................... 531
France Timeline of Events.......................................... 533
Conclusion and Merci................................................ 544
Let's Discover Paris Together...................................... 546
Let's Connect ........................................................... 547
Thank You ................................................................ 548
Acknowledgments..................................................... 549
About the Author ..................................................... 550
About the Illustrator.................................................. 551

## 552 BONUSES

What Visa You Need to Moveto France....................... 553
Travel Budget & Tracking Tool................................... 553
French-Style Chicken Pot Pie Recipe.......................... 553
Travel Planning Timeline ........................................... 554
Steps for Downloading Google Maps Offline............... 554
Useful Travel Glossary Terms..................................... 554
All Things Parisian Bucket List................................... 555

# INTRODUCTION

# Bienvenue ! Welcome!

This interactive guide was born out of a love for Paris, the adopted city I've called home for 8 years and counting. It's not only my favorite place to be, but living here has become an obsession and thrill for me to share with others. Through my years of helping friends and family navigate their questions, curiosities, and dreams of visiting Paris, I've become used to making a complex city much easier to handle.

I saw a need to explain the intricacies in a fun and comprehensive way so that Paris dreamers like you can experience and live out Paris for yourself.

This is more than just another travel guide; it's a personal handbook and masterclass on Paris and all things Parisian. It's your lifeline and bible of Paris— YOUR Ultimate Paris Survival Guide.

I feel entrusted and privileged to give my advice and suggestions on where to go, eat, shop, relax, and indulge. This is Paris, after all, so indulge your little heart out!

This guide provides practical help as well as recommendations and anecdotes on life in the City of Light as an expat turned local.

I wish that I had it as my guide when I first arrived!

Even if this isn't your first time in the French capital, this guide will allow you to dive deeper and discover hidden gems beyond the city's facade. It's for the traveler and the new Paris resident alike.

As for me, I fell in love with Paris back in 2011 and decided to move two years later as soon as I had my college diploma in hand. I've never looked back.

## BOOK REVIEW ☆ ☆ ☆ ☆ ☆

*"Paris is a challenging city - but this thorough and well-organized guide is the ideal planning tool to help you tackle it. There are more good tips here than most Parisians can offer!!"*

**Oliver Gee**
Host of The Earful Tower podcast

## BOOK REVIEW ☆ ☆ ☆ ☆ ☆

*"This guide completely eliminates the need to invest in endless hours of research when planning your first trip to Paris. The best tips and secrets are revealed, and you don't need to look elsewhere!"*

**Julie Fine**
Property Consultant, Iconic Paris Immobilier

## BOOK REVIEW ☆ ☆ ☆ ☆ ☆

*"This is the most comprehensive, thorough presentation of Paris, written with passion and love by Selene. I wish I had this Parisian handbook and roadmap when I arrived in August 2021....but with all of the things I haven't seen and done yet that are featured in this survival guide, I will need to keep coming back again and again. A must-have for any global citizen like me! Congratulations Selene for a masterpiece and masterclass of all things Paris!"*

**Kelly Culver**
Director, The Culver Group Inc
and dedicated client of Céline Concierge

## BOOK REVIEW ☆ ☆ ☆ ☆ ☆

*"The mix of storytelling, stunning illustrations, helpful resources, and time-saving tips and tricks to get the most out of your experience in the City of Light makes this a must-read for travelers coming to Paris. While comprehensive, the book is cozy and comforting. With Selene by your side, you can almost feel the magic that's in store for you when you finally do arrive."*

**Erin Cafferty**
Freelance copywriter + Co-founder of Remote ID

## BOOK REVIEW ☆ ☆ ☆ ☆ ☆

*"This book is at the image of the Celine Concierge company founder : warm, passionate, knowledgeable and reliable."*

**Célia Ouali**
Professor at La Sorbonne
and founder of Speak French for Real

## BOOK REVIEW ☆ ☆ ☆ ☆ ☆

*"As an expat for 13 years, I can confidently say I have never seen such a comprehensive, useful and enjoyable Paris guide. Fantastique !"*

**Alexander Martin**
Agent Immobilier | Paris Real Estate Agent

## BOOK REVIEW ☆ ☆ ☆ ☆ ☆

*"Wow! Where to start? I am just loving every bit of this book, it is insanely rich, practical and exhaustive, at the same time so pretty and fun to read through. But on top of all that, what strikes me the most is at the very beginning: Where My Paris Story Begins: Céline à Paris. I was almost in tears while reading this part, because I saw myself, it was also MY story. I guess it must be the story of so many people who came to Paris without knowing one word of French but stayed forever. Paris changed our lives and set us free, it will also change yours and help you to find your true self. Next time when you are about to come to Paris, make sure you have this book with you, that will be a magical trip..."*

**Nikki Wang**
Co-founder of TheWaysBeyond
An agency of cultural discovery for curious minds

## BOOK REVIEW ☆ ☆ ☆ ☆ ☆

*"Reading Selene's guide brought me straight back to when I first fell in love with this enchanting city 8 years ago! As a fellow adopted Parisian, I can truly say that she captured this city perfectly, packaged it up beautifully with a big bow, and then delivered it directly to your inbox. A gift I wish I had when I first arrived! Selene's guidance is invaluable, highly detailed, and spot on for both travellers and new Parisians alike!"*

**Gillian Tibbo**
Co-Founder of THE VEIL | PARIS
Boutique Content Creation Agency

# BOOK REVIEW  ☆ ☆ ☆ ☆ ☆

*"I pride myself on knowing Paris like the back of my hand...but Selene is the one person I'll call for the scoop I know I'm missing. Though I've done my research and spent a good period of time running around the City of Light, I still wanted to take notes on all the places Selene recommends that I didn't know about...and there were a lot! Whether you're just looking for a taste of the real Paris or want a curated experience (long or short term), she'll make it happen."*

**Marissa Wu**
Writer + Photographer

# Where My Paris Story Begins:
# Céline à Paris

*This is a love story.*

*And not just any love story.*

*No. This is a love story about a girl— a dreamer— who falls in love, not with a boy, but with the city.*

*A city she's only dreamed about.*

*She visits. She falls in love.*

*The girl realizes she's the star of her own film entitled* **Céline à Paris***.*

In the summer of 2011, I was on a plane with Andrea, my closest cousin. She's about two years older than me and had just graduated college. I had just finished my sophomore year.

We were on our way to London to begin our Eurotrip of four weeks. First, we hopped around from London to Frankfurt where we met Johanna. Johanna was the German exchange student my parents took in two years prior, and we were reuniting on her turf this time. We crashed with Johanna and her folks in Darmstadt a few days before the three of us boarded our train to Paris. Johanna was our unofficial, French-speaking tour guide.

To be honest, I arrived in Paris with no expectations or goals for the city other than wanting to see a French movie at the cinema and visit the Eiffel Tower. But when I arrived, it felt like I was the star of my own movie; there always seemed to be music playing in the background whether at the corner cafe or in front of Notre Dame—serving as a natural and charming soundtrack to the trip.

From the olive green chairs at the Jardin des Tuileries, to my ears perking up when I heard the French language whispered between lovers at the cafe, to the taste of the banana and coconut Nutella crepes fresh off the griddle, to the sensation of the gush of air that pushes past as the Parisian metro zips by, every part of my being was invigorated. I felt like a kid at Disneyland taking it all in.

The first few days we did the usual tourist things. We went to the Eiffel Tower at sunset, walked down Rue Mouffetard, and picnicked in the Jardin des Plantes with stinky French cheese, bread and wine. We went to Montmartre and sat on the lawn near the steps.

We bought some contraband beers from the vendors at Montmartre and itched for trouble. We wanted a Parisian adventure, and there seemed to be plenty to go around. We checked out the boys, inviting them over with our coy glances.

Soon, a group of three French guys came over to us and started chatting. A few beers in and they invited us to dinner at this tiny French bistro in Montmartre.

Each of us girls paired up with a guy and they became our dates for the night. There was Paul-Louis with the striking green eyes and outgoing personality, then Paul, the tallest of the three who always seems to be wearing a smile, and finally Jean, the shy blond one of the group. Jean spoke to me the most throughout the night and made me feel like he wanted to get to know me.

We were all so inebriated on beer and French wine, but I remember smoking cigarettes outside between courses and kissing Jean at different points in the night. It was a dreamy cliché— French kissing a French lover in Paris.

Paul-Louis and Paul invited us to their place and mentioned that they had access to their rooftop. They didn't have to ask twice— we were there!

That night was a mix of many crazy vignettes: us girls on a slippery rooftop in Paris, my heart beating swiftly from the excitement of a new adventure, kissing a French boy and the touch of his unshaven beard against my cheeks, the smell of Yves Saint Laurent cologne on my clothes, cute French accents trying to speak English, the six of us squeezed in a taxi, and a cool summer breeze drifting through the cracked windows.

I remember being in said taxi riding past the pyramids at the Louvre. The three of us girls screamed out in excitement because monuments that had only been seen through movies where coming to life for us!

This was it— the dream of going to Paris was here and now. We were enamored by the night, the guys, and their hospitality. How could three wild girls connect with these French guys and let the Parisian night carry us away without a care in the world? This night forever changed my life, whether it was the company, the Parisian night, or the emotions, some part of me felt like I was home.

We ended up at Jean's apartment at the end of the night sharing our umpteenth bottle of wine, bringing in the morning. We spent our first **nuit blanche,** as the boys educated us, an all-nighter.

With blue skies and the early morning sun beaming through the apartment, they offered us **un café** as two of the boys smoked out the window with bed hair.

After a few more kisses and giggles, we decided it was time to go. We slowly made our way back, taking the aerial metro scattered with a few early-morning commuters, to our temporary Parisian **chez nous**.

Johanna left on a train back to Germany that afternoon, leaving Andrea and I to continue the party without her.

Paul-Louis and Jean continued to guide us around the city the following days in what I can only remember as a magical and dreamy time for me. In that week, I felt like I was living a black and white 60s Godard film on the cobblestones of Paris.

## WHY DO I TELL YOU ALL THIS?

It's because Paris can have this magical effect on people. Of wooing them, of charming and romanticizing them.
I wouldn't say it happens to everyone, but it happens to many.

For me, I was out of my element, I felt like the more fun version of myself. I was unrecognizable to myself and my cousin.
I was willing to try anything at least once. Something about the Parisian air helped me feel free, brave, and adventurous. It almost felt like the rules that I was used to back home didn't apply here. Here, those rules could be bent, so I dared bend them.

If you yourself have felt this way about Paris and want to go back, you're in for a ride.

If you haven't been, but dream of going, this is a great start to your Parisian journey. Either way, you're in the right place for an abundant dose of travel inspiration, tips and tricks, Paris know-hows, and French lifestyle. Let's begin your perfect getaway of All Things Parisian.

# Why Paris? What is Paris All About?

"

*Paris is for lovers, artists, and dreamers. Behind every love, artistic vision, and dream, however, is a bucket load of determination and elbow grease. Paris is not for the faint of heart, even if you do speak French.*

**-Marissa Wu, photographer and creative**

You can meet people from all over the world in Paris. As my friend Hope Curran once said, "You'll find the United Nations in Paris." And it's true, as nearly every country in the world is represented in Paris.

In my time in this city, I have encountered hundreds of people. Some of those stay, many of those go. Paris is a transitory city and the longer you stay, the more you see that swinging door turn round and round with people coming and going. What's so beautiful about the community in Paris is that the people who you have presently in your life are all the more special and precious because of this.

A couple of years ago, I was between apartments and staying at a friend's place near Pigalle. My friend, Hannah, was visiting then and every day, our eyes caught the neighbor boys across the **vis-à-vis** who were about our age. Every time we looked out the window, they seemed to always be playing an instrument.

One Friday evening, Hannah and I were drinking beers while looking out the window. They saw us and waved. We waved back. They yelled to us in their very cute accents, "We're going to Montmartre, do you want to join us?"

How could we refuse? We hopped down to the street, bringing them each a cold beer from the fridge, and a new friendship was formed...

They turned out to be musicians collaborating on an album. One boy was Lucas from Argentina, and the other was Hugo from France. They ended up taking us to a friend's house party where we spent the evening listening to music as each artist took turns picking up an instrument and playing while singing.

It was my most Edith Piaf moment I had had living in the city. It was artistic, spontaneous, and pleasant. I felt a true connection to these artists and to the city that brought us together for one magical night.

Paris is all about the people. Paris is all about spontaneity and it has something for everyone. The key to Paris is to have an open heart. And it's ultimately what you want it to be.

But don't take my word for it, see what other travelers and expats say about the city and their first impressions.

# What was Your First Impression of Paris? Quotes from Other Travelers & Expats

 *So, I landed in Paris, got into a taxi and I gave the address, in Montmartre, of the apartment I was renting with some girls. And I remembered driving down the highway and arriving in a north exit of the highway, near Saint-Ouen.*

*And as we came over a bridge and off the highway, there I saw Sacré Cœur and I just started crying because I felt so happy to be in France and I felt like it's where I should be. I had this sensation of "I'm home", just from the taxi ride!*

**Eliza** from Melbourn, Australia

*It's an amazing and historic city.*

*For the people that live in Paris, it's really important to them that they always leave room for life and do what they value and enjoy any given day. Whether that's going to see something beautiful or spending time in cafes or parks.*

**John** Wisconsin, USA

*When I was 12 years old, I came for a family vacation. We flew into Paris, and I fell in love with everything French. I loved art and fashion and it left a lasting impression.*

*And when we went back home, I told my mom I wanted to learn French, so I did because I was homeschooled.*

*What shocked me the most when I came here as a 22-year-old to live here was winter. I came with the emoji heart eyes, the "Ah, Paris!", and it was January. Winter.*

*Winter is really hard for me as a Californian because of the lack of sunlight. Paris is hard in the winter.*

**Hope** from California, USA

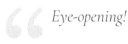

*Eye-opening!*

**Jim** from Arizona, USA

*Surprised by how dirty it is. It's not pristine the way that you think it is. Real people live there; it's a very real place.*

*At the time, the trash men went on strike, which is apparently a very big part of French culture, so that was pretty funny. I guess I didn't realize how rebellious the people are.*

*I was also surprised by how transient it is. People there are in and out so much that I think that it was a little more challenging to connect than I hoped it would be.*

*You come into it with your expectations so high that you almost don't expect the realness of it. And in that way, the grittiness and frustrations of Paris can be a negative— but they're also the things that make it a complex, authentic place.*

**Hannah** from Texas, USA

*Paris was intimidating the first couple of days...but after my third or fourth day, the sun came out and I was able to walk around more and I thought "Ok, this is what I was expecting." Little by little, I relaxed and I started feeling more comfortable, truly absorbing where I am, what I was experiencing.*

*After a week, I didn't want to leave. It really grew on me. It felt like possibility, opportunity. Not feeling hemmed in by things that I had constructed for myself. What life is supposed to look like or what life is going to look like.*

*I kept saying to myself, "Oh wait, life can be different; it can feel different."*

*You can tell and feel it by the pace. It's not New York; it's not this hustle-bustle place.*

**Eric** from Louisiana, USA

# PLANNING YOUR TRIP

*"If you fail to plan,
you are planning to fail."*

-Benjamin Franklin, allegedly

# Planning to Visit Paris
## (or anywhere else you wanderlust)

So, you're coming to Paris? The best advice I can lend is this— plan ahead! **At least** 6 months ahead of your arrival. Nothing is more disappointing than getting somewhere only to miss out on crucial bucket list experiences because things are booked up.

**Or** spending precious hours waiting in line for the Eiffel Tower, when skip-the-line tickets could have been purchased ahead of time online or through an agent or concierge, like me.

**Or, even worse**, you arrive at your hotel only to find out that your booking was never reserved because your confirmation got lost in translation (which happened to my parents on their first visit to Paris) — I spent the whole evening scrambling to find them an affordable, yet nice, hotel. My dad thought he had reserved it, but in fact hadn't. He and my mom were stranded and certainly wouldn't fit along with my brother in my tiny studio apartment.

I get it! Planning a trip to a place you've never been to is hard and can be overwhelming. This is why I'm going to give you some resources and a Travel Planning Timeline (to break down the steps) on how to make everything as easy as possible.

If you're a self-proclaimed international traveler like me, of which I have been for a decade, I want to help you understand the intricacies of traveling to Europe, and more specifically to Paris, so that you don't make the same mistakes I've made.

The internet has never made travel so accessible (thank God!) — but it's still a jump into a lot of unknowns. Where to start? Don't feel overwhelmed by the task— the key is to take it step by step.

Let's plan out your dates, places you want to go, and most importantly, your Travel Budget (I've included a template resource for this, too).

Let's do this before we get into the good stuff (like where the locals eat, adventures worth doing that are off-the-beaten-path, day-trip ideas with practical how tos, museum guide, etc— you get the idea)!

Check out the Travel Planning Timeline & Travel Budget & Tracking Tool in the chapter Bonuses.

# How To Plan a Trip The Smart Way + Travel Hacks For Finding Great Airline Tickets

As a traveler for the last decade as well as having visited 20 countries and lived in three, I can say with assurance that when it comes to traveling, planning is the key to a successful trip.

I've made many mistakes along the way in my travels (like not purchasing medical travel insurance on my first trip to Europe back in 2011 and then proceeding to sprain my ankle in Barcelona), but I've also found some great tricks and efficient ways to plan and carry out a trip abroad.

There is no right way to plan, but there are some guidelines that can help keep the stress to a minimum and guarantee a safer and more enjoyable experience.

Here are my 8 tips to help you plan your future trip the smart way.

**1  Plan as Far in Advance as Possible**

I highly recommend that you start planning at least 1 year to 6 months in advance of an international trip. A 1-year timeframe is a great ballpark for planning a trip to a place or places that you've never been to. Download my free Step-By-Step Travel Planning Timeline PDF. This great tool helps you have a big picture idea of the steps to focus on in every stage of your planning.

Planning with as much time in advance allows you to have the chance to steal great travel deals, too!

## ② Select Your Destination(s) & Create a Blueprint Itinerary Before Securing Travel Dates

By putting it down on paper and down in your calendar, you can start to build the blueprint of your travel plans. This framework will give you an idea of how many days you plan to spend in each city. It's important to figure out because that will help you assess your potential costs and budget. For instance, a pint of beer in London won't be as cheap as in Sevilla and this can add up quickly when you're in good company, having a great time.

If you're traveling on a tight budget, try taking a smarter approach to travel by staying longer in cities that are less expensive in order to stretch your dollar! This blueprint builds the foundation of your travel budget which I will discuss next.

## ③ Create A Travel Budget Based on Your Cities, Transportation & Accommodation Costs

Use my Travel Budget & Tracking Tool to work out, line by line, the travel costs you should consider in your budget. This also can help you figure out an estimated travel savings plan leading up to your trip start date. Nothing will put you more at ease than having an assessment of how much your trip will cost and then putting a savings plan into action to start saving for that coveted dream holiday!

With your travel budget all set, you'll want to seek out the best deals which takes me to my next tip!

## ④ Sign Up for Flight Alerts & Email Notifications from Websites Offering Up Great Deals

Take advantage of sites like Skyscanner[1] and Scott's Cheap Flights[2]. These websites will send you email alerts and

---

[1] www.skyscanner.net
[2] scottscheapflights.com

notifications for deals. For example, with Skyscanner, you can enter your flight city and dates and will get day-to-day email notifications when the price of your tickets drops or increases. With Scott's Cheap Flights, they send you email alerts with mistake fares, summer and holiday deals as well as rare price drops on traditionally expensive destinations.

If you know where you want to go, but don't have your dates set in stone yet, sign up for as many email alerts and flight deals as you can. You never know what's gonna drop from the travel heavens!

I mean, who doesn't love saving money whenever possible? Do you hear that **cha-ching** in savings coming your way?

**Did you know that flight fares can change up to three times a day?** If you've been monitoring fares for a while and see a dip in the price, act quickly on them before the price jumps back up!

### 5 Book Your High-Cost Transportation First (International Flights) Followed by Hotels/ Accommodation, Then Regional and Local Transportation & Entertainment

Finally, with all the leg work behind you of figuring out cities, dates and your budget, you'll be relieved when you can begin booking the big-ticket items like the international flights and hotels. From there, it will be easier to book the regional flights within the continent followed by all the smaller reservations such as skip-the-line museum tickets, entrainment, and restaurants.

The order of booking you want to follow is:

A.  International flight (because these are harder to change later on, unless you have no-fee changes or business class that often times allows you flexible fares)

B. Intercontinental flights & trains / Domestic Flights
C. Accommodations: Hotels / Airbnbs / Homestays
D. Entertainment / Private Tours / Museums tickets / Tickets available online for monuments
E. Restaurant reservations (book 1 to 3 months in advance for hard to book restaurants, especially in high tourist season).

## 6  See layovers as opportunities to visit multiple countries

For example, Icelandair[3] offers layovers from mainland Europe to the US with a stop in Iceland for up to 5 days. Likewise, Turkish Airlines[4] presents a similar overture with a minimum layover of 20 hours. They propose a **free** two-night stay in a 5-star hotel if booking your flight through their Business Class.

This trick allows you to travel through while taking a few days to enjoy another city on your way to or out of Europe, adding extra pizzazz to your trip.

## 7  Be aware of Hidden Fees

If you have a low to medium budget, seek out deals with budget and economy airlines, but be aware of extra fees and hidden fees for food, luggage, and seat selection. Budget and economy airlines like Ryanair[5], Easy Jet[6], Transavia[7], etc are great for booking low-cost flights, but these airlines come with a catch: if you have a lot of luggage, beware of the checked baggage fees; they can add up quickly! Airlines, no matter if they're budget or high-end, have to make their profits somewhere!

---

[3]  www.icelandair.com/flights/stopover/adventures/
[4]  www.turkishairlines.com/en-int/flights/stopover/
[5]  www.ryanair.com
[6]  www.easyjet.com
[7]  www.transavia.com

### 8 Look out for flights into smaller airports, not just the hubs

You sometimes, but not always, get better deals on flight fares from arrivals into lesser-known airports. With many European cities occupying at least two airports (Paris has three commercial airports), you are bound to find alternative deals for flights into and out of these airports.

There may be a catch, however. Beware of airports that are very far from the city center or in complete opposition of where your accommodations are— you may end up paying more in taxi fare or inconvenience that makes it not worth the trouble.

## BONUS TIPS:

When flying internationally, fly into the capital cities in Europe, but throughout your trip, try taking alternative regional transportation like intercontinental trains, bus and eco-flights when traveling within the continent.

## BONUS TIPS:

If you're short on time for your Europe trip, you can maximize your time by booking two one-way tickets (with differing arrival and departure cities) instead of a roundtrip ticket that flies in and out of the same city. This way, you can start in one place and end in another rather than circling back to the city you flew into so you can spend more time exploring and less time traveling on a plane or train.

Book positioning flights to get huge savings on international travel via travel agent sites and travel saving newsletters like Scott's Cheap Flights. A **positioning flight\*** is one that you take from a main hub city to another city for a long-haul flight (i.e. you book a money-saving flight from New York to Paris, but you live in Dallas, so you book an additional flight from Dallas to New York to take off on your international flight).

\* www.scottscheapflights.com/glossary/positioning-flight

# How Long Should You Visit Paris?

This is a very subjective question. There's so much to do and discover in Paris that 2 days is definitely not enough (but you can work with that if that's all the time you have). On the other hand, you may get bored on a 10-day trip if you don't know any locals or have a good sense of the place. I would suggest somewhere in the middle.

The first time I came in the summer of 2011, I ended up staying 8 full days and it still wasn't enough, so I decided to move here after college!

As you can tell, I'm biased towards the city that has become my home, and I'll always want to spend more time here. Paris is an infinite labyrinth of discovery and wonder waiting to be tapped into, but the true answer for you will be different.

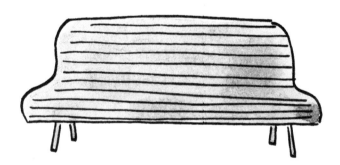

## HOW LONG DO YOU WANT TO STAY IN ONE PLACE?

If you are the kind of traveler who has tons of energy and wants to tick monuments and museums off your bucket list, you can probably get a lot done in 2-3 days. If you are a medium paced traveler— keeping the activities and sightseeing going, but making room for spontaneity, 5-7 days would be more your speed. And if you're here to relax, stroll off-the-beaten-path, and don't care much about lists, your best bet is to wander through Paris in 7-10 days or longer.

The general guideline I tell friends and clients coming for the first time is that there's enough to do for 5 days, but they may feel restless after 6. If you sense that your time wasn't enough, that's a good thing which says you'll come back on another trip. If you're coming back a second, third or even 10th time, take it slower and visit for a full week. Try to stay longer if you can to really allow Paris to charm you **à la française**!

# When Should You Visit Paris: Broken Down By Season

There are many different versions of Paris, and if you can't experience all of them, which one would you like to experience most? Winter in Paris can be delightful, with cozy food and Christmas decorations lavished throughout the city. Summer in Paris can be lively and joyful, and even empty if you're there at the right time. While coming at the optimal time for you can be magical, coming at the wrong time can ruin your trip if you're not careful.

Let's explore the different times, and the different versions of Paris, available to you!

 **TIP:**

Try to visit Paris in the shoulder peak seasons, like in the beginning of Spring and end of summer/ beginning of Autumn. You'll get the most out of your trip this way, as you'll experience the most pleasant weather, the least amount of tourists, and the bustling energy of Paris.

The city has a certain **je ne sais pas quoi** during this time. You'll smell wood burning from the chimneys and find that the city is covered with a hazy **gris**, or grey, tone. The greyness can be rather dreadful but can also inspire coziness. A sense of cocooning draws out hot chocolate or **vin chaud** (mulled wine) enjoyed in warm **cafés**. Scarves, boots, coats and gloves adorn adults, children and babies alike.

You'll want to check some winter-inspired experiences off of your bucket list like drinking **chocolat chaud** from the famous Angelina Cafe or better yet, eating high-calorie French comfort food, including lots of bread and cheese. **Raclette** and fondue parties are common events because you can use all the calories you can get. All of these tokens embody Paris in the winter.

You won't leave your home without several layers— wool scarves, cotton beanie, rain boots and a coat that keeps you toasty. You should never leave the house without the mandatory umbrella, because you never know if it'll rain. For at least two months, Paris is overcast, and its weather is bipolar, with grey skies that waffle between drizzle and rain.

While it isn't personally my favorite season, there's something special about the winter months. Like when you look out your window and see tiny snowflakes falling from the sky to land on the Parisian rooftops.

This past winter, locals were blessed with two snow days in the city. I happened to be with a few girlfriends who ran outside to start a dramatic snow fight. The open-air markets had never looked so sweet with snow enveloping all the fruits and veggies. And we ended up doing a spontaneous photoshoot against the backdrop of the snow-covered Jardin du Luxembourg. Winter can pleasantly surprise you in Paris when the streets are generally quiet and then all of a sudden, you're living in a Kodak moment.

Likewise, fashion is a statement the minute you walk out of your doorway. You're comforted by a coffee in a frosty window among the thousands of Parisian cafes you can stop by to escape the cold. The season just makes you want to cuddle under the blankets in your cozy Parisian home and stay there until the ice thaws.

As romantic as the winter months are, they can be equally challenging for locals. Paris is depressing for most of this harsh season, but quite lovely and escapist for others. If you're visiting Paris for the first time, I don't recommend coming in this season unless this weather and scene is just what you're looking for.

## MARCH, APRIL, AND MAY

Everyone is coming out of hiding from the colder months, the weather is starting to warm up, and the days are longer. The locals are happier as the weather improves. You can start to change your wardrobe by going for lighter jackets instead of heavy wool coats and choosing dresses with tights and flats instead of pants, thick socks and boots. Paris Fashion Week demands it!

The **jardins**, or gardens, are blooming colorful flowers all around and the city is in splendor. From the bright pink cherry blossoms to the white magnolias, to the dark purple wisterias that bloom all throughout this season, you'll experience a bright and vivid city. The first picnics in the green spaces under the warm sun bouncing on your cheeks are what define the start of this season.

I've had many a spontaneous picnic with friends, as we all gather around a few blankets and quilts. We still wear spring sweaters and light jackets to stay warm on the cool grass. Each person brings a couple of food staples to share like cheese and baguettes, red tomatoes, **rosé**, **charcuterie** (deli meats), and any other random snack we find on the shelves of the Franprix. Paris in March belongs to the locals before the tourist season picks up again around late April and early May.

And, if you get caught in the rain, you can duck into an art exhibition now that the new art season has arrived. There are more concerts and culture events to invite people out of their homes and into the streets.

I highly recommend visiting Paris during the spring. Plus, the fact that tourists aren't yet on their summer breaks makes this the ideal time to visit without the crowds.

## JUNE AND JULY

I personally LOVE the summer months in Paris because this is the time that the city is at its brightest and most relaxed. The locals can happily sit on cafe terraces without getting chilled, enjoy clear blue skies, walk or cycle all over Paris without the threat of rain showers. They can sit on the Seine River with friends and a bottle of wine to have what other than the Parisian staple: a picnic.

The cafes, parks, and streets are packed with people, but no one seems to mind all that much. We're happy it's warm and sunny. And since Paris is located high in latitude, the sun doesn't set until 10 PM in mid-June!

The first time I visited Paris was in the summer, so I have very fond memories of long summer days sitting beside the Seine watching the boats jaunt past which led to cool nights strolling the side streets of Paris. Summer in Paris is always an adventure, especially if you're looking for one. Locals and tourists alike are enamored with spontaneity, and people are just more festive and ready for a party whether it's planned or impromptu, in private or on the streets in public.

One such occasion to embrace is the annual Fête de la Musique, internationally celebrated as the day of music welcoming the summer solstice. Paris turns into a party town with live music around every corner and accepted public drinking.

A few years back, a large crowd of a few hundred blocked an intersection in the Châtelet area while a DJ jammed out to a mix of French and American pop singles, 80s music, and dance hits. My boyfriend and I bought cheap beers from the cafe across the street while we danced under the Parisian night. That moment was a rare but beautiful wish captured in a time capsule of life.

And who can forget the most magical of all Parisian nights— La Fête Nationale (the National holiday). Every year, on the 14th of July (**le 14 juillet**), every French man, woman, and child celebrates the biggest French holiday with friends, usually around a meal. The holiday commemorates a turning point of the French revolution, the storming of the Bastille prison, as well as French unity and patriotism. This day is filled with celebrations, concerts, and parades in the city. And if you have **le courage** (or bravery) to be amongst a dense crowd on the Champ de Mars, you'll be able to find an optimal spot to watch the music and firework show on the lawn in front of the Eiffel Tower. As the fireworks pop and burst, glitter and sparkle, the Eiffel Tower lights change color all while synchronising to a curated musical melody. You may even find yourself a little sentimental and feeling French (if you aren't) in spirit for one night. Nothing is more romantic than fireworks adorning the Iron Lady herself on this special evening.

As you can sense, summer can be a mix of joy and laughter, whim and impulse, magic and amazement. The days are long and tourists, like the locals, are more open to letting Paris take them places they have never been. It feels like through the summer heat, we are all in a spell of wonder that help us discover Paris anew.

Tourists are rampant but seeing Paris in the summer is definitely worth it if you don't mind the crowds. The city is at its liveliest.

## AUGUST

August deserves its own mention. Paris in August is a particular time of year. Anywhere from mid-July to the end of August, Parisians are more or less taking time off to enjoy **les vacances d'été** (or summer vacation). In their annual exodus, Parisians take off in hordes to the south of France or to their second homes somewhere **en province** (the provinces of France not deemed the capital). If they themselves don't own property, they bunker up with friends or family to enjoy weeks of the Mediterranean, Pastis, **pétanque** and St. Tropez.

Back in August of 2013, I stepped off of a plane in Paris and discovered the strange phenomenon that is Paris in August. I discovered that Paris was somewhat of a ghost town with many cafes, shops, bakeries and restaurants closing shop for several weeks to go on holiday, do renovations, or both before la rentrée, or the back-to-school season. Even the friends I was staying with at the time gladly gave me their keys for three weeks so I could house and cat sit while they were away.

During the month of August, there are likely to be more tourists than locals in Paris. It can either be a blessing or a curse.

If you prefer a bustling city then I don't recommend visiting in this season, especially if you know that you have some local mom & pop shops and cafes you are dying to visit while there— these are likely to be closed in August.

Don't be disappointed to see signs like this one taped to business doors:

I also wouldn't recommend a stay in August if you love AC. August is the hottest month in France and we experience what is called les canicules, or heatwaves. Many establishments now have modernized to offer AC, but there are still others that haven't. Just keep in mind that AC is not a universal feature in France, so don't expect it everywhere.

Nevertheless, if you like the idea of visiting an empty Paris, it could be your ideal time to visit. So do it! It's the time to enjoy just the right amount of Parisian inspiration without dealing with the moody Parisians themselves. The locals that do stay are laid back and without a care in the world— this is summer after all!

It could be a wonderful time for you to come as many museums stay open. Paris Plages welcomes you along the Seine and Canal St. Martin, and cinemas are in full swing to help you escape the hot weather. Not to mention that in mid-July to early August, les Soldes, or summer sales, are in full swing and les grands magasins, or department stores, are also a great way to entertain and evade the heat outdoors.

As you can see, Paris in August is a peculiar time of year. There are positives (less crowds, less cars) and some negatives (shops closed for weeks at a time and the intense heat waves). But with the rhythm of life running at a slower pace, Paris can be a fun place to enjoy the vacation, the warmer weather, friends at a bar terrace and quieter streets.

Paris is both pleasant and calmer during these months. There is a routine to the city as residents enjoy or dread **la rentrée**, or the back-to-school/back-to-work season.

The autumn season is truly an enjoyable time to visit. You will start to see the changing color pallet as the trees in the city gardens transition from summer pinks, purples and greens to oranges, yellows, and reds. The weather is cooler, and the tourist wave is dwindling. You'll actually be able to go all around and visit museums and events with less crowds than in the summer months.

The local food menus in restaurants and bistros adapt as the seasons change to hardier veggies and warmer meals. You'll start to notice that you'll need to bring out your light autumn jackets and scarves, and even your **imperméable**, or raincoat, to adjust to the chillier climate.

Friends often visit me from abroad in autumn months as my schedule opens up and the weather is still warm enough to venture outside and do activities off-the-beaten path. I've always found that the autumn seems to invoke mystery such as when we plan weekend getaways to nearby cities like Chartes with its medieval **château**. Or like when I take friends to visit the region of Champagne, just in time for the grape harvest called the **vendange**. There is something so romantic about Notre Dame against a grey sky and the overgrown ivy turning yellow and orange as you admire her from the quai in autumn.

Not to mention, one of my favorite festivals, Nuit Blanche (White Night), that takes place in early October. This art and culture festival takes place at various venues across the city to show off new and local artists into the long hours of the night, hence the reference to **une nuit blanche**, which can also imply an all-nighter. Performances, expos, and events take place anywhere from on the street to tiny galleries serving champagne to the Pont des Arts for performance artists to express their artistry.

Oui, Paris in the autumn is a delightful and pleasant period to embark on a visit if you can hit up **Nuit Blanche** and dress warmly throughout this season as Paris can tend to get chilly come night fall.

## DECEMBER

Despite the colder weather, Paris in December can be true magic, if done right.

Pack warm clothes, but not too many, as you'll want to enjoy shopping at the **grand magasins de Paris**, or department stores, that are all decked out with holiday embellishments. Many businesses adorn their storefronts with Christmas decorations and lights; streets and avenues are dressed to the nines with colorful lights and festive banners.

If you love Christmas markets, I recommend going on a day trip, or better yet a weekend trip to the region of Alsace, in the east of France, during December. There, you can get lost in some of the original Christmas markets whose towns look like they came straight out of a children's storybook such as Obernai, Colmar, Ribeauville and Riquewihr. If you don't have the time to go away, you can get a taste of these markets that are scattered in a few areas of Paris from early December to early January.

One of the most romantic experiences I've had with my boyfriend was spontaneously getting off the metro at the stop Trocadero, the plaza that faces the Eiffel Tower, during the holiday season. We strolled through the Christmas market, stopping to snack on handmade Alsacian-style pretzels and grabbing spiced **vin chaude** (mulled wine) to keep us warm all while admiring the ice skaters spin round and round in the rink overlooking the Eiffel Tower.

Even if you're single, this is one of the most picturesque moments during this season that you will truly enjoy. There's seasonal food and drink, as well as shopping for local products against the festive backdrop of the tiny cabin-like stalls that sit side by side throughout the market.

If you're visiting during December for winter holidays, you can truly have a marvelous visit. Another tidbit I recommend before you arrive is reserving a Christmas and New Year's Eve (**La Révéllion** or the Saint Sylvestre) dinner far in advance in order to get a table for your holiday meals. Not all restaurants are open, but a few around the city will welcome you to spend the special evening with them. Of course, if you need restaurant recommendations or help reserving, contact me[8] for trip assistance.

---

[8] www.celineconcierge.com/contact-us/

# Travel Resources — Airlines, Travel Websites, etc.

 **MY RESOURCES\***

 Travel Budget & Tracking Tool

 Step-By-Step Travel Planning Timeline PDF

 Steps for Downloading Google Maps Offline

 Useful Travel Glossary Terms

\* Download these useful Resources in the Bonuses chapter.

## OTHER RESOURCES

### FLIGHTS

**SKYSCANNER**
www.skyscanner.net

Sign up for email notifications for specific flight alerts for your travel dates.

**SCOTT'S CHEAP FLIGHTS**
www.scottscheapflights.com

Get email notifications for cheap flight deals, mistake fares to top destinations. Free 14-day trial, $49/year

## RYAN AIR
www.ryanair.com

Low-cost flights across Europe

## EASY JET
www.easyjet.com

Economy flights across Europe

## TRANSAVIA
www.transavia.com

Economy flights across Europe

# ACCOMMODATION

## BOOKING.COM
www.booking.com

For hotels, boutique hotels, flights and car rentals.

## VERY CHIC
www.verychic.co.uk

For luxury hotels at affordable prices

## PLUM GUIDE
www.plumguide.com

For highly vetted homes in major cities

## AIRBNB
www.airbnb.com

For local accommodation and experiences.

# TRAINS

## TRAIN LINE
www.thetrainline.com/trains/europe

Economy train tickets

## INTERRAIL
www.interrail.eu

For country to country train passes and deals

## OUI SNCF
www.sncf-connect.com

Inexpensive trains throughout France and Europe

## CAR RENTALS

**RENTAL CARS**
www.rentalcars.com

Rental car comparison

**KAYAK**
www.kayak.fr

Flights, hotels, travel packages
and rental cars

## TRAVEL INSPIRATION SITES

**CONDE NAST TRAVELLER**
www.cntraveller.com

**TRAVEL + LEISURE**
www.travelandleisure.com

**CREATE YOUR OWN TRAVEL MAP**
www.mytravelmap.xyz

**CREATE YOUR OWN TRAVEL ITINERARY**
www.inspirock.com

# YOUR ARRIVAL

# Airport Info and How to Get From the Airports to Paris City Center

"

*The last time I flew back to the States from France, I trusted a company to book me a car from my hotel to the airport. I went in with total trust as if I haven't traveled around the world consistently for the last 15 years.*

*When the driver arrived at the airport he shows me a bill of 180 €.*

*I told him I wouldn't pay him that until I spoke to the police. So, we waited in front of the airport for two hours for them to arrive. And while they were likewise shocked at the price, the officer simply said, 'In France, everything is a game. Today, you lose.'*

**-John Arndt, musician and world traveler**

There are 3 main commercial airports you can fly into to get to Paris. The most popular is Charles De Gaulle Airport in the northeast of Paris (this airport is known as **Roissy** to locals). You also have the smaller but just as busy Orly Airport, just south of Paris. Finally, the perplexing and lesser known little brother of the two is Beauvais Airport. Beauvais is 53 miles northwest of the city.

**TIP:**

Before booking a transfer to the airport, ask for the price upfront, no matter if you're taking an Uber, Parisian Taxi, or a private chauffeur company. Additionally, be sure to vet the company before hand and know what their payment policy is— how will you pay, and whether that amount includes tax or not. Don't be shy about asking questions before committing to private transfer to and from the airport.

A very important resource that is available for you at all the Paris airports is the Paris Tourist and Convention Office. The kiosk that is waiting for you at the exit of the arrivals terminal can give you on-the-spot information and guidance for how to get into the city. This is for those just-arrived needs, such as where to purchase train tickets, museum passes, and where to immediately get ahold of your own physical Paris map. Don't hesitate to make this your first stop upon arrival to Paris.

The taxi system is highly regulated in France, so don't risk high fees or getting into a car with an unlicensed driver. This has happened to me before, and I know it sounds dumb to say that I was duped, but they get you because you are tired after a transcontinental-flight and possibly disoriented from the foreign language and onset of jet lag. I ended up getting in the car, and on the drive realized that he didn't have a meter running, but was driving a regular car. I admit I was frightened into thinking I was just "taken". But he did drive me to my destination in Paris and asked for 80 € (which I could have paid 53 €). There are fixed rates for taxi drivers to and from the airports into Paris city limits (whether you're on the left bank or right bank), so before you get into a taxi, check the rates against the taxi company G7[1].

**TIP:**

Never get in an unmarked car or taxi in Paris, and especially from the airport. If anyone ever comes up to you, refuse and say you don't speak French. This is a scam where unmarked taxi drivers will come up to you in the airport and offer to help you with your bags, they take you to their car (usually parked in the garage) then drive you into Paris, but demand a very high rate, usually.

Here is the breakdown of each airport with details on how to get to and from the city with prices of local transportation at the time this was written (May 2021).

## CHARLES DE GAULLE AIRPORT - CDG

This is the largest international airport of Paris and the second busiest airport in Europe. It is located 23 km (14.29 mi) Northeast of Paris in the city of Roissy-en-France. You may often hear the locals refer to CDG airport as Roissy Airport.

You can go to and from the airport by luxury car service, Parisian taxis, ride share app services called VTC in French (like Uber, Bolt, and Kaptain), by bus (RoissyBus has services from CDG airport and Paris-Opéra), or by a regional train system called the RER.

---

[1] https://www.g7.fr/en/paris-taxi-fares

## Getting to the airport from the center of Paris by train:

The RER line B (the blue line) has direct trains from the center of Paris at Châtelet-Les Halles and usually take around 45 mins one way. You will want to get on the RER line B in the direction Aéroport Charles de Gaulle. The train stops at terminals 1 and 3 first, then terminal 2 (the terminus) at CDG airport. There is also a shuttle called the CDGVAL that can shuttle you between the terminals in case you get off at the wrong terminal.

Tickets from Paris to CDG airport cost 11.40 € (free with a Navigo card, charged up to Zone 5) and can take upwards of 1 hour from the center of Paris. There are direct trains to the airport both from Bourg-la-Reine (South of Paris) and from Gare du Nord that can reduce the journey time by about 30 minutes. So, look out for a train "**sans arrêt**" on the marquee.

---

 **NOTE:**

A Navigo Card is the rechargeable ticketing card for public transportation for locals. They offer student pricing as well as options for tourists (**Navigo Easy**). The Navigo Card helps you effortlessly travel between Paris' five transportation zones that make up **Grand Paris**, or the greater Parisian metropolitan area. You can find out more information on **Ile de France Mobilités\***.

———————————

\* www.iledefrance-mobilites.fr/en

---

# ORLY AIRPORT - ORY

This airport is 14 km (8.69 mi) south of Paris. It is the second largest international airport in Paris.

Options to and from the airport are: by luxury car service, Parisian taxis, ride share app services like VTC in French (like Uber, Bolt, and Kaptain); Orly Bus, and the Orlyval.

The Orlyval is the train shuttle taken from the city Anthony (12 km, or 7.4 mi, south of Paris) with its own train station of the same name located on the RER line B (a regional train system).

## Getting to the airport from the center of Paris:

If you go for public transportation, the ticket costs as low as 12.10 € for a combination ticket of the RER B train (a regional train system). You would purchase your ticket, hop on the RER B from Paris in the direction to Anthony (south) then transfer to the airport shuttle called the Orlyval. The journey from Châtelet-Les Halles can take 30-45 mins, so be sure to plan plenty of time in advance!

---

 **NOTE:**

The Orlval's regular service runs from 6 AM to 11:35 PM every day.

---

For the Orly Bus option, you can catch a 30-minute shuttle ride from Place Denfert-Rochereau to Orly terminals 1, 2, and 3. Service frequency is every 10 to 15 minutes. You can likewise catch the shuttle from Orly terminals 1, 2, 3, and 4 into Paris with a drop off at Place Denfert-Rochereau. The fare costs 9.50 €. The fee is free and included with your Navigo Pass if you pay for Zones 1-4.

## BEAUVAIS- BVA

Paris-Beauvais Airport (BVA) is 85 km (53 mi) northwest of Paris.

This is the smallest of the three international Paris airports and serves low-cost and charter airlines like RyanAir and Wizz Airlines.

Transfers to and from this airport can be made by shuttle bus, called a **Navette**, via taxi, car rentals, ride shares, or by TER train (another regional train system that extends further than the RER. It is also called the Transilien train).

Parisian Taxi and rideshare apps Uber and Bolt are available at Paris–Beauvais Airport.

**NOTE:**

Be aware that a taxi is an expensive option to and from this airport (starting at around 150 €) and the drive is about 1h 20m.

The average cost of a one-way ride to Paris with Bolt is 151 € and with Uber X is 180 €.

**TIP:**

I don't personally recommend flying into this airport unless you are traveling on a small budget, and you have time on your hands. If you're looking for convenience, this is not the airport for you. It is probably more hassle than it's worth!

# The Paris Train Stations

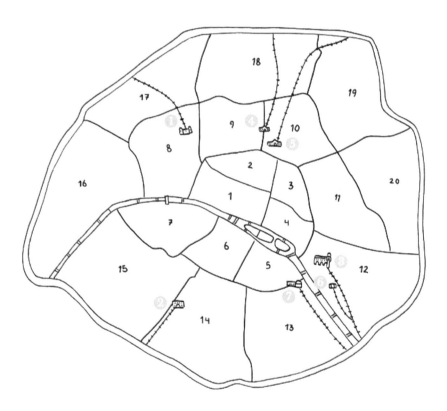

There currently exist seven primary SNCF train stations, or **gares**, in French. **Une gare** means train station and is pronounced "Garh". **SNCF (Société national des chemins de fer français)** is France's public national railway company.

The positive about the system of **grande lignes**, or main train lines, is that the ticket prices are supplemented by the government, so travel is affordable to its citizens. The downside is that the system is fairly centralized in Paris, so to get anywhere outside the city, you may have to take a connecting train or two. For instance, say you're in Strasbourg and want to go down to the South, chances are, you'll find a ticket from Strasbourg to Paris and another from Paris to Biarritz, rather than cutting directly across the nation.

Despite this, train travel across France and Europe is, as I mentioned, very affordable and fast.

In 1966, the SNCF introduced France to a high-speed electric train and rail network. With this novelty, passengers can now effortlessly go from Paris to the South in a matter of hours. It takes 3 hours and 6 minutes to go from Paris to Marseille at its peak speed of 320 km/hour (198.83 mi/hour).

Here's a breakdown of each train station and where they can take you!

##  Gare Saint-Lazare

If you're looking to go to/from Normandy and the northwest regions surrounding Paris, like Rouen to visit its stunning cathedral or the upscale coastal town of Deauville, head over to the Gare Saint-Lazare. Likewise, you can catch a train from this station for a day trip to the delightful town of Giverny.

The station situated in the 8th arrondissement is the second busiest station in the city. The Paris metro also has 5 lines connecting at Saint-Lazare as well as servicing the RER train line E, Transilien (intercities rail line), and 14 bus lines. The train station remains a hub of activity with a bustling shopping center underground in the station itself.

## Gare Montparnasse

Say you're heading to Bordeaux or Spain, you will find yourself departing from the Montparnasse train station. It's located south in the 15th arrondissement of Paris. The station serves the west and southwest parts of France, including favorite cities like, Rennes and Nantes.

There's a commercial shopping center connected to the station as well as the conspicuous Montparnasse Tower. Being one of the oldest mainline train stations in Paris, it's curiously the only one not connected to a RER train line.

 ## Gare de Lyon

If you're a fan of beautiful historical architecture, you may want to pay a visit to the Gare de Lyon, whether you're taking a train or not! Seen as one of the prettiest train stations in Europe, the Gare de Lyon was completed in 1900 to celebrate the 1900 Paris Exposition, which showcased the architectural and technological innovations of the past century. The renowned Le Train Bleu restaurant attracts tourists as well as locals to dine in the majestic train-inspired dining hall, accompanied by a luxurious lounge bar (see also Traditional French Restaurants & Bistros to Take You Back in Time). You'll pass through this station for trains to and from southeast France, including the eastern French city of Lyon— which the station was named after— as well as Germany, Switzerland, Italy and Spain.

 ## Gare du Nord

Are you planning on heading to/from the UK? Then you'll probably be transiting through Gare du Nord. Gare du Nord is most notably known for servicing the EuroStar, which travels to/from the UK by the English Channel Tunnel called the Chunnel. It's an international train station, servicing the Netherlands, Belgium, Germany as well as parts of Northern France. The station is also a hub of activity connecting metro lines 2, 4, and 5 just like RER lines B and E along with several Transilien (TER) intercity train lines.

## NOTE:

Passengers traveling through Gare du Nord to the UK via the EuroStar have to clear two border checks. Before travelers board the EuroStar, they get screened by the French Border Police for leaving the Schengen Area as well as a second conducted by the UK Border Force for those entering the UK.

 ## Gare de l'Est

If you're looking to head east for a day trip or to continue your travels, you'll be transiting through Gare de l'Est , appropriately translated as "east station". True to its name, the station services trains departing to the east, including French cities Mulhouse, Nancy, Strasbourg and additionally, Basil, Switzerland. Located in the 10th arrondissement, the station was built in 1849, facing the Boulevard de Strasbourg. The station also houses metro lines 4, 5 and 7 as well as a myriad of buses and night buses.

 ## Gare de Bercy

If you have an itch to visit Italy, you can jump on a slow, but low-cost, overnight train via the Gare de Bercy to cities like Milan and Venice. This unique station specializes in auto-trains which transport passenger vehicles along with them. In 2002, the station upgraded to allow four sleeper-trains that travel to/from Italy for overnight journeys. It's located in the 12th arrondissement of Paris, near the Bercy (AccorHotels Arena) indoor sports arena and concert hall.

##  Gare d'Austerlitz

For those heading over to the city of Orleans, 120 kilometers (75 mi) south of Paris, you'll head to Gare d'Austerlitz. This understated train station that had more prestige in the late 19th century shows off a Belle Epoque style façade and underwent renovations in 2020. In its prominence, the station mainly served trains to/from Orléans, but once the refurbishments are complete, the station will double its capacity, adding four new TGV platforms and new routes to the regions of South France.

Book your trains directly via the SNCF site or on other partner sites such as Train Line, Interrail, or OUI SNCF.

## TRAINS

TRAIN LINE
www.thetrainline.com/trains/europe

Economy train tickets

INTERRAIL
www.interrail.eu

For country to country train passes and deals

OUI SNCF
www.sncf-connect.com

Inexpensive trains throughout France and Europe

# Late Night Spots to Check Out When You're Jet Lagged

So, you've arrived in Paris from abroad and your circadian rhythms are off, so you want to sleep during the day and you're up at night. What do you do!? Nothing but embrace it! You can just as easily take advantage of Paris at night as much as during the day.

Here's a list of late-night hangouts and getaways where you can pass the time, meet up with the locals, and even feel like a local at all hours of the day.

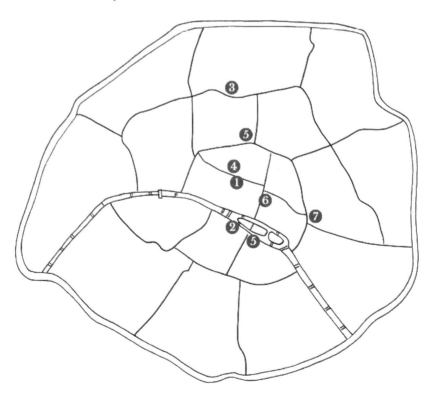

## TIP:

Some ways to beat jet lag are by staying hydrated and drinking lots of water. When you arrive in Europe, don't nap upon your arrival or in the middle of the day. Try to stay awake as long as you can and go to bed when the locals do. You can even try setting your clocks to the local time a few days before your trip to adjust your bedtime to prepare your body.

 **AU PIED DE COCHON**
6 Rue Coquillière, 75001 Paris
01 40 13 77 00

You can get anything from beef bourguignon to a croque monsieur past 2 AM at this traditional French restaurant, open 24 hours. Au Pied is centrally located at the footsteps of Châtelet-Les Halles.

 **LE CASTOR CLUB**
14 Rue Hautefeuille, 75006 Paris
09 50 64 99 38

For a truly charming experience, you can skip over to Le Castor Club for specialty cocktails in their club that has bluegrass vibes written all over it. On weekends, until 4 AM, their basement bar turns into a club with a dance floor for you to boogie the night away.

### MADAME ARTHUR / LE DIVAN DU MONDE

75bis Rue des Martyrs, 75018 Paris

07 68 78 68 01

You can enjoy a late-night dinner and cabaret show at Madame Arthur and then hop next door to Le Divan du Monde to continue the dance party. Both are open late and welcome you if you need a hangout to get over that jet lag.

### LE TAMBOUR

41 Rue Montmartre, 75002 Paris

01 42 33 06 90

This cafe/restaurant is a rustic hangout open 24 hours with a lively and eclectic wait staff. It's the perfect hideout to pass the night in good company with a glass of Bordeaux or a full-on French meal.

### LA CRÈME DE PARIS - CRÊPERIE

**Location 1**

4 Rue du Faubourg
Montmartre,
75009 Paris
01 48 24 89 50

**Location 2**

1 Quai Saint-Michel,
75005 Paris

If you have an early morning or late-night craving for anything from homemade **crêpes** to waffles or ice cream, La Crème de Paris is your one-stop-shop! Their two shops, one on the left bank and one on the right bank are open from 8 AM to 2 AM, 7 days a week.

## 6 BARBEROUSSE PARIS

60 Rue Quincampoix, 75004 Paris

07 66 39 63 66

Whether you're a fan of rum or just need a late-night getaway to help you get over that lingering jet lag, Barberousse is your stop. The ambience will surround you with Pirates of the Caribbean vibes. They produce their own house rum—over 200 flavors— carefully crafted and aged on location.

## 7 BADABOUM

2 bis Rue des Taillandiers, 75011 Paris

01 48 06 50 70

Badaboum offers an exciting music scene in a split-level club open late nights— until 5 AM on Thursdays and 6 AM Fridays and Saturdays. You won't want to miss this place if you're near the Bastille area where you'll get great sound in a modern yet futuristic setting. The drinks are pricey, but good and worth the late-night atmosphere.

# Interview with
# **John Arndt,**
# a musician and
# France newcomer

John

John moved to Paris after experiencing the "**coup de foudre**", or love at first sight, and moved here in 2020.

John is a music producer/composer, originally from Marshfield, Wisconsin. He grew up in this small town with dreams of going out into the larger world. He first visited Paris in the fall of 2019 on an invitation to play music at the American Church in Paris. He was so impressed with Paris' beauty that on his second day, he decided to move there after being without a permanent address the previous three years.

In early 2020, I met John through a current client who owns one of the apartments that I manage.

He was preparing to move to Paris and rent out my client's home, but before doing so, he needed a piano. He is, after all, a fledging musician.

My client put us in touch and John hired me to help him research piano rental companies and source the perfect piano for him and his music needs. Not only did I help coordinate the piano rental and delivery, but I made sure that it was delivered to the apartment before John's arrival so that he could settle into his new Parisian home without a hitch and do what he does best: music.

John and I became friends, staying in touch throughout his stay even as things progressively got worse in Paris and the number of Covid cases was on an upsurge.

I sat down with John, though we felt the distance through the Zoom call. COVID was in full-force, and both John and I were living through a locked-down Paris for the first time ever. However, he was in good spirits as he munched away at his minimal lunch of home-made French fries and a Coke. I wondered to myself if he was so passionate about his music that he didn't waste time on banalities such as lunch, but rather focused everything he had on playing tunes on his new piano.

As we began talking, we laughed at how ridiculous the lock down seemed, yet John mentioned that he would rather be right here in a locked-down Paris than anywhere else in the world. Shining through the uncertain circumstances was an obvious love for Paris.

He's interested in plugging into the beauty, the culture, and the inspiration of Paris. This is his inspiring story.

## Why did you move to Paris?

I moved here to have more day-to-day experiences with beauty. To wake up every day and be able to say, "I can't believe I get to live here."

It's the first time in my life that I've felt lucky to live somewhere.

So when I was living in Minneapolis, I never woke up in Minneapolis and said, "I'm so lucky to be here." No! But here, all the time, I look out and I go, "oh my god, this is my life; I can do this." This is the thing that is actually possible.

So to be able to live in and to make things in that frame of mind is really important to me and I feel like Paris is a good zone for that.

In Paris, I'm always a little afraid and just trying to soak things up because it's a new situation. I like that, just by living here, I will be expanded over time. Every time I go out it's sort of a learning experience.

It's so cheesy, but when the Eiffel Tower sparkles every night, I have this feeling of beauty. It starts with a feeling.

My hope about moving to Paris was that I would make more time to make beautiful things just for the sake of making beautiful things.

### What was your first impression of Paris?

It's an amazing and historic city.

For the people that live in Paris, it's really important to them that they always leave room for life and do what they value and enjoy any given day. Whether that's going to see something beautiful or spending time in cafes or parks.

### What do you love about Paris?

I love the smallness of it; I like the fact that the buildings are not built super high. You can see the sky, yet I'm in the center of a great city!

I like that there are beautiful sculptures and beautiful things everywhere.

### Did you know French? If yes, where did you learn the language? If not, how did you learn?

I didn't know any French in October and I literally got DuoLingo after I got home from France after my first trip.

I thought, I'm going to move to France, so I need to start learning the language.

I'm not like most people who have studied French since sixth grade and have always wanted to go.

For me, I was interested in it, and I've always liked it in movies and music, but I've never studied it. It's a new thing.

### What kind of visa/resident permit do you have?

When I got asked to do a show at the American Church in Paris (ACP), it came with an apartment, like an artist residency for two weeks. So I blocked out that time and went.

The second day I was here in October, I fell in love and decided to move here. And that's how I met Daniel. He was wrapping cables at the concert at ACP. I said, "Dude, I'm moving to Paris." And he said, "I'm an immigration attorney." I was like, "You're hired!"

Daniel is now helping me apply for the artist visa that will be good for four years. It will be such a cool thing to have the artist visa to be able to do what I love.

## What are your plans now?

I'm going to go back to the States because I have to apply there for my visa. Then, I'm going to come back in September once I have the artist visa.

This summer, I have a few recording projects and will go on a road trip across America.

## How did you find housing in Paris this time?

I knew an artist friend who knew someone who referred me to an apartment owner.

I kept looking around, but when it came down to it, she was able to offer what I needed, including getting a piano.

And with these other anonymous places, it would be a big problem for me to ask to get a piano moved in.

You turned out to be a godsend as well, helping me find a piano rental and get it moved in before my arrival. Everything worked out so magically.

## What was your biggest challenge with moving to Paris?

It has been two months since my iPad was mailed to me from Indiana... so receiving packages from the States has been a challenge in that instance.

Outside that, the only challenge has been confinement which comes naturally to me.

**What's your biggest frustration with Paris?**

No, spicy food! Where are the jalapenos?

**Speaking of food, what is your favorite French meal?**

Crêpes and nutella.

**How has Céline Concierge helped you in the past?**

I couldn't believe that getting a piano in Paris was possible; I thought it was going to be the deal breaker for the apartment. I thought the owner was going to say there's no way you're going to get a piano in there.

Turns out, there's Céline Concierge, who was able to take care of all the details about the piano. You helped look up all the different piano options, interfaced with the stores, got me all the pricing, and made sure the piano got moved in and was intact.

And so, I arrived with the piano that I needed already in the apartment, and it was beautiful and ready to go. It felt like a miracle.

**Would you recommend Céline Concierge in the future?**

Yes, unequivocally. You made everything so much easier for me, especially the first week or so of moving in.

In what can be a lonely and confusing experience, knowing that I had someone who could help me figure out any detail that confused me made such a huge difference.

I couldn't recommend working with you more.

*John applied for a long-term artist's visa in late summer of 2021 and moved back to Paris in October 2021 to start a new chapter of his life.*

*Find John's music at The Brilliance.*

# YOUR STAY

You'll find all you need to know about hotels and accommodations, how transportation works, an arrondissement guide, as well as the best neighborhoods to stay in during your visit (with my personal recommendations) in this section.

Likewise, I wanted to give you some fun facts and tidbits that can help you to connect with the French people, their culture, and lifestyle all the more.

Let's get started with some know-hows that are going to help win you extra brownie points with the French.

# Key Facts You Should Know
# About Paris and France

I't's all in a name: Paris is the capital of France, and its nicknames include **Paname**, the **City of Light**, and the **City of Love**.

Everyone knows that Paris is the most romantic city in the world, so the city of love is a no-brainer, but why the City of Light? It could be because of a combination of two things. First, is the Enlightenment period, which saw intellects, artists, and writers becoming "enlightened" with knowledge and thinking differently than the Roman Catholic Church from the late 17th to early 19th century.

Second, Paris was one of the first cities in Europe to install and illuminate a network of gas lanterns at night along the streets in the late 1600s, a consequence of the high nocturnal crime rate. Eventually, an electrical street lighting system replaced gas lamps with a first test on the avenue de l'Opéra and the Place de l'Étoile in celebration of the Paris Universal Exposition. From then on, it wasn't long before the whole city to was lit up at night by the same incandescent electrical system street by street.

Meanwhile, during the Roman rule, the city was named Lutetia, or in French **Lutèce**, and you can see traces of its past such as in the historically named Hôtel Lutetia that sheltered Jews after the Nazi occupation or in Julius Caesar's memoirs where he mentioned Lutetia.

So then why was Paris nicknamed Paname? The clues of this nickname come from the iconic hats that hail from Panama and became famous among travelers and Parisians in the early 20th century. To listen in on a historical journey elaborating on the subject of Paris as Paname,

I highly recommend this podcast episode "Paname" by the Amber Minogue who produces the podcast of the same name.

Among these nicknames, Paris is also known as one of the fashion capitals of the world as well as the capital of Haute Couture for obvious reasons.

## GEOGRAPHY:

France has regions, departments, and arrondissements. Regions are large areas of France which are broken up even further into departments. Within a region, there can be many departments. Within a department, there can be many arrondissements, or districts. Thinking in American geographic terms (not political or governmental terms), regions are similar to states, departments are similar to cities, and arrondissements are similar to counties.

France is made up of 18 regions. Thirteen of these are mainland regions (such as Normandy), and five of these are overseas regions. These regions are broken up into 100 departments (one of which is Paris), four of which are **départements et territoires d'outre-mer (DOM-TOMs)**, which are overseas departments and territories. The overseas departments are: Martinique, Guadeloupe, French Guiana, Mayotte and La Réunion. These are all governed by the French government, similar to governance of mainland France.

The overseas territories, or the TOMS, are an administrative division of France, but not considered France proper. They are neither considered part of the European Union but do serve political objectives. The French territories and collectives are: French Polynesia, Saint Barthélemy, Saint Martin, Saint Pierre and Miquelon, Wallis and Futuna, and New Caledonia.

It is important to know this because these departments and territories echo what once was French colonialism. The good news for us today is that travel between the DOM-TOM departments and territories doesn't require a visa for French nationals. That means you can get away to the Caribbean while resting within French sovereignty.

With all this talk of regions, departments, and arrondissements, where does Paris fall? Paris is defined as a department within the region of Île-de-France. Notably, Île-de-France translates in English as the "Island of France" and includes eight administrative departments. The name fits well as Parisians notoriously think themselves to be the Island of France and the only significant part of the country.

The three departments bordering Paris (le Hauts-de-Seine, la Seine-Saint-Denis, and le Val-de-Marne) are called **La Petite Couronne**, or The Little Crown. After La Petite Couronne, there are four more departments (Seine-et-Marne, Yvelines, Essonne, Val-d'Oise). These are the eight departments that make up Île-de-France, arranged in two rings, with Paris at the center.

There are 20 different arrondissements, or districts, within Paris. Each of the numbered arrondissements corresponds to its zip code. All zip codes in Paris begin with 75 and end with the number of the arrondissement. For example, if you live in the 5th arrondissement, your precise zip code will be 75005, and so forth for all the other arrondissements.

Check out the quick guide on the arrondissements in the next chapter.

## L'HEXAGON

The French's playful name for the mainland country is **l'Hexagon**, or the Hexagon. This metaphor is frequently used to refer to the country whose geographic form looks like a 6-sided hexagon. It symmetrically has 3 land sides as it does 2 sea sides. Next time you're talking about **La France** to your French peers, refer to the country as **l'Hexagon** and you will really impress them if you're a foreigner.

## POPULATION:

The population of the department of Paris is estimated at about 2.1 million. In the whole of Île-de-France (Paris and its 7 surrounding metropolitan departments), the population is estimated at 12.2 million (2019). France's overall population is 67 million and the top three largest cities after Paris are Lyon, Marseille, and Toulouse.

## HERE'S A BRIEF LEXICON RELATED TO GEOGRAPHY:

**une commune** | a town, municipality, village, city

**une ville** | a city

**département** | department or area

**région** | region

**lieu dit** | specific place or locality (to a small extent)

**le banlieue** | the suburb

**le périphérique** | outer highway ring surrounding Paris

**DOM TOM (départements et territoires d'Outre-Mer)** | Overseas Departments and Territories

# A Quick Guide on the Arrondissements of Paris

## What is an arrondissement?

**P**aris is made up of 20 districts, or neighborhoods, called arrondissements (arr. for short) that spread outward from the center in a clockwise motion and spiral out like the shell of an **escargot**, or snail. Another note about the geography of Paris is that the Seine river splits it into halves— the right bank (**Rive Droite**), which is north Paris, and the left bank (**Rive Gauche**), which is south Paris.

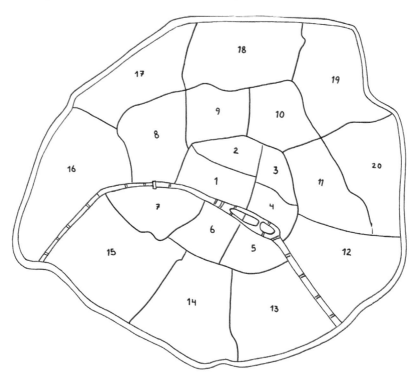

Here are the 20 arrondissements of Paris in a nutshell. Consider it your digital wine tasting of each area of the city to whet your palate for your next trip.

Every Parisian neighborhood is one of a kind. Each embodies its own reputation and emanates a personality of its own. Visiting the City of Light is a subjective and very personal experience. From the Latin Quarter to Montmartre, you will have different experiences when walking, visiting, and booking accommodation. There is no perfect neighborhood of Paris, yet they each have something to attract and delight you. It's not surprising that the locals have their lists of secret spots and favorite hangouts.

### For a taste of what Paris resembled when kings ruled the land, go to the...

 1st arr. – The 1st arr. is iconic for the Louvre Museum, Jardin des Tuileries, and the Jardin du Palais Royal, and being in the smack center of Paris. It's also one of the most bustling (and by consequence, noisy and crowded) districts with the biggest underground commercial center Westfield Forum Des Halles. If you're in the 1st arr. you're at the footsteps of Paris and can go anywhere by foot quickly.

### If you're looking to immerse yourself in the local sentiment, you have to check out the...

 2nd arr. – It's like a discreet little brother north of the 1st arr. You will find the famous Parisian passages tucked away here and the well-known streets Rue Montmartre and Rue Montorgueil. If I was to choose a perfect location to stay in Paris, I would choose the 2nd arr.! I would say it's in the heart of the city and a great balance between locals and non-locals. The area surrounding Sentier has proven a modern and hip place to hang out, shop, and eat.

## If you want local and trendy vibes, head over to two of the coolest districts...

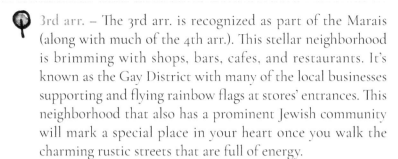

**3rd arr.** – The 3rd arr. is recognized as part of the Marais (along with much of the 4th arr.). This stellar neighborhood is brimming with shops, bars, cafes, and restaurants. It's known as the Gay District with many of the local businesses supporting and flying rainbow flags at stores' entrances. This neighborhood that also has a prominent Jewish community will mark a special place in your heart once you walk the charming rustic streets that are full of energy.

**4th arr.** – This district encompasses a part of the Marais and the two islands that rest on the Seine: Île de la Cité where Notre Dame sits and Île Saint Louis. This charming and picturesque area is prime real estate and a favored choice for a **séjour** in Paris. The 4th arr. is fun and active, a winner if you're in Paris to experience the local mood.

## If you're looking to stay out late, head over to the...

**5th arr.** – You can find many locals here in this secluded district. It consists of the Latin Quarter and is most famous for the Panthéon and the lively Jardin des Plantes, not to mention the unforgettable cobblestone Rue Mouffetard. This neighborhood is one of the hidden gems of Paris. You'll find quaint cafes and bars, and tranquil streets that transform into the hub of nocturnal life in the city.

## If you want a picturesque setting for an afternoon walk, head to the...

**6th arr.** – Reputed for the Jardin du Luxembourg and the alluring Boulevard Saint-Germain, this district is one of the most coveted in Paris among tourists. It blends luxury, charm and aesthetics perfectly. With its streets lined with designer shops, and grand cafés and brasseries, travelers flock to sit on the rival terraces of Café de Flore and Les Deux Magots. Definitely check out the Odéon area, including Rue de Buci, Rue de Seine and the gorgeous Saint Sulpice Church. If I was looking to buy property in Paris, this is the place I would explore.

## You're one-stop-shop for the Iron Lady herself is in the...

 7th arr. – The Eiffel Tower makes this district the most famous of them all. Visitors picnic on the lawn of the Champ de Mars as they admire the view of the tower. Other famous landmarks like Invalides, the Musée Rodin, and Musée d'Orsay are crowd pleasers here, too. You can also expect stunning architecture to ogle at and robust streets like the delightful Rue du Bac and the Beaupassage (a hidden courtyard and passage that's a must-see!). Nonetheless, you'll find quiet streets, making this arrondissement an ideal oasis for travelers to stay, whether in a hotel or homestay.

## For a regal visit with stunning architecture, head to the...

 8th arr. – This district is the emblem of sophistication, business and government all blended together. It's very business-oriented with banks, creative agencies, national embassies, and of course, the Champs Élysée running through the arrondissement. You can wander over to the famous Place de l'Étoile that borders the neighborhood and features the Arc de Triomphe. The French President's home can even be found in this corner of Paris. Additionally, there are stunning hotels and 5-star restaurants that exist in the 8th arr., but I don't recommend staying in this neighborhood as it can become quiet and impersonal, especially after dark.

**If you truly want to live like a local, do not hesitate to go to the...**

 9th arr. – This district is famous for the Opéra Palais Garnier and the distinguished Rue des Martyrs leading up to the Montmartre area. I would argue that the 9th arr. is Paris' best kept secret for travelers; it's like a hip and quiet Marais. This lovely district is full of locals and strategically placed as a buffer between the chaos of the city center and the vibrant 18th arr. If you can, stay somewhere near Saint Georges— this area is a dream.

**For a dynamic and contemporary take on the city, go to the...**

 10th arr. – The 10th arr. is one of my absolute favorite areas of Paris, especially if you're under 40. This area tends to attract young adults as well as hip and trendy folks looking for authenticity in Paris. People tend to be slightly more open and friendly in this corner of Paris. Expect more of an urban vibe along the colorful Canal Saint Martin. Finally, this neighborhood is ever transforming and changing, so definitely go at least once every time you visit Paris to see how it evolves.

**For more nightlife and a taste for the local go-tos, head over to the...**

 11th arr. – Equally trendy, you can find a myriad of culinary options, and if you're looking for an off-beat side of Paris, this is your neighborhood. Plus, if you're looking for a night scene, you'll find fun streets like Rue de Lappe and Rue Oberkampf. These are Paris' version of Austin's 6th street.

**If you want to further immerse yourself in the French scene, go to the...**

 12th arr. – An understated neighborhood, the 12th offers great green spaces like La Coulée Verte and Parc de Bercy. The Cinémathèque Française is found here for all the enthusiastic cinephiles out there. This cool and calm area is mostly residential with fun and unique places to hang out in, like the popular open-air market Marché d'Aligre and Bercy village which features an open-air commercial center, cinema, and plenty of cute cafes and restaurants.

**If you're looking for an urban and eclectic taste of the city that doesn't look like the rest of Paris, head to the...**

 13th arr. – This is an unconventional neighborhood that looks unique to the rest of Paris. You have tiny maisons in the charming Butte-aux-Cailles neighborhood and street art that colors the buildings. Expect a residential ambience as this is one of the few areas of Paris where you'll see the buildings higher than 8 floors. You should not go to the 13th arr. without peeking into Station F, the world's largest start-up facility that connects popular bars, cafes, restaurants and of course, plenty of entrepreneurs and business creatives.

**To see how real Parisians live, head to and stroll around these two residential areas...**

 14th arr. – The 14th arr. is like the inconspicuous cousin of all the arrondissements. Not many exciting things happen here except ordinary Parisian life that is, in and of itself, the essence of its existence. It's a residential area with many Parisians living here. The infamous Catacombs are within its borders as well as the large and stunning Parc Montsouris. Some noteworthy streets to go for a stroll and even take advantage of a photo op are Square Montsouris and Rue des Thermopyles, both located in the 14th arr.

 15th arr. – Like the 14th arr., this is a very residential area and offers wider streets than you'll find on the Rive Droite (Right Bank). Gare Montparnasse sits in this district as well as shopping areas like Beaugrenelle and green spaces like Parc André-Citroën. Along the barges of the Seine River, near Javel, you'll discover a laid-back party scene where eating street food and drinking beers along the river's edge is the norm.

**For an opulent time in the city that's also residential with stunning architecture, head to the...**

 16th arr. – The 16th arr. is a very posh and rich area of Paris. It's also residential and well-known for Place du Trocadero, which faces the Eiffel Tower across the Seine. It is still considered one of the bourgeoisie areas of Paris with world renowned sporting stadiums like Roland-Garros and Parc des Princes. If you want a quite stay in Paris while remaining true to the Parisian fabric, you may consider a stay in this neighborhood.

**If you want to go back in time, visit the humble yet lively...**

 17th arr. – This area is off-the-beaten-path and a hip side of town where you will find lots of young restaurant owners and cool cafes. Located on the northwest edge of the city, this district is undiscovered by tourists and even many locals. It seems like a forgotten part of the city, yet it's bustling with Parisians going about their business. This is one of the reasons that visiting the 17th arr. will feel like walking into Paris 20 years ago. Walk along the Rue de Lévis and definitely pop into one of my favorite bakeries, Pâtisseries Boulangeries Marques.

**For a sense of a Paris stuck in the past, check out the…**

 **18th arr.** – This district is notorious for the Moulin Rouge – and what once was and still kind of is Paris' red light district (Blanch and Pigalle areas). It's also known for Montmartre, where the beautiful Sacré Coeur Basilica lies. A favorite among tourists, the 18th district is also a **mélange** of cultures, cuisines, and nationalities. But don't let it fool you with its beauty, there are some questionable areas in the patchwork of the 18th arr. Don't miss out on the starving artists' square, Place du Tertre, the lively Rue des Abbesses and Rue Lepic for a feel of the true Montmartre scene.

**For a change in the Parisian pace, head to an urban oasis full of culture in the…**

 **19th arr.** – Escape from the tourist crowds to the 19th arr. to discover secret alleyways and street art in this animated, metropolitan neighborhood. The popular Parc de la Villette sits nestled north of the 19th arr., a hub to celebrate culture, cinema, theatre, live music and science. Couples, friends, and families can all enjoy picnics or bike rides near the waterfront promenade along the Canal de l'Ourcq. Sitting on a hill, the Parc Des Buttes-Chaumont is also widely known as a great spot to get a rooftop view of Paris. If you do go here, don't miss a trip to the famous Rosa Bonheur tapas bar— a local crowd pleaser.

**For diversity in cultures and people, there is no other than the humble...**

 20th arr. – The cosmopolitan 20th arr. is most known for the Père Lachaise Cemetery where many renowned people are now buried. It's definitely off-beat, but if you happen to be in the area, you will get a sense of a quiet, peaceful and upcoming Paris. You'll want to check out the Ménilmontant neighborhood as well as the Parc de Bellville, which also boasts another great panoramic view of the city that is less known to the tourists.

# Accommodation in Paris: Luxury Hotels, Boutique Hotels, Home Stays and Apartments

**A**s I've already mentioned, Paris is what you make it! That includes your accommodations.

Imagine, your experience can go from low-key, fitting-in-like-a-local to extravagant and luxurious depending on a few things: your budget, who you're traveling with, and your personal bucket list. Now, I'm not saying you have to break the bank in order to stay in a ritzy place. Many first-time or inexperienced travelers think their stay options are either a hostel, a hotel, or a crappy Airbnb (with all due respect). But in reality, there are a myriad of other affordable alternatives you can undertake that are just as lovely.

Here are some questions to consider before booking and ideas to guide your path to the perfect place for you:

## What is your a budget for accommodation?

One of the biggest determiners is your budget— how much are you willing to spend on accommodation per night?

What do you want to spend per night? Now multiply that by the number of nights you're planning to travel— it's that easy to create a budget for your trip accommodations. I also walk you through creating a budget for your entire trip with my Travel Budget & Tracking Tool in the Bonuses chapter.

If you're on a student budget or are an economy traveler, you should consider hostels and boutique hotels. Some of the best resources I use when booking on a tight budget are hostelworld.com for student rates, booking.com for bargain steals, and hoteltonight. com for competitive last minute fares.

On the other hand, if you're coming to Paris to splurge, find comfort and style, and you have a comfortable budget, Paris is just the place to indulge in whatever fantasy you can image. If a 4 to 5-star hotel or luxury apartment are a no-brainer, I recommend using plumguide.com for exceptional homes to make you feel like you're a local in the city of love. Likewise, you can always take a gander over to my Favorite Luxury Hotels chapter down below for the best luxury hotels you are going to fall head over heels for!

## Where to stay?

Where do you want to stay in Paris?

Out of the 20 arrondissements, each with their own personality, it's hard to choose an area. You may be imagining something along the lines of the charming Montmartre area with its tiny cobblestone streets, the trendy Maris neighborhood, or even the expat favorites: the Saint Germain area or the Latin Quarter. You may be thinking that you want to stay off-the-beaten-path in the Oberkampf neighborhood or in the urban and hip Canal Saint Martin district.

In the chapter coming up, I give you Where to Stay in Paris: My Top Neighborhoods to Stay in Paris.

## Who are you visiting with?

Are you traveling with kids on a family trip or maybe with your parents? Maybe you're on your honeymoon or a girls getaway. All of the alternatives will lead you to different possibilities, **bien sûr !**

## What kind of experience do you want to have?

Are you going to be out of your hotel room most of the day and are looking for a modest crash pad? Or are you coming to Paris for a relaxing, extravagant retreat?

Starting on the low-end, hostels provide students and those on a shoestring budget with eco-friendly rates while providing a clean place for travelers to rest their heads and a community of other travelers at your disposal.

Next, you have low-cost Airbnbs and cheap 2-star hotels if you want more privacy than a hostel at very competitive fares.

Maybe you're adamant about booking a comfortable hotel or cozy Instagram-worthy Airbnb with many amenities. Or maybe you want a charming boutique hotel; you can do a luxury apartment if you want to have that "I'm a Parisian for the week, living in the city" vibe.

This is where the mid-range accommodations come in with countless boutique hotels (Favorite Boutique Hotels chapter below), 4-star hotels, and higher-end apartment stays that can be found with the likes of Plum Guide, Airbnb (I consult you in more detail in the How to Find Homestays chapter below).

Lastly, you have the luxury, high end (**haute-gamme**) hotels and homestays (Airbnb Luxe Homes). This is for those wanting the **crème-de-la-crème**. These are the likes of The Ritz and Plaza Athénée hotels which I touch upon in the Favorite Luxury Hotels chapter.

# Where to Stay in Paris: My Top Neighborhoods to Stay in Paris

So you've booked your flight— congratulations are in order! You're one step closer to **Par-ee** and now you're doing your research on **where to stay in the city**. The hotel/apartment search can be daunting considering the myriad of options you have out there. Keep reading for my recommended arrondissements to stay in so you can make an informed decision. I also give you a couple of my favorite hotels that will make booking your accommodations a breeze.

I also want to suggest some alternatives to reserving hotels and offer you my insider secrets to booking luxury apartments in Paris. See the next chapter: How to Find Homestays & Luxury Apartments.

Not every neighborhood in Paris is the same. From the Latin Quarter to Montmartre, you'll have different experiences when booking accommodation. The neighborhood you choose to stay in will depend on your preferences, **bien sûr**! I usually encourage friends and clients to stay as close to the center as possible, so they are within walking distance of all the Parisian highlights.

Encompassing the core of Paris, the 1st through 7th arrondissements are where most of the action happens.

As explained in the chapter A Quick Guide on the Arrondissements of Paris above, Paris is made up of 20 districts, or neighborhoods, called arrondissements (arr.) that spread outward from the center in a clockwise motion and spiral out.

**Voilà**, here are my top neighborhoods you should stay, in order of personal preference.

### Stay in the 2nd arr. for a walkable and bustling neighborhood...

Elaborating on my brief description of the 2nd arr., this area is perfect for walking around and people watching as it's bustling and active. You can easily hang out on a terrace, either for summer cocktails or a cozy winter hot chocolate. You must visit and stroll down the two popular streets: Rue Montorgueil and Rue Montmartre. The intersecting streets have a lot to offer from up-and-coming restaurants, trendy clothing boutiques (like Rouje and the Sézane Apartment), and plenty of terraces to choose from.

Look into The Hoxton, Paris hotel for a stylish and modern place for your next stay. Its 172-bedroom hotel boasts comfort, design, and Parisian flair while staying contemporary. It is equipped with an all-day brasserie serving up French favorites, a classy wine bar serving up the famous French "**planche**", or meat and cheese boards, and the upscale Jacques' Bar. You won't be disappointed when you visit!

Book online at: thehoxton.com

## Stay in the 6th arr. to be at the center, while enjoying a backdrop of elegance...

It's no wonder foreign tourists, especially Americans, flock to the 6th arr. for the perfect Parisian vibes— terraces, shopping, and a taste of culture. The 6th arr., with its share of private art galleries and museums attracts the art buff as well as the fashionista. The streets between the 6th and 7th arr. are abounding with designer shops, including Armani, Hérmes, Céline, Louis Vuitton, among others.

If you're considering the 6th arr. for your next trip, look no further than the reputed and newly renovated Hôtel Lutetia. This 5-star hotel is a stone's throw away from Le Bon Marché and the high-end grand magasin (department store). It is in the epicenter of all the action whether you're into shopping, art, culture, or just looking to be a **flâneur**, or wanderer, around the city. Among the hotel's amenities include a luxury spa, wellness center, pool, and gym, as well as the Lutetia Brasserie, which is known for its friendly staff, and the opulent Bar Josephine— the perfect spot for evening cocktails in Paris.

Book online at: hotellutetia.com

## Stay in the 3rd and 4th arr. aka, The Marais, for a taste of the local, trendy Parisian life...

You can't have the identity of the 3rd without the 4th's and vice versa— each is nearly inseparable from the other. When you step foot in the Marais, you will get both the hustle and bustle of the city at the Saint Paul intersection as traffic, pedestrians, and cafe patrons mesh and intertwine. Just as well, the Marais is an oasis of quiet streets and secret passages and courtyards that are waiting to be discovered (like the discreet Village Saint-Paul). This quaint area is inviting with its fun pop-up boutiques and restaurant staples like L'As du Fallafel. There's no doubt that this neighborhood steals hearts with all visitors!

If staying in this neighborhood is a must for you, check out the charming boutique hotel Monsieur Saintonge in the heart of the Marais. This 4-star hotel boasts a modest 22 rooms, an **épicierie**, or delicatessen, and is a carefully designed space that is within walking distance of all the best designer shops in Paris, the Picasso Museum, and the stunning Place des Vosges.

Book online at: monsieursaintonge.com

## Stay in the 9th arr. to escape the crowds and mingle with the locals...

I used to live in the 9th arr. and I knew it as a village within Paris. It is truly a go-to if you want to delve deeper into the city and its residents. This is the neighborhood where many neo-bistros (see the Contemporary French Restaurants & Neo-Bistros to Try chapter) and high-end contemporary restaurants are popping up. Fashion boutiques are popping up as well to rival those of the left bank. The street not to miss here is Rue des Martyrs, as you can enjoy a stroll any day, rain or shine. The street features all the staple food vendors like your cheesemonger, butcher, fishmongers and veggie vendors as well as up-and-coming jewelry and clothing boutiques. If you follow this street north, it will lead you to Montmartre.

For a romantic stay **au couple** in the 9th arr., check out the classic choice Hôtel Amour, appropriately named for promoting all things love and romance. This tiny, 29-room boutique hotel features a lovely cityscape garden courtyard, which is perfect for intimate meals with your partner from their Restaurant Amour. The hotel's playful design dallies between sex and innocence as the hotel showcases bright pink tones, a disco ball in each room, as well as pin-up photos that induce foreplay.

Book online at: amour.hotelamourparis.fr

Another hotel line that I'm passionate about that features two hotels in the 9th arr. is the Touriste collection hotels. Hôtel Panache and Hôtel Bienvenue are both 4-star hotels that are memorable for their interior design, friendly and down-to-earth staff, as well as contemporary and elegantly styled rooms. Each hotel possesses a restaurant and bar, a small library for patrons' reading pleasure, and they are both perfectly located a few blocks away from the lively Grands Boulevards area.

Their 3rd and 4th hotels are located in the 10th arr.: Hôtel Beaurepaire and Hôtel des Deux Gares.

## Stay in the 5th arr. to unfold the secrets of the city...

Known as being an expat hangout, the 5th arr. is full of hidden gems that reveal history like the notable landmark Le Panthéon as well as being the student headquarters of the city. You'll be thrilled to discover the 5th arrondissement's cafes and international food options. You can eat out in this area without breaking the bank. One of the best parts about the Latin Quarter is its late-night tendencies; from the Saint Michel corner to the Rue Mouffetard, you won't be disappointed to find yourself here after sunset because Paris is a moveable feast, after all!

To experience a secluded getaway, stay at the Hôtel Monte Cristo Paris, a beautifully designed 4-star hotel with its own private indoor swimming pool— a rare gem in Paris. The hotel exemplifies elegance and fine taste, even featuring its own scent box with perfumes created specifically for the hotel. If you love rum, you're going to love the Bar 1802, showing off a selection of over 700 bottles. Finally, the hotel serves patrons a buffet of fresh **petit déjeuner** options, or you can likewise enjoy a private dinner in your room from the restaurant Le Grand Dictionnaire.

Book online at: hotelmontecristoparis.com/en/

## Stay in the 7th arr. for a relaxed and restful visit where art and culture are within walking distance...

Visitors, like expats, love the 7th arr. for its access to the most famous monument La Tour Eiffel, one of the myriad of reasons travelers come to Paris. It is also one of the more quiet neighborhoods, probably because it feels more spacious than some of the others; the streets are longer and wider, and the green spaces are bountiful and lush. Take for instance, Champ de Mars, the vast green space at the footsteps of the Eiffel Tower or the lawn adjacent to the avenue Breteuil, both places welcome picnics.

Le Narcisse Blanc Hôtel & Spa is a 5-star hotel with a rooftop overlooking the famous Parisian rooftops. It has a cozy and relaxing indoor swimming pool and spa center, as well as an exceptional restaurant. It is nothing other than elegance at its finest. This sophisticated hotel is a mere 15 min walk from the Eiffel Tower, where along the way, you can explore the walkable 7th arrondissement's Rue Saint Dominique, Rue Cler and Rue Malar. Don't hesitate to book at this hotel for an exquisite and memorable time!

Book online at: lenarcisseblanc.com/en/

Of course, this list is subjective, based on my experience of living in Paris as well as advising travelers. I endorse these specific arrondissements for travelers wanting to maximize their time while visiting Paname.

There are boundless wonderful hotels, fun hostels, and stunning Paris apartments that can serve as your resting place in **all** of the arrondissements. These, however, are my infallible go-tos when consulting friends and clients. They have proven successful in the past like I'm sure they will on your next stay.

# How to Find Homestays & Luxury Apartments
## (An Alternative to Hotels: Luxury Apartments)

I've been working in the real estate sector for over four years as a concierge and property manager of second homes and emphasize that while hotels in Paris can be your launching point, it doesn't have to end there. Maybe you're considering an Airbnb or short-term apartment rental for your next trip. These are great options, but what if you want to try something even more exclusive?

Paris has a hidden luxury apartment business just waiting to be tapped into. This route is for people looking to feel like a local during their stay rather than a simple tourist. Below, I show you how to book a luxury apartment from anywhere from a week to several months.

Finally, if you're a seasonal traveler to Paris for business or pleasure, I can go a step further and help you find long-term accommodation in the form of a second home, or a *pied-à-terre*[1]. I do this by partnering with some of the best real estate agents who specialize in short to long-term apartment rentals to find the best fit for you. Imagine yourself staying in Paris in your very own **pied-à terre** or co-owned property! I can help make these dreams become reality.

---

[1] A **pied-à-terre** is a temporary or second home, but does not imply "vacation home" per se. This phrase literally translates as "foot on (the) ground" and pronounced **pi-ette-ah-tair,** using a pronunciation technique called a liaison where the phrase sounds like one word. It often refers to a flat you call your own and where you may **place your foot** on the ground for occasional short-term purposes. Put simply, it's the home you pass through and stay, stopping and going whenever your heart pleases.

## WHY BOOK LUXURY APARTMENTS INSTEAD OF A LUXURY HOTEL?

- Because you want to feel like a local and like you fit right into the city
- An apartment can be more cost-efficient than a hotel
- The comfort of space: you aren't restricted to the hotel lobby and your room as the living quarters
- Apartment amenities like a kitchen, living room, washer & dryer, which most hotels are limited on (even in the hotels with extended amenities)
- Privacy: who can argue with having a whole apartment to yourself
- If you're traveling with friends or family, an apartment can offer more intimacy and togetherness
- Apartments are also ideal for couples traveling together
- Your very own personal & private on-call concierge during your trip to have the benefits of a hotel concierge at your service (**contact me**\* to find out more)
- Optional housekeeping service so you can always have a spotless apartment— don't miss out on this coveted amenity
- Designer, cozy, and luxurious apartments in the best neighborhoods of Paris for your personal taste and pleasure.

---

\* www.celineconcierge.com/contact-us/

# MY RECOMMENDED WAYS TO BOOKING SHORT TERM APARTMENT RENTALS:

## 1. SHORT-TERM BOOKING WEBSITES

| | |
|---|---|
| **Booking.com**<br>www.booking.com | **Haven In**<br>www.havenin.com |
| **The Plum Guide**<br>www.plumguide.com | **Paris Perfect**<br>www.parisperfect.com |
| **Airbnb**<br>www.airbnb.com | **Homeaway**<br>www.vrbo.com |
| **OnefineStay**<br>www.onefinestay.com | **Paris Attitude**<br>www.parisattitude.com |

## 2. PROPERTY MANAGEMENT COMPANIES & LONG-TERM RENTALS

**For luxury homestays**

### CÉLINE CONCIERGE

I have local connections and partnerships I turn to when I need to find unlisted, exclusive luxury homes. You won't find them anywhere else in the urban jungle of Paris. I personally manage second homes in Paris as well as know other property managers, so I can place you in the perfect spot for you to experience that true Parisian vibe!

You name the neighborhood and budget, and I can comb through Paris real estate to find anything you dream up. Don't hesitate to contact me[2] if you're looking for a unique treasure.

---

[2] www.celineconcierge.com/contact-us/

## SETTLESWEET[3]

Settlesweet is a personal home matchmaker who will accompany you in every step of finding your future **long-term** home rental in Paris. They offer extensive accompaniment and a comprehensive apartment search from your customized home selection, to viewings, to application filing, to home subscription assistance for the English-speaker as well as the newbie to Paris. Don't forget to mention Céline Concierge if you go this route— they will, no doubt, take good care of you!

## 3. LUXURY VACATION PROPERTY RENTALS & OWNERSHIP

### Co-Own Property in Paris

## ELITE DESTINATION HOMES[4]

This company provides a way for avid Francophiles and repeat visitors to the city to actually put their names on a property deed in Paris. Next to their specialty in vacation home rentals, they equip keen owners to own shares in a home in what they coin as "fractional ownership". This is a practical and affordable way to actually invest in luxury real estate in the 75 zip code. I would be more than thrilled to put you in touch with them because I have personally worked with them, managing their homes in Paris.

## 4. REAL ESTATE AGENCIES

### Own property in Paris

## ICONIC PARIS[5]

They are one of the best real estate agents who can show you first-rate properties available in Paris on both sides of the river. Besides sales, they also specialize in long-stay apartment rentals so they can home match you with your future Parisian home. Contact me[6] for more details about this luxury real-estate agent!

---

[3] www.settlesweet.com
[4] www.elitedestinationhomes.com
[5] www.iconicparis.com
[6] www.celineconcierge.com/contact-us/

## A+B KASHA[7]

This real estate and design company focuses on real estate with a twist. Their mission is simple; they transform real estate in Paris curated into your very own luxury **pied-à terre** in the city. Their focus is on bringing new life by renovating homes and flipping them into your all-time Parisian dream home!

## BARNES INTERNATIONAL REALTY[8]

Barnes is another partner I work with who specializes in luxury apartment rentals and sales. They have a passion for real estate and serving the international community with their wide network of homes and agents across France and the world.

## INDEPENDENT BUYER'S AGENT[9]

I partner with buyer's agents in Paris who can show potential home buyers any property across all the different real estate listings. They are the **crème de la crème** of realtors in France such as my friend and real estate expert Alexander Martin. As a buyer's agent he brings together realtor services– the ability to not only source, but to translate– all the while helping people navigate the system.

If you feel overwhelmed considering all your options and don't know what the next step is, get in touch with me. Don't wait! I'll connect you to Alexander or other buyer's agents I partner with depending on your needs. Just tell me what your dream home looks like and let me guide you in securing the perfect Parisian apartment without the hassle!

I offer FREE consultations to all my clients. I'm here to assist you— from **dreaming** about your ideal Paris trip to helping you relocate into your newfound **chez toi**. I can assist you in whatever part of the journey you find yourself; just contact me[10] today to get started in making your dreams come true.

---

[7] https://kasha.paris
[8] www.barnes-international.com
[9] www.celineconcierge.com/contact-us/
[10] www.celineconcierge.com/contact-us/

# Favorite Luxury Palace Hotels

Luxury accommodation can provide unimaginable comfort and elegance during your stay in Paris. From beauty spas, to fine dining restaurants, to incredible views, luxury hotels are experts at catering to your needs and desires, and your best Paris experience.

For top-notch comfort and a 5-star experience, look no further than my recommendations for luxury stays in Paris.

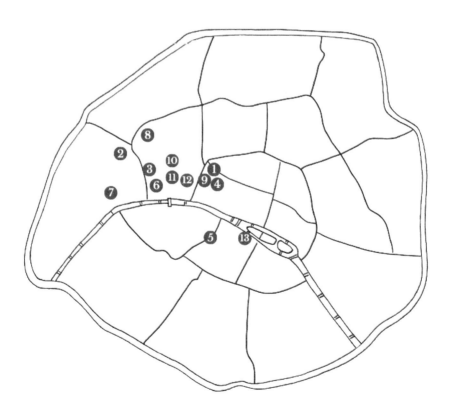

## 1 THE RITZ

15 Pl. Vendôme,
75001 Paris
01 43 16 30 30

**Notable Amenities:**

- Beautiful veranda and courtyard
- Indoor Pool
- Spa
- Afternoon Tea Experience
- Newly renovated in 2016

Representing luxury at its best, you can't go wrong with a stay at the Ritz. It's located on the internationally renowned Place Vendôme, a square known for its prestigious brand-name jewelry shops. That gives you a sense of what you'll find when entering the equally majestic Ritz where walking in is like stepping into Heaven. It's recognized for its luxury beauty spa, one of the best in the country, as well as the Hemingway Bar, a fun spot to grab a drink before hitting up the town. Its Salon Proust offers up a delectable Afternoon Tea experience from the Pastry Chef François Perret.

## 2 THE PENINSULA

19 Av. Kléber,
75116 Paris
01 58 12 28 88

**Notable Amenities:**

- Spa & Wellness Center
- Rooftop bar (Le Rooftop)
- Enclosed Terrace (La Terrace Kléber)
- Indoor pool
- Fitness center
- Car collection available to guests, upon request

Located in the prestigious 16th arrondissement, this high-end hotel offers warm hospitality and exquisite rooms that are inspired by Haute Couture. Guests can ride around the city in a stylish car from their collection of luxury vintage cars. The spa offers an urban retreat in the city and is a favorite among individuals and couples alike. Visitors can enjoy an unforgettable view of the city and the Eiffel Tower from Le Rooftop, the hotel's chic and romantic rooftop bar.

## 3 THE FOUR SEASONS HÔTEL GEORGE V

31 Av. George V,
75008 Paris
01 49 52 70 00

**Notable Amenities:**

- Indoor and Outdoor Pool
- Spa
- 3 Michelin Star Restaurants: Le Cinq, Le George, L'Orangerie
- Penthouse and Eiffel Tower Suite

This grand hotel is a treasure trove of beauty and excellence. It boasts Michelin dining and decadent decor that is for the dreamer in you. Its opulent terrace is the center of the hotel where you can relax over a glass of red or celebrate with a bottle of champagne. Its signature service and hospitality will make you feel right at home.

**LE ROYAL MEURICE**

228 Rue de Rivoli,
75001 Paris
01 44 58 10 10

**Notable Amenities:**

- ► In-room dining menu
- ► Pet friendly
- ► Two restaurants and a bar (Bar 228)
- ► 3 Michelin Star restaurant Le Meurice Alain Ducasse
- ► Spa
- ► Jardin des Tuileries at the footstep of the hotel

Facing the lovely Jardin des Tuileries on the bustling Rue de Rivoli, this luxury hotel makes for the perfect couple getaway. If you're fortunate enough to get a room facing the south side, you'll get to see the Eiffel Tower sparkle as you celebrate with that special someone with champagne directly from your room. Le Maurice has an exceptional afternoon tea service curated by top chef Alain Ducasse that is worth a try even if you're not staying at the hotel.

**5 HÔTEL LUTETIA**

45 Bd Raspail,
75006 Paris
01 49 54 46 00

**Notable Amenities:**

- ► Hair Salon
- ► Indoor Pool and Spa
- ► Art Deco style Bar (Bar Joséphine)
- ► Upscale Brasserie (Brasserie Lutetia)
- ► Kid Friendly

Just a stone's throw from the iconic Le Bon Marché, this newly renovated self-proclaimed luxury palace hotel is the epitome of sophistication and class. Opening its doors in 1910, it's a hallmark of history with famous patrons ranging from De Gaulle to Josephine Baker. The stunning hotel made its bold transitional facelift from Art Nouveau to Art Deco, reopening its doors in 2018 to re-welcome guests. This beauty offers something for everyone. Whether a sole traveler on business, a family stay, or a lovers getaway, it truly is an ideal place to spend your time in Paris.

 ## PLAZA ATHÉNÉE

25 Av. Montaigne,
75008 Paris
01 53 67 66 65

**Notable Amenities:**

▸ Located in the heart of the fashion district
▸ Courtyard Garden
▸ Two haute-cuisine restaurants and a bar (Le Bar)
▸ Dior Institute Spa
▸ Fitness studio
▸ Family friendly

This dream of a hotel was made for the perfectionist in us all. It's perfectly nestled on the prestigious avenue Montaigne, where Paris meets fashion and style. From the Dorchester Collection, you can only expect extraordinary taste in every detail. You can't go wrong by staying here! From its iconic bright red awnings and lush flower gardens draped over windows to the inviting secret garden terrace, its exceptional service, and 3 Michelin Star restaurant led by world famous chef Alain Ducasse, this is your dream come true. You will become a part of history as you enter the legacy of so many who have stayed before you.

## 7 SHANGRI LA HOTEL PARIS

10 Av. d'Iéna,
75116 Paris
01 53 67 19 98

**Notable Amenities:**

- Spa
- Indoor Pool
- 2 restaurants, one of which has a Michelin Star
- Suites with exquisite views of the city and Eiffel Tower

Elegance and sophistication defines this world-renown hotel with an optimal view of the Iron Lady herself, the Eiffel Tower. Its two restaurants showcase fine-dining at its best: La Bauhinia and its one Michelin Star Shang Palace. A fun fact: the Shang Palace is the only Chinese restaurant in France awarded a Michelin star (awarded in 2012). You will feel right at home with the unmatched suites that offer exceptional views of the City.

## 8 HÔTEL LE ROYAL MONCEAU RAFFLES

37 Av. Hoche,
75008 Paris
01 42 99 88 00

**Notable Amenities:**

- Cinema
- Library
- Art Gallery
- Private Apartments
- Spa & wellness center

This 5-star luxury hotel is a culture lover's paradise. They have an in-house art gallery and cinema. Offering rooms and suites alike, the most noteworthy is the distinguished Presidential suite. The hotel's overall style is defined as sublime, contemporary elegance. They really offer something for the whole family whether it's a familial Saturday afternoon brunch atelier, sushi classes, shopping at Le Royal Boutique, or a Royal Tea Time with pastries from Pierre Hermé, the famous French Pastry Chef.

## MANDARINE ORIENTAL

251 Rue St Honoré,
75001 Paris
01 70 98 78 88

**Notable Amenities:**

- ▸ 2 Gourmet Restaurants
- ▸ Chic Bar
- ▸ Indoor Pool
- ▸ Spa & wellness Center

A plush and vibrant hotel, the Mandarine Oriental is nestled in the fabulous shopping district of Rue Saint Honoré. This contemporary and elegant hotel invites you in for a Parisian getaway of a lifetime. Its rooms and suites offer unique views of the city; you have the choice of city or garden views, and you can upgrade to enjoy a room with your very own terrace. It's two restaurants, Camélia with its traditional French cuisine, and Sur Mesure with its haute cuisine, offer two memorable dining experiences from recognized chef, Chef Thierry Marx.

## LE BRISTOL PARIS

112 Rue du Faubourg
Saint-Honoré, 75008
Paris
01 53 43 43 00

**Notable Amenities:**

- ▸ Spa & Wellness Center with eight treatment rooms (Spa Le Bristol)
- ▸ Indoor, rooftop pool
- ▸ Panoramic View Suites, Penthouse Suites, and Honeymoon Suites available
- ▸ Hotel Bar (Le Bar du Bristol)
- ▸ Beautiful Garden Terrace
- ▸ Ball and functions room for events

Past guests are always returning guests at Le Bristol. They swear by this hotel because they treat their guests like family. The hotel is perfectly situated in the 8th arr. with views of Sacré Cœur, Le Grand Palais, and the Eiffel Tower depending on which suite you're in the mood for: Penthouse, Honeymoon, or Imperial Suite. It also features the cuisine creations of Chef Eric Frechon, the 3 Michelin Star chef of the Épicure restaurant at the hotel. You'll feel like you're in your own palace the moment you step foot in this Parisian oasis that has access to almost anything your heart desires.

 ## 11 LA RÉSERVE PARIS HOTEL & SPA

42 Av. Gabriel,
75008 Paris
01 58 36 60 60

**Notable Amenities:**

- ▸ Two prestigious hotel Restaurants, Le Gabriel and La Pagode de Cos
- ▸ Hotel Bar (Le Gaspard)
- ▸ Indoor pool
- ▸ Spa & Fitness Center
- ▸ A library reserved for guests (The Duc de Morny Library)

If you're looking for luxury in a quiet and private setting, La Réserve is for you. This self-proclaimed "private apartment" is exactly what it feels like when you arrive onto the premises and enter your very own chez toi in the form of a spacious suite the hotel calls apartments. Plus, it's conveniently located just at the edge of the prestigious Avenue des Champs-Élysées in the 8th arr., a neighborhood notorious for business and politics among fashion and gastronomy. Its 25 suites offer a dedicated butler for your chambers that reflects 20th century Parisian beauty. You've arrived at home in this poetic dream that is fit for kings and queens.

## 12 HÔTEL DE CRILLON

10, Place de la
Concorde,
75008 Paris,
01 44 71 15 00

**Notable Amenities:**

▸ One Michelin Start Restaurant, L'Ecrin, from Executive Chef, Boris Campanella
▸ Private Dining Room (La Cave)
▸ Indoor Pool
▸ Spa & Wellness Center
▸ Fitness Studio
▸ Bar, lounge, gastronomy restaurants
▸ Afternoon Tea Menu

This elegant space, part of the Rosewood Hotels, located in the Place de La Concorde is just a stone's throw away from the Jardin des Tuileries. The hotel features rooms, suites, and signature suites that are Grand Appartements designed by Karl Lagerfeld. These residential-style mini-apartments are perfect for the traveler who is staying awhile. Likewise, the suites with connecting rooms are perfect for families. Besides being a gorgeous luxury hotel on the footsteps of the stunning Place de la Concorde, for refined travelers and guests, this grand hotel is un-refuted stomping ground in Paris.

## 13 RELAIS CHRISTINE

3 Rue Christine,
75006 Paris
01 40 51 60 80

**Notable Amenities:**

- Spa Guerlain
- Pet-friendly
- Self-Service Bar
- Complimentary Breakfast
- Located on the footsteps of Saint Germain neighborhood

This is a hidden gem tucked away in Paris' left bank with one of the best breakfasts in Paris. It's a breath of fresh air if you want a more private, intimate experience with the one you're traveling with, even if that's just with yourself! The discreet hotel in the Saint Germain neighborhood is ready to offer you a memorable getaway that will make you feel like a local rather than a tourist. This hotel promises comfort and rest while enjoying the little pleasures of the French lifestyle. You won't want to miss out on drinks on the cobblestone garden courtyard that feels like an urban refuge in the city.

# Favorite Boutique Hotels

If you're a traveler that loves style and sophistication, one-of-a-kind experiences and prefers to retreat to places with intimate settings, then a boutique hotel is probably your best bet for accommodation. They are refined in style, yet reasonably priced compared to luxury palace hotels. Many boutique hotels in Paris and France still fall within the category of luxury without a heavy price tag.

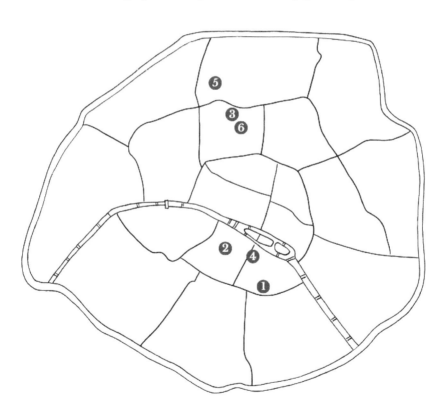

Boutique hotels are smaller hotels with no more than 60 rooms—sometimes there can be as few as 3 rooms— and they are usually located in trendy neighborhoods. They pay attention to detail in the design of the hotel as well as offer great amenities and personalized service.

Below, I've touted some of my favorite boutique hotels that are foolproof and awaiting your visit to the City of Light!

 ## HÔTEL MONTE CRISTO

20-22 Rue Pascal, 75005 Paris

01 40 09 09 09

This place defines chic with its beautifully designed rooms, suites, polished bar and lounge area, and stunning indoor pool. You can get a steal if you book in advance. You won't want to leave the hotel as this place is a village within the city. It offers a stunning indoor pool and great lounge bar to hangout, keeping you entertained, happy, and satisfied sipping your favorite rum libation. The bar hosts rum tastings and has over 700 kinds available in house.

 ## HÔTEL LUXEMBOURG PARC

42 Rue de Vaugirard, 75006 Paris

01 53 10 36 50

This idyllic boutique hotel is perfectly located on the edge of the Jardin du Luxembourg, right in the heart of the 6th arr. The lovely rooftop patio gives you a privileged view of the garden and you can relax in its quaint library, available for patrons. Its 17th century decor will make you feel like you've time traveled on a romantic escapade.

### ③ HÔTEL AMOUR

8 Rue de Navarin, 75009 Paris

01 48 78 31 80

From its racy reputation of once being a love hotel for ladies of the night, this place has transformed into quite a stylish and hip place to stay at for Millennials. This modern hotel has a knack for making you feel relaxed while you enjoy a romantic getaway with your lover. You'll feel like you're miles away from a busy city when dining in the secret garden terrace. You'll feel rejuvenated as you stay in this fun, playful hotel whose rooms are as unique as the people who work here.

### ④ HÔTEL LE LAPIN BLANC

41 Bd Saint-Michel, 75005 Paris

01 53 10 27 77

Journey through this Alice-in-Wonderland-esc boutique hotel in the 5th arr. that is famous for its calming and soothing pastel color palette. This elegant and chic hotel is the epitome of peace and simplicity. It's located four minutes from Jardin du Luxembourg, is in the heart of the Latin Quarter and is accessible to many restaurants and bars near the Saint Michel area.

### 5 HÔTEL PARTICULIER MONTMARTRE

23 Av. Junot Pavillon D, 75018 Paris

01 53 41 81 40

This charming hotel awaits couples for a romantic getaway in the bustling Montmartre neighborhood. Its ritzy cocktail bar receives guests in its prime location for nightlife in Paris. This rare gem that once belonged to the Hermès family continues welcoming guests in a contemporary and romantic setting.

### 6 HÔTEL BIENVENUE

23 Rue Buffault, 75009 Paris

01 77 37 02 95

If you're looking for design and comfort without breaking the bank, you're welcome at this hotel whose name exemplifies hospitality. Its charm and trendy vibes will leave you feeling refreshed after just one night's stay. The outdoor terrace is the perfect spot to unwind and recharge. Its sister location, just a five-minute walk south, Hôtel Panache, also reflects the unique tasteful style of its designers and is a solid choice for a great night in Paris.

# Transportation and How to Get Around Paris

Paris offers countless ways to get around. And luckily for us, Paris city limits are all but 34.45 km square (21.40 mi sq) in area (excluding the Bois de Boulogne and the Bois de Vincennes). From its extremities, north to south, it's 9.2 km (5.5 mi) long and would take you 2 hours to walk from Porte de la Chapelle in the north to Porte d'Orléans in the south. If you wanted to walk east to west, it's a short 11.2 km (6.59 mi) wide and would likewise take a mere 2 hours and 22 minutes from Porte Maillot in the west to Porte Dorée in the east.

The city itself is surrounded by a notorious highway called the **Périphérique** which spans a length of 35.04 km (21.77 mi). For obvious reasons, the Périphérique is detrimental to city planning because it acts as a physical barrier to Paris' growth beyond this ring, but on the bright side, it is a fast route you or your taxi driver jumps on when you have to go across town or to the airports quickly.

The actual Parisian city limit is only what you get inside this ring, and you immediately spill over into the lesser areas known as **le banlieu**, or suburbs, the place where the city and population are actually able to grow.

The city's population is 2.148 million, so as you can imagine, the city possesses a plethora of choices when it comes to transportation. Here are the top ways to get around and how to access them.

## WALKING

Paris is probably one of the most walkable cities in the world. Walking is one of the best ways to get around because it allows you the time to admire the architecture and really get a feel for the ambience, the people, and the soul of the city. By foot, you can stop and go at your leisure, even popping into a cafe or shop every now and then. Walk if you have time, not if you're in a hurry to get somewhere.

Did you know that Paris is planning to be the most green, sustainable city in Europe by 2030? It is currently undergoing a city-wide facelift in preparation for the 2024 Summer Olympics.

## BICYCLE

If you're here to stay, it's worth purchasing your own bike, new or second hand, at these recommended bike shops throughout the city. If you're coming to Paris for a short time, you can rent from a bike rental shop with rates starting at 12 € for half a day.

The shops I recommend are Paris Bike Tours, A Vos Vélos, and Holland Bikes where you can find different offers like Dutch-style bikes, electric and non-electric options, as well as kids bikes— and storage accessories depending on your needs.

## PUBLIC CITY BIKE HIRE

I recommend the Vélib city bikes for short-term stays and for short distances. They have affordable prices, too. You can quickly check out a city Vélib bike at any of the hundreds of kiosks around the metroplex with a credit card and by accepting a hold of 150 € for the deposit on the bike.

**Public City Electric Bike Hire** (for French or foreign residents of Île-de-France)

You can do an electric city bike rental with VéliGo Location (long-term electric bike rentals).

This eco-friendly mode of transportation costs 40 € per month for a subscription of six months to a year. They provide a helmet, insurance, and bike training for the newbies in town.

## ELECTRIC SCOOTER

These have become the craze in the last year as the city renovates to make Paris more pedestrian and bike friendly. You can order these online or rent them on demand. Among the for-hire options, you have Uber, Lime, and Dott.

**Uber, Lime, Dott and other Electric Scooter Options**

These have their conveniences but can be a dangerous due to the one-way streets and uneven pathways like cobblestone streets. Paris is getting better with providing bike lines for bicycles and scooters to travel on, but it still doesn't minimize the danger of these scooters.

They have been known to put people in the hospital and I don't personally recommend them, especially if you are traveling. One of the dangers to be aware of are other cars, buses, pedestrians, and bicycles. If you do opt to take these around town, please respect the traffic signals.

## PUBLIC METRO

The Parisian metro company RATP (Régie autonome des transport Parisiens) is an extensive, inexpensive and popular way to get around.

You can zip through the city in a matter of minutes on its 15 lines and the wonderful thing about the metro is that there are metro stops nearly every 300 meters from each other. The system's density is also its strong point.

I recommend you buy a Navigo Easy Travel Card with 10 metro passes if you plan to take it a few times during your stay. At the time of writing this (November 2021), the Navigo Easy card with 10 metro tickets (**carnet de 10**) costs 16.90 €, while the individual price of a ticket costs 1.90 €.

Available Metro Lines: 1, 2, 3, 4, 5, 6, 7, 7bis, 8, 9, 10, 11, 12, 13, 14.

### TIP:

Download other useful transportation apps in the **Useful Apps to Download When in France chapter.**

## RER TRAIN

The **Réseau express régional d'Île de France**, or RER, is a regional rail system that serves Paris and its metropole consisting of 5 lines labeled A, B, C, D, and E. The rail system is co-managed between RATP and SNCF. You'll take this train to traverse longer distances within Île-de-France (IDF) and if you're going to the suburbs. It also includes some newer lines:

H, J, K, L, N, P, R, U. Think of the RER as a broader and faster train system than the metro.

The Paris metropolitan area encompasses five zones that starts at one, then expands out up to five, and your RER ticket fee is based on the distance you travel within these zones.

## TER TRAIN

Similar to the RER train, the train system called Transport Express Régional (TER) services between the different regions of France and can get you further than the RER trains. They are run by SNCF and their rail system extends beyond the Île-de-France (IDF) area, which are denoted by Transilien (TER trains serving the IDF).

All you need to know is that you can book your tickets online and you'll be able to get to where you're going without worrying too much about the names.

## TRAMWAYS

Where you have the Parisian metro and the RER rail system intersecting throughout the city, the Parisian tramway lines are typically on the outskirts of Paris and in the suburbs.

The tramway lines consist of: 1, 2, 3a, 3b, 4, 5, 6, 7, 8, 11 express, and future 12 and 13 express lines.

## BUS

Paris has a sizeable bus system. It is as expansive as the metro system, if not more. The RATP bus system branches out from Paris into the suburbs (**banlieue**).

You must be aware that there are day buses as well as night buses called the Noctiliens.

An RATP metro/bus ticket is valid for the metro, bus, and travel on the RER within zone one of Paris. You should be aware that if you purchase a ticket directly on the bus, it's a solid 2.00 € ticket, slightly more expensive than a ticket purchased from a kiosk or from a booklet.

Day buses and night buses work similarly except that night buses run less frequently. Lastly, a good tidbit to know is that Google Maps will accurately route bus itineraries, so feel confident if you prefer to take the bus— I do. I just don't recommend taking the bus if you are pressed for time, because they could be a slow method of transportation compared to the metro that runs more often, or a taxi.

## PARISIAN TAXI

The Parisian taxi is a foolproof way to get around, but one of the more expensive ways. Like in the films, it's always fun to yield a black **taxi Parisien** with a, more-times-than-not, grumpy French taxi driver who is grumbling about politics, the weather, or the mayor, specifically.

The most widely known taxi company is G7.

Taxi ride fares from CDG airport to Paris are fixed at a price of 58 € or 53 € depending on if you are arriving or departing from the left or right bank **(see A Quick Guide on the Arrondissements of Paris)**.

Fixed rates for transfers also apply to and from Orly Airport at 32 € (Left Bank) or 37 € (Right Bank).

If you're being charged anything more than this for a regular Parisian taxi, it could be a scam, unregistered taxi, or someone posing as a taxi driver.

## TIP:

Before getting in a taxi, always request the price when going to and from the airport. You want to be upfront with the driver about your destination and the price and avoid a nasty surprise when you arrive at your destination.

## NON-PARISIAN TAXIS, OTHERWISE KNOWN AS VTC IN FRENCH (UBER, FREE NOW, ETC.)

A VTC means "**Véhicule de Tourisme avec Chauffeur**" or simply put, a vehicle for hire with a driver. There are several vehicle for hire companies operating in Paris, including but not limited to the following: Uber, Bolt, Free Now, Caocao Mobility.

# Interview with
## Jim Le,
## seasoned expat turned French national

Jim

Jim is an American who obtained his French nationality after living in France for five years. Since moving to France in 2010, Jim has built a career in the film industry, has found love, and gotten married.

Jim is a production and event manager, originally from Phoenix, Arizona. He first visited Paris in 2004 on a summer trip before subsequently returning to France as a study-abroad student in Aix-en-Provence. He later taught English in Normandy and has since worked as a freelancer in Paris.

Jim and I met through a mutual college friend back in 2013. I invited Jim to a meet-up event for expats somewhere in the 8th arrondissement where we exchanged stories and our reasons for moving to France. The thing about Jim was that he was a few years ahead of me on his France journey.

Not only did we connect over our love for film and Paris, but he was someone who was transparent with me about the difficulties and challenges of moving to and integrating into society here. From our conversation, I could tell that he was resourceful and passionate about making it work and being a success in France.

He had done everything I dreamed of for myself: obtained an artist visa to stay in France, found work in the film industry, and he even directed his own short film that he wrote.

Jim and I have remained friends and he has proved to be such an invaluable friend and guide to me along my own journey to staying in France. This is his courageous story about how he made Paris his home.

**Why did you move to Paris?**

I studied Media Arts (aka Film Production) and French, so having degrees in both, I figured Paris was the perfect fit for someone like me!

I also always wanted to shoot a film in Paris, and I did so with the 2012 short film "L'Americain" about a young, reserved Parisian who takes in a mysterious American backpacker for a few days.

It was to illustrate the inadvertent effects we have on the people we come across and the lasting impressions they can leave on us. I'm also a fan of French New Wave, so I wanted to do an homage to that.

**What was your first impression of Paris?**

Eye-opening!

**Did you know French? If yes, where did you learn the language? If not, how did you learn?**

I spoke ZERO French and knew nothing about France or French culture until I met my friend Galaxie, who moved to Arizona after growing up in Normandy, France. As I became more and more curious about her and her culture over the years, I decided to take French 101 just for fun. But I ended up loving it so much that I continued to take French classes throughout college, and Galaxie and I eventually took a summer trip to France together a few years later.

During my undergrad, I did a semester abroad at IAU (Institute for American Universities) in Aix-en-Provence where I did an intensive French curriculum. So, I would say I got the basics and phonetics down at that time.

But I didn't really become fluent until I did TAPIF (Teaching Assistant Program in France) because I spent an entire year in a small village in Normandy where nobody spoke English. So, I was pretty much forced to learn and speak French every day.

Fun fact: I ended up teaching in the same village where Galaxie grew up, and I even taught at her former primary school— if that's not destiny, I don't know what is!

**What do you love about Paris?**

The food! Bread, cheese, charcuterie, pastries, wine...

I also love the Haussmannian architecture— that never gets old.

**What challenges did you face with moving to Paris?**

Finding an apartment!

I spent my entire first year in Paris subletting short-term rentals, crashing at friends' places and even spending four months in a hotel (don't worry, I got a sweet deal)!

As a freelancer, it's really difficult to lease an apartment because they always turn you down unless you have a full-time work contract. I found better luck through Le BonCoin and going directly through the landlords themselves rather than apartment agencies.

**What is a lesson you have learned from living in Paris?**

I learned that moving to a different city like Paris doesn't automatically change your life for the better.

You can't just pack up your bags, move to a new city and think that your life is going to be better for it. If you're looking for a positive change in life, YOU need to change as well.

In my case, I had to let go of my bad habits, grow up, learn to take risks, and be fearless if I wanted my life in Paris to be any different than what it was back home. By doing so, my life here vastly improved both professionally and romantically. The year I decided to make drastic changes was the year I actually met my French husband!

Biggest lesson— get out of your comfort zone.

## What kind of visas/resident permits did you have to be able to stay in France?

The first visa I got was for the Teaching Assistantship Program in France (TAPIF). It's a program run by the French Ministry of Education and the Cultural Services of The French Embassy that places Americans as assistant English teachers in schools throughout France. That visa lasted an entire school year.

When I returned to the States after that program, I did some research to see how I could come back to France. At the time, the French Consulate in the U.S. offered an "artist" visa called the "Skills and Talent Card," which allowed artistic professionals to come live/work in France and pursue their own personal projects.

I sent in my application and got approved to move to France at the beginning of 2010— and I've been living here ever since!

## What's one major difference between the U.S. and France that not many people know about?

By working in the film industry in France and accumulating a certain number of declared hours each year in your specific line of work, you can obtain this status— like I did— called "intermittent du spectacle", which allows people working in the theatre/cinema/television industry to strictly do what they do for a living as their primary income.

Since some of these jobs usually aren't the normal "Monday through Friday, 9-to-5" type of job, people with this status receive financial aid from the government during periods of unemployment, since they're always working on a project-by-project basis.

For example, if you're an actor in the States, you're maybe working at a restaurant or depending on two jobs just to get by. But in France, if you're an actor, you're strictly an actor. That's the only thing people expect you to be doing.

And that's one of the best things about France— they are very supportive of the arts and respectful of the people who do the work.

I've been "intermittent" since 2011.

## So, you're a dual French and American citizen. Tell me how you eventually got your French nationality?

I arrived in Paris with the "Skills and Talent" Card in 2010. It was a three-year visa, and I was able to renew it for another three years after that. So, after five consecutive years of living in France, I was finally eligible to apply for French citizenship.

However, I didn't realize that the entire process would take so long (between 12-18 months)! With my "artist" visa about to expire and no word yet about citizenship, I was left with no choice but to apply for the new "Passeport Talent" (which had replaced the previous "Skills and Talent Card").

But my dossier kept getting bounced back and forth between the different offices because no one knew who was actually approving this new visa!

So, the lady at the Préfecture candidly asked me about my love life (awkwaaard!) and suggested I just get married because even she thought it was the simplest solution!

Shockingly, I took her advice! My French boyfriend and I got hitched 3 months later while I waited for word about my nationality. It wasn't until a year later that I finally got approved, so I'm now officially French AND, yes, still happily married! 🩶

## What is your biggest frustration with Paris?

French bureaucracy...

It's astonishing how long and complicated it is to do paperwork or get anything official done here. It's almost like they're trying to discourage you from living here.

It's never easy and you need to have a lot of resilience and patience.

**What would you tell someone who is like you and wants to move to Paris?**

Keep track of everything that you do while you're in France because the French government will probably want proof of it years later!

If I was to do anything differently, I would have studied abroad longer. Or taken French classes earlier, probably in high school so that by the time I moved to France, I would have spoken better French by the time I moved here.

**If you had known about a lifestyle service like Céline Concierge, would you consider using our services, why or why not?**

Yes, I would have needed help finding an apartment as a freelancer. I had a lot of trouble finding a place.

But back then, there weren't a lot of concierge services like that. I didn't even know that those kinds of services existed.

So, if I had known that there was a service like that, I would have seeked help to find a place to live because I was struggling. I was looking everywhere!

Even French people have a hard time finding a place to live; it's not just expats. It's a universal problem for everyone. It's a competition; it's a war.

**Do you have a favorite book, film, or song about Paris?**

The film Les 12 travaux d'Astérix (aka "The Twelve Tasks of Asterix") is a great epitome of French bureaucracy and summarizes the frustration I endured while trying to remain in Paris, albeit in a very humorous way!

*Jim is still living in Paris and is happily married...*

# WHAT TO DO IN PARIS

Jump into this section for the best activities to do in Paris at any level of adventure. Do you want to stroll through the emblematic covered passages of Paris or walk down the most Instagrammable streets for a photo op? Discover some lesser-known museums because you've been to the Louvre ten times already? Perhaps you want to immerse yourself in the Parisian scene and live like a local.

In this section, there is something for everybody, whether you want to laze around reading French literature in the Jardin des Plantes, have an ultra-relaxing spa day, venture out on a solo day trip to Giverny, or visit a charming **château** only 30 minutes from Paris by train.

Dive into this section for the best things to do in Paris from a local's point of view.

# The Must-See Monuments and Landmarks

**D**id you know that the city has an overwhelming 2,185 monuments? Yikes! As an expat living in France, over the years I've been asked time and time again, besides the Eiffel Tower, what are the best things to do and see in Paris...so let's start with the basics.

Below, I've included my picks for 10 highlights to visit in Paris for first-time visitors. In the chapter Secret, Underground Paris Spots and Adventures I write about places to visit that are more unique and experiences off-the-beaten path. This initial list is not at all exhaustive, but rather a jumping off point to get your feet wet in the magnificent **Ville Lumière**.

I know 10 highlights seems underwhelming but believe me, as an 8-year resident of Paris (at the time of writing this), you will end up overwhelmed by these initial 10. These visits will leave you craving more and may even convince you to make a move to the French capital before you can say, "*Comment allez-vous ?*" three times in a row.

I hope these places will charm your hearts as much as they have my very own!

 **LOUVRE PYRAMID**
Musee du Louvre,
75001 Paris
01 40 20 50 50

▸ **Kind of Landmark**: Glass pyramid structure
▸ **Built in**: Commissioned by President François Mitterand in 1984, and completed in 1989
▸ **Arrondissement**: 1st

This is one of the most iconic landmarks of Paris and was designed by architect I. M Pei. This structure consists of one large pyramid and three smaller surrounding ones made of glass and metal. The largest pyramid gives access to the Louvre Museum (which is also a Paris highlight!). The **pyramides** sit in the Cour Napoléon, surrounded by the Louvre that was the former royal palace.

## 2  SAINT EUSTACHE

2 Imp. Saint-
Eustache, 75001 Paris
01 42 36 31 05

- ► **Kind of Landmark**:
  Catholic Church
- ► **Built in**: 1534
- ► **Arrondissement**: 1st

Saint Eustache is one of Paris' largest churches and features the largest organ in France. It was strategically built in the center of the city. Every Sunday afternoon, there are organ rehearsals and you can even catch one of the many classical choirs performing. Visits are free and as with all the churches in Paris, there are various mass services throughout the week and weekend. It sits next to Les Halles— a notorious site for shopping and recreation.

## 3  NOTRE DAME DE PARIS

6 Parvis Notre-Dame
- Pl. Jean-Paul II,
75004 Paris
01 42 34 56 10

- ► **Kind of landmark**:
  Catholic Church
- ► **Built in**: work began
  in 1163, completed and
  opened in 1345
- ► **Arrondissement**: 4th

This beauty is truly the most stunning Gothic Cathedral from the inside and out. Since the cathedral's fire that took place on April 15th, 2019, it has been closed to the public. The city of Paris has been continuing the reconstruction effort since 2019. You can still visit it from the outside but expect the site to be closed for a few more years.

## TIP:

I recommend visiting the equally beautiful Église Saint-Paul-Saint-Louis du Marais (in the Marais neighborhood) or the stunning Église Saint-Sulpice as two alternatives.

 **LE PANTHÉON**
Pl. du Panthéon,
75005 Paris
01 44 32 18 00

▸ **Kind of landmark:** Church and burial place
▸ **Built in**: work began in 1160, completed in 1260
▸ **Arrondissement**: 5th

Originally built as a church and dedicated to St. Geneviève (the patron saint of Paris), the Panthéon is now a monument and mausoleum where distinguished French citizens are buried. Visit the permanent exhibition that explores the lives of those who helped shape French history, many of whom are buried there such as Voltaire and Rousseau.

## 5 EIFFEL TOWER

Champ de Mars, 5 Av.
Anatole France,
75007 Paris
08 92 70 12 39

- ▸ **Kind of Landmark**: Tower
- ▸ **Built in**: 1887-1889
- ▸ **Arrondissement**: 7th

Constructed from 1887-89, the Eiffel Tower was originally built as a temporary installation for the entrance of the 1889 World's Fair. It stands at an impressive 324 meters (1,063 ft) tall. It was supposed to be torn down after 20 years, but the City of Paris kept it after it proved a valuable asset for communication and tourism. Tickets up the beauty start at 10 € for adults, then bump up depending on which level you want to explore and whether you will do so by foot or by elevator access. Contact me[1] for details on private tours for your next visit!

## 6 ARC DE TRIOMPHE

Pl. Charles de Gaulle,
75008 Paris
01 55 37 73 77

- ▸ **Kind of Landmark**: Arch
- ▸ **Built in**: 1806, opening in 1836
- ▸ **Arrondissement**: 8th

This is the largest arch positioned in the center of the most famous roundabout in the world, Place de l'Étoile, overlooking the most famous boulevard, Champs-Élysées. Did you know that the Arc has 12 streets leading to it? And they say all roads lead to Rome... Visits up to the top cost 12 €. Visits are free for those 18 years or younger.

---

[1] www.celineconcierge.com/contact-us/

## 7 PALAIS GARNIER OR THE OPÉRA GARNIER

Pl. de l'Opéra,
75009 Paris
0 1 71 25 24 23

▶ **Kind of landmark**: Opera House
▶ **Built in**: 1861
▶ **Arrondissement**: 9th

This famous and inspiring opera house is gilded with gold, enamored with stucco and marble interiors, and surrounded by elegant statues. This magical place will take your breath away the moment you step in! The interior tour of the Paris Opera house is only 12 €, plus 5 € for the audio guided tour— I highly recommend paying extra for this one; you won't regret it! Tours include the Grand Staircase, the Chagall ceiling, and the auditorium (but it is not a guaranteed entry as it may be restricted to visitors for rehearsals or artistic consideration). Check out the site for exceptional closures before visiting.

## 8 CATACOMBS[2]

1 Av. du Colonel Henri
Rol-Tanguy,
75014 Paris
01 43 22 47 63

▸ **Kind of Landmark**:
Ossuary (a place which
the bones of the dead
rest)
▸ **Built in**: The creation
of the quarries was
commissioned in 1777
by Louis XVI. In 1786
The Catacombs was
consecrated to become
the resting place and
Ossuary of the Cemetery
des Innocents
▸ **Arrondissement**: 14th

As an underground landmark where six million bones rest, it's not a visit for the faint of heart. This unique tour of the guts of Paris will certainly grip you, but it's not one to miss. Where else can you visit the literal bones of your ancestors? This is the ultimate tour that you won't find elsewhere around the world. Make sure to dress warmly as it's chilly below the surface. Tickets are 13 €, plus 5 € for the audio tour (recommended).

---

[2] **This is A City of Paris museum** - A City of Paris museum is a collection of 14 museums carefully curated by the city of Paris cultural team. This collection represents 'a record of the history of Paris' and many of which are of zero charge. Take advantage of this selection of lesser-known museums where you'll experience more intimacy with the art and history of the city itself.

## 9 MONTPARNASSE TOWER

33 Av. du Maine,
75015 Paris

- ▸ **Kind of Landmark**: Skyscraper
- ▸ **Built in**: Construction took place from 1970-1973 and it was inaugurated on June 18th, 1973.
- ▸ **Arrondissement**: 15th

The first skyscraper erected in Paris and the second tallest monument within the city limits is our Montparnasse tower stretching 210 meters (689 ft) high. You can check out the 360° view from the top of the Panoramic Observation Deck for 18 € for an adult ticket. It is true what they say— you can discover the best view of the Eiffel Tower from here!

## 10 SACRÉ COEUR BASILICA

35 Rue du Chevalier de la Barre,
75018 Paris
01 53 41 89 00

- ▸ **Kind of Landmark**: Basilica
- ▸ **Built in**: Construction began in 1875 and was completed in 1914.
- ▸ **Arrondissement**: 18th

At 130 meters high, this adored basilica sits in the neighborhood of Montmartre, overlooking the city. Check out the inside of the basilica for impressive stained glass windows— visits of the inside are free. You can visit the basilica tower where you will catch another 360° view. Purchase tickets directly at the basilica for only 6 €, and 4 € for ages 16 years or younger.

## NOTE:

An arrondissement is a district or neighborhood of Paris. Within the city limits, there are 20 arrondissements or districts with the first starting in the center point of the city and each consecutive one circling around like the shell of a snail until you end up at 20. But the real question is: did the arrondissement come before or after the escargot?

Check out the chapter A Quick Guide on the Arrondissements of Paris.

# Museum Guide

You can't come to the land of art and culture without visiting at least one museum, whether large or small. Paris alone has over 130 museums ranging from contemporary, modern art museums like the MAM or Pompidou Center, historical museums like the Museum of Natural History, to specialized museums like the Cinémathèque Française, with a focus on cinema, and the European House of Photography, with an emphasis on the art of photography.

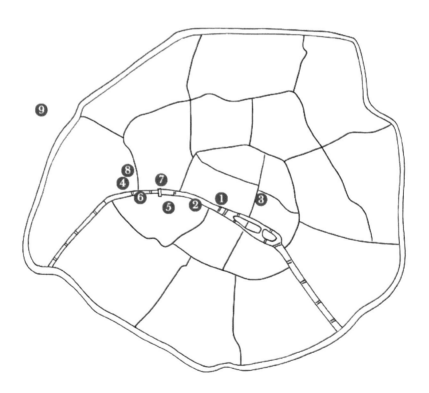

If your interests and passions are set on art, fashion, history, or gastronomy, you are sure to find a museum that fits the bill. Explore one or all of these wonderful museums on your next trip! Get in touch with me[3] for private museum tours with licenced tour guides as well as visits that are not open to the public.

 **MUSÉE DU LOUVRE**
Rue de Rivoli, 75001 Paris
01 40 20 50 50

The mother of all museums, the Louvre, is a must-see for art-lovers and Paris visitors alike. Even if you aren't particularly a fan of art per se, the Louvre has something to impress everyone. From ancient Egyptian artwork, a Medieval collection, to modern day art, it also houses La Joconde, more commonly known as the Mona Lisa. But be warned, it takes days, even weeks to see everything in this monumental museum—it is the world's largest, after all, at 72,735 meters square (23,8632 sq ft)!

 **MUSÉE D'ORSAY**
1 Rue de la Légion d'Honneur, 75007 Paris
01 40 49 48 14

Situated in an old train station, the Orsay Museum features artwork dating mainly from the mid-19th to early 20th century. You'll find statues, painting, frescos, and photography to gaze at. It's a pleasant museum to visit, especially for its cultural events like its cinema expos and classic music concert lunchtimes held throughout the year.

---

[3] www.celineconcierge.com/contact-us/

### **3** CENTRE POMPIDOU

Place Georges-Pompidou,
75004 Paris
01 44 78 12 33

For a taste of modern and contemporary art, come here! The Pompidou Center is a museum, public library, and architectural wonder of Paris with the restaurant George on the rooftop of the museum. A visit to the Pompidou is anything from the ordinary, from the tube-like features of the building to the strange and sometimes bewildering art, this place is all about discovery and reinvention of the norms.

### **4** MUSÉE D'ART MODERNE DE PARIS (MODERN ART MUSEUM OF PARIS OR MAM PARIS)[4]

11 Av. du Président Wilson,
75116 Paris
01 53 67 40 00

Another modern and contemporary art museum, the MAM of Paris displays a profound collection of over 13,000 works from its permanent collection dating from the 20th and 21st centuries up to the present day. The collection represents artists such as Picasso, Matisse, Chagall, Dufy and many more! A visit and walkthrough of the permanent collection is reasonable at no more than 2 hours (depending on your pace).

---

[4] A City of Paris museum

## ⑤ MUSÉE RODIN

77 Rue de Varenne,
75007 Paris
01 44 18 61 10

The Rodin museum is housed in an old mansion named The Hôtel Biron that was finished in 1937. The museum showcases a beautiful assortment of statues, paintings and artifacts throughout the museum and a garden escape spanning a lush 3 hectares. Auguste Rodin's most noteworthy masterpieces The Kiss, the Thinker, and the Gates of Hell are found at the museum as well as a life-size replica of the latter two, amid many more.

## ⑥ MUSÉE DU QUAI BRANLY – JACQUES CHIRAC (QUAI BRANLY MUSEUM)

37 Quai Branly,
75007 Paris
01 56 61 70 00

For a rare gem of indigenous art from Africa, Asia, Oceania, and the Americas, pay a visit to this extraordinary place. The Quai Branly Museum displays nearly a million unique pieces of photography, art, and artifacts. The museum and research center is an homage to the past French president, Jacques Chirac, who completed it during his tenure in office. Dine in at Les Ombres restaurant, located in the museum, for an exceptional view of the Eiffel Tower and Parisian rooftops.

## 7 LE GRAND PALAIS

3 Av. du Général Eisenhower,
75008 Paris
01 44 13 17 17

The Grand Palais is a huge exhibition hall and museum. It showcases exhibitions, **salons**, or trade shows, and events like Paris Fashion Week throughout the year. The west wing of the Palais holds the science museum, the Palais de la Découverte. It will hold the fencing and taekwondo events in the upcoming Paris Summer Olympics in 2024.

## 8 YVES SAINT LAURENT

5 Av. Marceau,
75116 Paris
01 44 31 64 00

Hosted in an iconic **hôtel particulier** on avenue Marceau, where the designer spent many years designing his work, this museum offers a rotation of retrospectives and thematic exhibitions. It's a must see for the new designer or the fashionista as the museum explores the design and work of the famous Saint Laurent as well as the history of the **haute couture** traditions of the 20th century.

## 9  LOUIS VUITTON FOUNDATION

8 Av. du Mahatma Gandhi,
75116 Paris
01 40 69 96 00

This architectural wonder opened in 2014 and is a cultural center, museum, and exhibition venue that houses a permanent collection from 120 artists. Patrons can view the pieces in person, but they are also accessible online. The foundation prides itself on showcasing work from innovative and outside-the-box-thinkers while bringing art and culture to the masses.

Here is an exhaustive list[5] of Paris museums.

---

[5] https://en.wikipedia.org/wiki/List_of_museums_in_Paris

# Noteworthy, Lesser-known Museums

Going off the beaten path can sometimes give you the best reward, and some of my personal favorite spots in Paris aren't on many tour companies' lists. Not only will you get to appreciate a deeper and more specific history to Paris, but you'll view sides of Paris many people don't prioritize. Check out some of the lesser-known museums below!

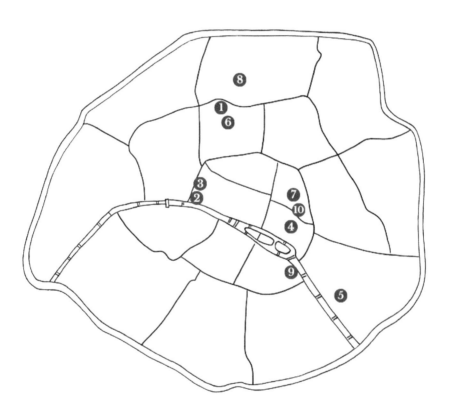

And as always, contact me[6] if you're interested in a private tour or visit after-hours to any of these museums. I have the key to put together any kind of unique experience that you're looking for!

 ## MUSÉE DE LA VIE ROMANTIQUE[7]

16 Rue Chaptal,
75009 Paris
01 55 31 95 67

It's a tiny and quaint museum in an old **atelier** of the painter George Sand. There's a tearoom and a lovely courtyard perfect for a photo op. You can definitely make it an afternoon adventure. Oh, and the best part is that the museum entrance is free—donations are welcome.

 ## MUSÉE DE L'ORANGERIE

Jardin Tuileries,
75001 Paris
01 44 50 43 00

This is a quiet and underrated gem and a favorite for impressionist artwork. Claude Monet's famous Water Lilies (**Les Nymphéas**) occupies the entirety of two oval shaped rooms. You can easily let time slip by as you ponder the genius and elegance of the pieces. L'Orangerie features a permanent collection as well as holds seasonal exhibitions.

---

[6]  www.celineconcierge.com/contact-us/
[7]  A City of Paris museum

### 3 JEU DE PAUME

1 Pl. de la Concorde,
75008 Paris
01 47 03 12 50

The Jeu de Paume is a tiny museum with a big heart and even bigger history. A depot for stolen artwork during the occupation of Paris during World War II, it is now a forerunner in modern and postmodern art, photography, and cinema.

### 4 MAISON EUROPÉEN DE LA PHOTOGRAPHIE (MEP) (EUROPEAN HOUSE OF PHOTOGRAPHY)

5/7 Rue de Fourcy,
75004 Paris
01 44 78 75 00

This place is a photographer's dreams! Not only is the MEP an exhibition center, but it also contains a library, auditorium, video viewing facilities, and a bookstore equipped with a cafe. Most notably, the *maison* facilitates a photographic restoration and conservation workshop for the preservation of photographs and archives of the museums of Paris.

## 5 LA CINÉMATHÈQUE FRANÇAISE

51 Rue de Bercy,
75012 Paris
01 71 19 33 33

La Cinémathèque is a cinephile's paradise! From the film museum with seasonal exhibitions rotating through filmmakers and auteurs of the past to the library holding the world's largest film archives to the movie theater, this place has something for any curious film fanatic.

## 6 MUSÉE NATIONAL GUSTAVE MOREAU

14 Rue de la Rochefoucauld,
75009 Paris
01 48 74 38 50

This artist's home turned art museum is a perfect stop for a serene escape from the city and offers an espresso shot of art and culture. Despite the small size compared to other museums, the walls are nonetheless brimming from top to bottom with portraits and tableaux from the symbolist artist himself.

P.S. there's a beautiful and very Instagram-worthy staircase in the house, inviting you to photograph it!

### 7  MUSÉE PICASSO
5 Rue de Thorigny,
75003 Paris,
01 85 56 00 36

This art museum filled with and commemorating Pablo Picasso is housed in the stunning Hôtel Salé in the Marais district of Paris. The gallery holds over 5,000 pieces ranging from paintings, sculptures, and drawings to the personal effects of Picasso. The visit is easily digestible as its focus is the sole artist and takes no more than a couple hours depending on your pace.

### 8  DALÍ PARIS
11 Rue Poulbot,
75018 Paris,
01 42 64 40 10

This permanent collection dedicated to Salvador Dalí features his extensive surrealist artwork in drawings and sculptures. The museum is small but comprehensive in the life of Dali and his art creations. You will escape the crowds of Montmartre for a few hours while immersing yourself in the artist's life and probably walk away feeling inspired. I highly recommend a visit if you have any affinity for the artist and love the fantastical world of surrealism.

### 9 MUSÉUM NATIONAL D'HISTOIRE NATURELLE (MNHN) (NATIONAL MUSEUM OF NATURAL HISTORY)

57 Rue Cuvier,
75005 Paris
01 40 79 56 01

The origins of this museum lie in royalty with King Louis XIII, when in 1635 he established the royal garden of medicinal plants at the current-day Jardin des Plantes, which was run by the physicians of the king himself. Later on, in 1793, during the French Revolution, the museum was formally founded by leading professors of the time in order to instruct the public and oversee scientific research. Today, the museum is a pandora's box of discovery of humankind and the animal kingdom alike. This museum is ideal for families with children due to its visual aesthetic.

### 10 MUSÉE CARNAVALET

23 Rue de Sévigné,
75003 Paris
01 44 59 58 58

Last, but certainly not least, Musée Carnavalet exhibits the history of Paris in a renovated space that took four years to complete. It's also the oldest City of Paris Museum and is located in the Marais neighborhood in a Renaissance building known as a **hôtel particulier,** or urban mansion. This gem of a museum is worth the visit because it immerses you in the history of **La Ville Lumière** in a visit that will take about two to three hours. The best part— it's completely free!

## HONORABLE MENTIONS:

Maison de Balzac*

Musée de l'Armée Invalides - Military Museum

Musée de Cluny: National Medieval Museum

Musée Marmottan Monet

Musée Maillol

Musée Jacquemart-Andre

Musée Guimet

Musée de l'Homme

Musée du Parfum Fragonard

Musée du Vin

Musée de la Mode de la Ville de Paris - Palais Galliera

Musée des Beaux-Arts de la Ville de Paris - Le Petit Palais

Musée du Luxembourg

---

\* A City of Paris museum

# Parks and Jardins

**P**aris may seem like a concrete jungle, but there are many more green spaces than the city reveals at first glance. Did you know that it has over 500 green spaces for you to stroll through and relax in? Paris' range of stunning parks includes everything from secluded, miniature squares overflowing with trees and urban gardens, to spacious, walkable city parks with whitewashed statues and olive-green chairs. There is the famous "**champs**" or fields like the lawn of the Invalides or Champ de Mars featuring the Iron Lady, herself.

By 2024, the year the City of Paris will host the Summer Olympics, it is planning to create even more urban spaces and parks, turning the city into a greener and more walkable capital.

For instance, the city is commissioning various architects and city planners to transform the Champs-Élysées into a more walkable, green space with fewer cars. Likewise, the Montparnasse area will get a facelift, as well as the city skyline with the installation of various rooftop gardens across Paris.

Continue reading for my top picks of the most stunning parks and gardens in Paris for any visitor or returning traveler to take advantage of the sun and maybe even a Parisian-style **pique-nique** with friends!

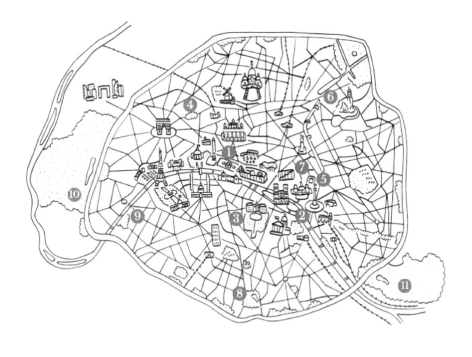

THE ULTIMATE PARIS SURVIVAL GUIDE

## 1 Jardin des Tuileries

Right in the heart of Paris, this historic garden ground with its iconic olive-green chairs is the perfect spot for a stroll and an afternoon pause. In the summer, you can have an adventure at the fair on the park grounds. It's also an excellent park for kids to roam around. Its family-friendly vibes, beautiful garden landscape, and the fact that it's tucked between the Musée du Louvre and Place de la Concorde make it a beautiful Paris park with a great view of the Eiffel Tower.

## 2 Jardin des Plantes

Known as the botanical garden of Paris, this special place houses the Muséum national d'histoire naturelle (National Museum of Natural History), a **ménagerie**, or zoo, greenhouses, libraries and archive buildings, as well as several galleries featuring botany, geology, and mineralogy. Not only is the Jardin des Plantes fitting for a stroll, you will find rare species in the plant life here that are the ideal backdrop for a picnic.

## 3 Jardin du Luxembourg

This spacious park has something for everyone. Whether you're a runner or a **flâneur** (wanderer), you're going to love this divine garden with its fountains and blooming flowers. Even if you've been to Paris already, it's a must-visit for locals and tourists alike.

## ④ Parc Monceau

This little oasis in the 8th arrondissement is a dream waiting to be had. The charming little statues, pathways, and manicured lawns are another great setting for a picnic and walk in the park. If you're a runner, it's a perfect paradise for a jog.

## ⑤ Place des Vosges

This secret enclave is a lovely getaway in the heart of the Marais neighborhood worth checking out. The stunning architecture of the buildings surrounding this green space makes it the quintessential picnic spot as well as a picturesque background for a photo shoot, or simply a stroll.

## ⑥ Parc des Buttes-Chaumont

If you want to experience a true Parisian day, take a picnic to the **Butte** (or hill) on any sunny day. The park will be teeming with locals on a run, picnicking, and sunbathing. What makes this spot a unique park to visit in Paris is its altitude. It's one of the highest places to get a nice view of the city while taking in the sun and just relaxing. A fun bonus is the after-hour drinks you can take pleasure in at Rosa Bonheur Bar and restaurant inside the park. That makes for a full day of amusement!

## ⑦ Anne Frank Garden

To truly experience Paris like a local, I highly recommend taking a moment of your travels to pop into the historical Anne Frank Garden. It's secretly tucked away between the Parisian buildings of the Marais and little-known to travelers. This city sanctuary, with lots of shade, is a wonderful park to gain refuge from the hustle of Paris as well as a nice spot for kids to play. The garden features an orchard and a graft of the chestnut tree that Anne Frank admired from her window. It also neighbors the Museum of the Art and History of Judaism— pay a visit if you have the time.

## 8 Parc Montsouris

Parc Montsouris is a charming and spacious park on the edge of the city, perfect for a morning jog. You will often see university students picnicking here as it's the go-to for young adults residing nearby at the Cité Universitaire grounds. Did you know, Emperor Napolean III commissioned Haussmann to create this 38-acre park in the late 19th century?

## 9 Parc André Citroën

This urban green space used to be a car factory and is now a vast park featuring a moored hot-air balloon. You can get one of the best 360-degree views of the city atop the Ballon de Paris Generali, starting at only 7 €. Besides the fantastic view this park offers with the balloon, it's a large green space that you are sure to relax in, play some frisbee, and find some solitude.

## 10 Bois de Boulogne

This large, wooded park is the second largest after the Bois de Vincennes and is located along the western border of the 16th arrondissement. It's home to the Château de Bagatelle, a small hunting lodge that was originally designed to house members of the royal family and friends while they hunted on the grounds. The Jardin d'Acclimatation is also a part of the **Bois** as a small children's amusement park. Lakes, waterfalls and wildlife are a part of this park and help you feel like you're far from the city when you step inside.

## 11 Bois de Vincennes

This is the largest public park in Paris, located on the east border of the 12th arrondissement. The Parc Floral, or the Floral Park of Paris, the Paris Zoo, and Lac Daumesnil (Lake Daumesnil) are a few of the unique features of the park that are worth paying a visit to. Visitors can rent row boats and picnic on them for an afternoon on the lake or simply stroll/bike through on the many footpaths and bike paths of the nearly 2500 acre park. One of the highlights of the park is the 14th century Château de Vincennes that is open to the public.

## 12 Parc de Sceaux

Last on the list, but definitely not least, is the stunning Parc de Sceaux! Visiting this oasis during the cherry blossom blooms is pure magic and nothing says spring in Paris more than cherry blossoms in bloom— they have two large orchards of them! This park ground is a mere 30 minutes outside of Paris and easily accessible on the RER train line B.

The backdrop of this park, with its impressive **château** in the background, is an ideal photo spot for engagement photos or selfies with friends on any given day! The Château de Sceaux once belonged to the royalty Duke and Duchesse of Trévise and you can say it's the little cousin of Versailles due to its many similar features and surrounding gardens.

# Must-Visit Streets in Paris

Why would I include a whole chapter on streets? These streets give an insight into local living. Some are lined with cobblestone, some are filled with local vendors that inspire the mood of the streets, while others are preserved by the City of Paris in order to maintain and help local small businesses to survive in the world of globalism. These streets are unique, charming, and scenic. Each one offers a clue into real Parisian life— these are the streets where the real locals live their lives and do business.

Enjoy the scenery when you walk along these must-see Parisian streets!

## RUE CLER - 7TH ARR.

 Local vendors and shops line this ideal street in the 7th arr. and is near two other charismatic streets: Rue Saint Dominique and Rue Malar. In the summer, it's a great street to peruse the green grocers and get your shopping done as you can find the butcher, wine cave, and cheese monger all within 5 minutes of each other. During the holiday season, this is one of the embellished streets you'll see filled with Christmas lights and decorations.

### WHY DO YOU NEED TO VISIT?

It's walking distance from the Eiffel Tower, so if you're planning a trip there, stroll the Rue Cler on your way to or from the Eiffel Tower— you won't regret it!

## RUE DES MARTYRS - 9TH & 18TH ARR.

 This street extends the length of two arrondissements (the 9th and 18th arr.) and is my absolute favorite street in Paris. I am biased as I lived just a street down from here back in the day. Everything about this street alludes to true Parisian life. From the fresh veggie and fruit stands to the cheese shops and cafes. Particularly fun is Le Dream Cafe with its friendly servers and its cheap beers at 3.90 € a pint at happy hour prices. As Elaine Sciolino writes in her book The Only Street in Paris, "Life on the Rue des Martyrs, life on this street is like a village."

### WHY DO YOU NEED TO VISIT?

If you walk up the street from Notre Dame de Lorette, you will eventually come upon the picturesque view of Sacré Cœur in the background.

## RUE MOUFFETARD - 5TH ARR.

 Located in the 5th arr., this eclectic cobblestone street is lined with restaurants serving up international cuisine, bars and boutiques, as well as local green grocers and boulangeries. You can truly find everything on this street without leaving the neighborhood. Rue Moufftard, like the Rue des Martyrs, has a very village-esc feel about it. One of the best coffee shops, Dose, as well as a great craft beer bar, Brewberry, are located off the street. The area is also a great late-night hangout where you'll find take-out of anything from crepes to Greek gyros to Lebanese.

### WHY DO YOU NEED TO VISIT?

It's so much fun to walk up and down this street— there's so much to see and take in. If you don't visit, you're really missing out. Take a stroll around the Place de la Contrescarpe for an ideal terrace to hang out on while drinking a beer.

## RUE DES ROSIERS - 4TH ARR.

 This cobblestone lined street perfectly located in the heart of the Marais is rustic and picturesque, with ivy overgrown on the sides of buildings and tiny sidewalks compelling pedestrians to take to the street itself. Jewish shops and food stores make up a large portion of the window shops as you are in the center of the Jewish quarter.

### WHY DO YOU NEED TO VISIT?

It's a small yet charming street, so visit for the experience and to taste the best falafels in Europe. L'As de Fallafel is self-proclaimed to be the Ace of Spades of falafels, but you really can't go wrong with any vendors cooking up street food here.

## RUE LEPIC - 18TH ARR.

 This ancient and historical road in Montmartre is packed full of history and historical figures who lived here throughout time. Besides featuring the famous cafe, Les Deux Moulins, where Audrey Tautou's character worked at in the film **Amélie**, this important street was home to some of France's top figures from the novelist Louis-Ferdinand Céline, the painter Van Gogh, to the carmaker Louis Renault.

### WHY DO YOU NEED TO VISIT?

In addition to the historical importance, this little street is charming as can be and full of life thanks to the local French vendors selling anything under the sun. It's a one-stop-shop as you can get anything you need for a dinner at home.

## RUE MONTORGUEIL - 1ST & 2ND ARR.

 Located in the Sentier neighborhood in the heart of Paris, Rue Montorgeuil is a fun and lively place to spend a day walking. Meet friends for a drink or meal at one of the many cafe terraces and brasseries, or simply do some shopping at the local boutiques. The street houses some well-known shops for sweets and desserts like À la Mère de Famille, the specialty chocolate shop, and Fou de Pâtisserie, cake shop.

### WHY DO YOU NEED TO VISIT?

It's the 'it' place to be on the weekend for socializing while you do your shopping. It's home to the oldest pâtisserie shop in Paris, Stohrer, where you must try its delectable Rum baba.

## RUE DES THERMOPYLES - 14TH ARR.

 If you can't get away for the weekend to a little village in Provence, the next best thing is to come to la Rue des Thermopyles. With its colored buildings and vibrant greenery, it has all of the charm with none of the travel! You may even recognize it from Instagram as it's pretty popular.

### WHY DO YOU NEED TO VISIT?

This quite, residential street is a pleasant discovery and escape in the bustle of the city. A walk down this street will transport you to a lush secret garden that feels miles away from the capital.

## RUE CRÉMIEUX - 12TH ARR.

 Listed as one of the most Instagrammable spots in Paris by every blogger, Rue Crémieux calls your attention because it is the most colorful street in the city. Set apart from the usual beige color palette of the Haussmannien architecture, the buildings on Rue Crémieux will magically transport you to Havana with its neon and vibrant hued homes.

### WHY DO YOU NEED TO VISIT?

This ultra-cute street with its buildings colored pinks, yellows, greens, and bright blue tones is a rare gem in the city. Plus, you're bound to find this street listed on every Parisian blogger's most Instagrammable spots.

## RUE DE L'ABREUVOIR - 18TH ARR.

 The cute street in Montmartre got its name in the late 19th century when it was considered as the "route to the drinking trough" (**abreuvoir**). Most recently, it was seen in **Emily in Paris** when she uses it to promote a client's product.

## WHY DO YOU NEED TO VISIT?

The curving street, with Sacré Cœur in the backdrop and two cobblestone sidewalks on either end of the road, makes this street very Instagrammable and appealing for a photo op. Do pass by or visit the equally coveted La Maison Rose, the picturesque pink house turned cafe that also sits on this street at 2 Rue de l'Abreuvoir.

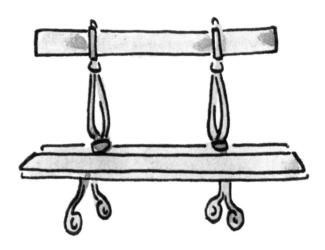

# Other lesser-known streets to inspire you:

 **LA COUR DAMOYE**
12 Place de la Bastille, or 12 Rue Daval, 75011 Paris

If you feel like a quick trip to a tiny French village but don't have time to get out of the city, try La Cour Damoye. This little cobbled street is pedestrian only and will make you feel like you're somewhere else entirely; when you walk down, you'll ask yourself if you haven't accidentally stepped into a luscious evergreen garden courtyard.

 **PASSAGE DES SOUPIRS**
49 Rue de la Chine, 75020 Paris

You'll find this street in the 20th arrondissement, near Place Gambetta. Walk up the steps and you'll be transported into the countryside, right in the middle of Paris! Perfect for a bit of peace and quiet.

## L'ALLÉE DES BROUILLARDS

Place Dalida
or Rue Simon
Dereure,
75018 Paris

Literally called the Alley of Mist, this pedestrian street in Montmartre has inspired many artists in its time. Jean-Pierre Aumont lived here; Auguste Renoir and Amedeo Clemente Modigliani painted here; Claude Nougaro wrote a book about it (**9, allée des Brouillards**). Whether you're an artist or not, this is a place to get inspired!

## COUR DU BEL-AIR

56 Rue du Faubourg
Saint-Antoine,
75012 Paris

This picturesque cobbled street is a little gem right in the middle of Paris. Picture courtyards of three-story buildings covered in vines, book shops and art galleries. As you enter the first courtyard, you will see that the pavement is wider in front of the green-fronted shop. Legend has it that this pavement was used as a gaming table by the Black Musketeers, whose barracks were next door. For a long time, the ancient wooden steps were referred to as the "Musketeers' staircase".

## LE SQUARE DES PEUPLIERS

68-72 de la Rue du Moulin-des-Prés, 75013 Paris

Don't be fooled by the name, Le Square des Peupliers is not, in fact, a square but a street. Located in the 13th arrondissement, this secret passage is full of different colors and flowers. You won't be disappointed!

## SQUARE DE MONTSOURIS

1 Square de Montsouris or 53 Avenue Reille, 75014 Paris

This is a rare street in Paris, near the Parc Montsouris, where you'll find individual houses overflowing with lavish vegetation that are all uniquely beautiful. It's a magical street that will remind you of summers in Provence. If you visit, do so discreetly as this is a private street.

## HONORABLE MENTIONS:

Rue Daguerre
(bustling, good nightlife)

Rue de Lappe
(lively, good nightlife)

Rue Cherche Midi
(good restaurants/bustling)

Rue des Francs Bourgeois
(shopping)

Rue Paul de Kock / Rue Émile Desvaux
(picturesque and village-like)

Passage Sigaud
(village-like street with individual maisonettes)

# The Most Instagrammable Spots in Paris

So you've made it to the sparkling city of light and how can you **not** whip out your phone for a few pics for **the Gram** against the stunning backgrounds that the city presents? Don't worry, you'll get those alluring Eiffel Tower shots and many more featuring the hundreds of monuments sprinkled throughout Paris. But, what I want to offer up in this list is a few of those famous Instragram-worthy shots as well as a few under-the-radar locales for you to add to your Instagram profile to make even your most well-traveled friends jealous!

Strike a pose and snap away with this list of the most Instagarm-worthy spots curated especially for you!

## FOR COVETED EIFFEL TOWER PICS

 Go to Trocadero

If you don't have a picture next to the Eiffel Tower, were you even in Paris? If you want one of the best views, Trocadero is a gorgeous hot spot for one of the best horizons of the city and the Iron Lady (aka the Eiffel Tower).

 Head over to Avenue de Camoens

Come here for a romantic photo where you'll feel like you're the only one in Paris. And if you're traveling alone, the Eiffel Tower will pose as your plus one!

 Stroll by Rue de l'Université (228 Rue de L'Université)

Get an up close and personal ET shot here. This is a magical spot that will make you feel like you live in an apartment next to the Eiffel Tower, if only for a few minutes. A guy or gal can dream, right?

## FOR A SURREALIST DREAM

 Wander over to Colonnes de Buren/Les Deux Plateaux

This square that's adjacent to the Jardin du Palais Royal is unexpected and a fun spot for a quick photo op. Hop onto a pillar and pose, standing, sitting or leaning - no matter how, your creative juices are bound to come up with a quirky way to photograph against this exceptional background.

 Take a ride to Arts et Métiers Metro (underground metro on line 11)

For a one-of-a-kind backdrop in which to photograph your beautiful face, jump on line 11 from Châtelet in the direction Mairie de Lilas, but get off at the Arts et Métiers stop. To your wonder you'll find a futuristic looking metro station decked out in steampunk style walls.

 Head to Bir Hakeim Bridge

The film **Inception** may have made this bridge hyper-famous, but you can turn your next photos or videos into a masterpiece when you shoot your content from the underbelly of the bridge. Or go for a more conventional POV and shoot this bridge from the side showcasing the aerial metro (line 6) passing by for a fun picture of the city.

## IN THE GARDEN

 Take a stroll through the Jardin des Tuileries

I could list all of the gorgeous parks and gardens on here, but my **top** choice for the most picturesque views are in the Jardin des Tuileries. From the fountains to the many statues you can pose next to to the rows of beautifully manicured chestnut trees, you're sure to capture a few pics for the Gram in this **jardin**.

Splurge at the Plaza Athénée Hotel Courtyard

A lunch at La Cour Jardin may be a dream of yours, so why not turn this heavenly garden escape into a mini-photo shoot? Make a reservation here ahead of time and dress to the nines because the lush garden courtyard will be sure content for your next post. That is priceless bliss!

## MONTMARTRE & PIGALLE

 Go Behind Sacré Coeur (30 Rue du Chevalier de la Barre)

For a fresh take on the Sacré Cœur Basilica, why not frame it from behind in your selfie? Find one of the most photogenic spots at 30 Rue du Chevalier de la Barre— enchanting cobblestone steps and sidewalks included.

 Walk over to 7 Rue de l'Abreuvoir

This spot was already on the map before **Emily in Paris** had a say. You're gonna love the winding cobblestone street, overgrown vines, the ever charming lamp posts as well as the Sacré Cœur Basilica in the distance for your next IG post. As a bonus, walk down the street one minute for a few shots against the famous La Maison Rose.

 Dine at Pink Mamma

Are pink backgrounds your thing? You're not going to want to miss a visit to Pink Mamma! The multi-story building's facade is gleaming with bright pink tiles that shout out "photo shoot!" But don't stop there, definitely eat here for a meal whether lunch or dinner. The Italian food is fresh, colorful, and delicious. And trust me, there will be plenty more photo ops on the inside from its bohemian, sky-glass staircase abounding in photogenic knick-knacks to the glamorous bars to the vibrant dishes.

## FOR SOME RITZY AND GLAM CONTENT

 Walk the Avenue des Champs-Élysées

Everyone who visits Paris, no matter if you're a fashionista or not, must stroll down this world famous avenue, if only once. Cross the street at any of its abundant cross walks (when it's safe to do so) and pause for a quick photo with the beautiful Arc de Triomphe making an appearance in the background.

 Jaunt over to Avenue Montaigne

With a myriad of beautiful designer shop windows at your disposal how can you resist taking a stroll on the Avenue Montaigne for intricately designed window displays? Snap some Insta-worthy pics for your feed here or against the backdrop of the stunning window displays at the Plaza Athénée featured on this street.

 Pay a Visit to the Opéra Garnier

How can I talk about glam and glitz without mentioning the elegant Opéra Garnier? For an optimal POV, get in front of the metro which is a gateway to this iconic landmark. And if you're inspired, get tickets to take a tour of the Opéra from inside for even more Instagram-worthy content!

## MAKE THE SEINE YOUR SCENE

 Walk over the Alexandre III Bridge

Whether this is Paris' most famous bridge is arguable, but what is for sure is that it's a gorgeous bridge. From its luminous rows of lampposts to its gold embellished statues it could be the backdrop to your next photo. This is a great spot to play around with angles, and focus, so have fun with your camera when you go.

Stroll along the Quai de Montebello (Riverbanks of the Seine in front of Notre Dame)

The riverbanks along the Seine River are already photogenic just by existing, but why not insert Notre Dame into your photos from its side along the lower decks of the riverbanks? For an intimate setting that will make you feel like a local, find the staircase that leads to the lower deck on the crossroads of Place du Petit Pont and Quai de Montebello.

 Go Behind Notre Dame de Paris

To get an unpredictable angle of Notre Dame, why not try photographing it from behind at the Square Jean XXIII? This viewpoint accentuates the gothic arches giving you a fresh take on Notre Dame and a fun addition to your IG feed. Heck, you may even want to create a reels featuring the Dame with French music playing in the background.

## UP ON HIGH

 Journey up to the Printemps Rooftop

Weather permitting, you can steal gorgeous Insta-worthy shots of Paris including the the Opéra Garnier, Madeline Church, and the Eiffel Tower in the distance. Lounge atop Perruche, Printemp's latests rooftop bar and restaurant with a beautiful outpost in the city. The summer vibes conveyed by the lush rooftop garden, colorful patio furniture, and the fresh cocktails will transport you to the south of France.

 Dine at Les Ombres

For one of the most breathtaking views of the Iron Lady, pay a visit to Les Ombres restaurant and terrace, which is atop the Quai Branly Museum. Here you'll capture a stunning view of the city and a glimpse of the Eiffel Tower — I highly recommend you go for a sunset dinner to seize that golden hour lighting.

## CUTEST STREETS & PARISIAN PASSAGES

 Wander through the Galerie Vivienne

Make this elegant covered passage your next backdrop for your Instagram stories, reels, or posts. Its stunning interior arches, sky-lit window roof, and dazzling mosaic tiles by the same artists who did the Opéra Garnier are features that merit the next selfie.

 Walk through the Passage du Grand Cerf

This luminous passage in the heart of Paris will capture your best light as you pose in this long corridor featuring a glass roof and specialty boutique shops with unique storefronts. Try posing in front of the myriad of a quirky storefront signs for a unique snapshot of daily Parisian life.

 Walk to Rue Crémieux

Whether you're an amateur or expert photographer, you'll love a pass at photographing the most vibrant street in Paris. Bursting with color, Rue Crémieux is the most colourful street in the city and if you're lucky, you may even get a cameo of one of the many neighborly cats that roam about.

 Visit Rue des Rosiers

Nothing is more charming and photogenic than a cobblestoned street overgrown with lavish greenery on old buildings. On the Rue des Rosiers, with its one-of-a-kind store fronts, you'll have plenty of photo opportunities including the bright yellow and green storefront of L'As du Fallafel, the world-famous falafel restaurant.

 Strike a pose on Rue de Birague & Place des Vosges

Last but not least, if you want to capture the sensational Parisian architecture, you must visit the Rue de Birague for a romantic background. Nestled through the archways you'll find the beautiful Place des Vosges with its dreamy garden and fountains.

You can of course visit all of these places solo and on foot, and I highly recommend that you do, but if you dream of someone curating a personalized photoshoot, I have just the thing— a perfect, personally curated half-day photoshoot of your dreams!

Imagine you're picked up at your accommodation in Paris by a private chauffeur in a luxury Mercedes van accompanied by your very own photographer who takes you around these Instagrammable spots while sipping champagne and snacking on macarons. If you're saying "Sign me up!" then let's chat[8]! I can coordinate all the details for your next Paris photo shoot for you and your girlfriends or your soulmate for those wedding or engagement photos.

---

[8]  www.celineconcierge.com/contact-us/

# Paris Passages

Few people know this, but under France's second empire there were roughly one hundred and fifty passages and arcades in Paris. Nowadays, only around thirty of them remain, but among them are some of the most original places to visit in the French capital. From Paris' renowned covered walkways, featuring the greatest names in fashion and fine dining, to little-known roads and **ruelles** with an other-worldly charm, you are sure to find your **bonheur** in one of these secret passages.

These are just some of my favorite passages for you to enjoy, but there are also many other streets (as seen in the previous two chapters) that provide a breath of fresh air in Paris, as well as the backdrop for your next Instagram photo!

## PASSAGE DES PANORAMAS/PASSAGE JOUFFROY/ PASSAGE VERDEAU (leading off one another)

 Let us begin where it all began, at the Passage des Panoramas. Built in 1799, and later classified as a historical monument in 1974, this is Paris' oldest passage and one of the first covered shopping arcades in Europe. It was built by an American ship owner and originally housed his paintings of panoramas of famous places, which, as you can guess, is where it got its name. The panoramas were a huge success, drawing in many Parisians who also enjoyed being able to shop in one of the sixty original boutiques without having to face the muddy Paris streets. Its exceptional location kept it a local favorite for many years to come, especially once the Théâtre des Variétés opened up next door in 1807.

Even now that the panoramas are gone, you can still get away from the hustle and bustle of the outside streets and experience the original charm of this passage by visiting one of its shops or eateries. It's particularly well-known to stamp collectors and is also an excellent place to pick up a vintage Paris postcard as a souvenir.

**Location**: 11 Boulevard Montmartre, 75002 Paris

**Metro**: Grands Boulevards

**Opening times**: Open every day of the year, 6 AM to Midnight

## GALERIE VIVIENNE

 The Galerie Vivienne is another of Paris' most notorious passages. It was built in 1823 by the architect François-Jacques Delannoy upon the request of Maître Marchoux. In fact, it was originally called Galerie Marchoux until its inauguration in 1826 when it was renamed Galerie Vivienne due to its location on Rue Vivienne. Maître Marchoux wanted to build the most beautiful covered arcade in Paris, and he pretty much succeeded! It truly is a sight to see and represents the finest of Parisian luxury, including a mosaic by Giandomenico Facchina (the same guy who did Opéra Garnier) that was added in 1880.

It was the arcade's location that allowed it to really gain popularity in the 19th century. It joined the Palais Royal arcades that were a notorious spot for parties, gambling and prostitution. New laws regulating these activities and the closing of the Palais Royal casinos meant that the passage saw some decline, which was only worsened by the opening of the large fashion houses on the Champs-Élysées and Madeleine. Nevertheless, business picked up again from around 1960 as newer fashion labels such as Jean-Paul Gaultier moved in, and the Paris City Hall helped restore the passage to its former glory in 2016. If you like traditional French opulence, it is definitely worth a visit!

**Location**: 4 Rue des Petits-Champs, 75002 Paris

**Metro**: Pyramides, Bourse, Palais-Royal - Musée du Louvre

**Opening times**: 8:30 AM-8:30 PM

## GALERIE COLBERT

 Galerie Colbert was built as a rival to Galerie Vivienne in 1823. Just as spectacular as its neighbor, the vast rotunda featured a glass dome at the center of which was a magnificent bronze

candelabra topped with seven gas-lit crystal globes, earning it the name "the light-up coconut tree" (**cocotier lumineux**). Unfortunately, the arcade fell into disarray and closed in 1975, only to be opened again in 1986 after it was purchased by the National Library.

Today, instead of high-end shops, it contains the National Institute of Art History (INHA) and the National Heritage Institute (INP). Completely restored, it is back to its previous glory, aside from the coconut tree, which has been replaced by a statue of Eurydice. It also houses the cafe Le Grand Colbert, which, decorated in Art Nouveau style, is a registered historical monument that you will surely recognize as it is often used in movies.

**Location**: 4 Rue Vivienne - 75002 Paris

**Metro**: Opéra, Grands Boulevards

**Opening times**: All day, every day

## PASSAGE BRADY

 Now for something a little different: Passage Brady. This little passage, built in 1828 is divided into two sections by Boulevard de Strasbourg and is open on one side and covered by a glass roof on the other. It is locally known as **Little India** and it doesn't take long to see why! Filled with Indo-Pakistani, Mauritian and Reunionese shops, you can get all kinds of exotic products here in this bazaar-style place. Culinary specialties, incense, spices, beauty products, traditional medicine and herbs, clothing... it's all here. And the best thing is, they won't break the bank as the prices are super cheap!

One of the most famous shops here is the Super Market Bazaar Velan. A fixture since 1973, this little boutique sells a range of Indian food products, including papadums, chutneys, spicy peppers, manioc, but in particular, spices of all kinds. Some say it has the biggest choice of Indian products in Paris. And speaking of food, there is nowhere better than here to eat a delicious traditional meal for reasonable prices.

**Location**: 46 Rue du Faubourg Saint-Denis, 75010 Paris

**Metro**: Château d'Eau, Strasbourg Saint-Denis

**Opening times**: Monday to Saturday 9:30 AM - 11:30 PM; Sunday 6 PM - 11:30 PM

## GALERIE VÉRO-DODAT

 Once a private road, the Galerie Véro-Dodat was opened to the public in 1826. It was constructed by two butchers by the name of Véro and Dodat **(quelle surprise !)**, who purchased the existing private house and tore it down to make way for their own residence and the covered arcade you see today. Built in the neoclassical style, this passage is a mix of dark wood, glass windows, copper ornaments, mirrors, columns and its famous black and white marble floor. The ceiling is relatively low and features paintings of landscapes and ancient goddesses. It was also one of the first places in Paris to have gas lighting installed.

Part of this arcade's success comes from the Lafitte et Gaillard transport company that was located opposite its entrance. At the time, this was one of the biggest travel companies in Paris, rivaling even the Royal transport company, which made this area one of the main places where residents left the capital. Travelers leaving Paris would wander around the passage while waiting for their coaches, keeping these streets alive at all hours of the day.

**Location**: 19 Rue Jean-Jacques Rousseau, 75001 Paris

**Metro**: Louvre - Rivoli, Châtelet-Les Halles

**Opening times**: Monday to Saturday from 7 AM to 10 PM.

# BEAUPASSAGE

This open-air passage and contemporary courtyard is a secluded sanctuary packed with cafes and gastronomical restaurants, art installations, and terrace space excellent for hanging out on a warm, sunny day. To give you a little bit of history on the newly renovated passage which opened in August of 2018, it used to be an old Renault Garage, a far cry from the gastronomical hot spot it is today.

The discrete passage that can easily be missed if you aren't looking for it, connects the Boulevard Raspail, Rue de Grenelle, and Rue du Bac. On your next visit to Paris, definitely get lost here. Stop by the coffee roaster and coffee bar %Arabica for a specialty coffee— they have a delicious flat white or if you want to change it up go for the Matcha Latte.

For lunch, I recommend the street seafood restaurant Mersea, and for dinner, the Peruvian-inspired restaruant Coya, on the Rue du Bac end of the passage. For a sweet treat, you won't want to miss the gourmet lounge Pierre Hermé, any sweet-tooth's dream come true. Finally, for the wine-lovers, you can step into the perfect setting: Allénothèque wine cave and restaurant. The place mixes the French savoir faire between cuisine, **le vin**, and the art of oenology, or the study of wine.

The accessibility of the Beaupassage and the blend of food, art, and the French culture make it a must-visit— that and the fact that you won't regret stumbling upon this alcove when you have time to spare getting lost.

**Location**:          53-57 Rue de Grenelle, 83-85 Rue du Bac, 14 Boulevard Raspail, 75007 Paris

**Metro**:             Rue du Bac, Sèvres Babylone

**Opening times**:     Every day, 7 AM to Midnight

## COUR DU COMMERCE SAINT-ANDRÉ

No list of Paris' passages would be complete without the Cour du Commerce Saint-André. Exquisitely picturesque, this passage was built along the 12th century walls that delimited the city at the time of King Philippe Auguste. Although the construction of the boulevard Saint-Germain cut this passage short by some 40 m, it is nevertheless home to a whole bunch of historical and cultural gems.

First up, you can see the remains of one of the wall's towers in the restaurant Un Dimanche à Paris, located at number 4. But that's not the only interesting restaurant on this street. Here, you will also find Le Procope, the oldest restaurant in Paris, dating back to 1686. Many of Paris' greatest minds met here, including Voltaire, Rousseau, Diderot, and Montesquieu. During the French revolution, Procope became the unofficial headquarters of Danton, Marat, and Robespierre. Danton even lived on this street at number twenty, but his apartment was destroyed by the building of boulevard Saint-Germain. Today, a statue has been erected in his honor where he was arrested before his death.

This isn't the passage's only tie to the revolution. Above the restaurant, you will see a large bell that was rung each time a new edition of Marat's political newspaper, **L'ami du Peuple**, came out, as he had set up his printing press on this street. That's not all, in 1792 a new neighbor moved in and opened Schmidt's carpenters. It was here that Joseph Ignace Guillotin put the finishing touches on his new invention: the guillotine!

The passage's inhabitants witnessed the first tests of this deadly machine, thankfully only on bales of hay and the odd sheep! It was later moved before it was used on anything more human.

If French history is your thing, make sure to check out Cour du Commerce Saint-André!

**Location**:     75006 Paris

**Metro**:     Odéon, Saint-Germain-des-Prés

**Opening times**:  All day, every day

## PASSAGE DU GRAND CERF

Here is a passage that you have probably seen in photos, the Passage du Grand Cerf, literally, the Great Stag Passage. You might wonder where it got its name, as many people have! The passage was built in 1825 on an old square that was home to a hotel by the name of **Le Grand Cerf**. So now you know!

The animal theme continues inside, and you will see various wooden animals on the shop fronts. What stands out the most, however, is the 12-meter-high glass roof, which makes the Passage du Grand Cerf the highest covered passage in Paris. In fact, its partly metal structure allowed them to build two levels of glass façades and apartments on the third floor.

This passage was never meant to house luxury brands but was always destined to showcase artisanal work and production methods. Unfortunately, the popularity of other passages and the lack of upkeep in the 1900s led to the Passage du Grand Cerf becoming unpopular and changing owners several times. It even closed for a while when its famous roof became unstable. Luckily, it was saved in 1985 by new investors that restored it to its former glory. Today, you can find a plethora of different shops there, selling everything from decorations, design, fashion, fabric, soap, perfume, and jewelry. It is also the only passage in Paris that accepts Bitcoin as a payment method and is known now as "Bitcoin Boulevard"!

**Location**:     75002 Paris

**Metro**:     Etienne Marcel, Arts et Métiers

**Opening times**:  All day, every day

## PASSAGE DE L'ANCRE

 Saving one of my favorite places for last, I just had to tell you about the Passage de l'Ancre. This one really is a secret to all but the most in-the-know of Paris' visitors. Even most residents have never heard of it! As you step through the blue door, you enter a world within a world: it's like finding a secret garden right in the center of Paris. The passage itself is short and sweet, but it is more than worthy of a photo shoot among the vines, potted trees, and plants. This place manages to find the right balance between green and leafy, bright and colorful, and vibrant and peaceful.

And in case you are wondering why it's called the Passage de l'Ancre (Anchor), it's because it used to be home to an inn which had an anchor on its sign. Sadly, this area was predominantly Jewish and was ransacked during the Vel d'Hiv raid of the Second World War in 1942. Most of its inhabitants were deported and the area closed for a long time. It was reopened again, however, in 1998, and has truly regained its splendor!

**Location:**        223 Rue Saint-Martin, 75003 Paris

**Metro:**        Etienne Marcel, Arts et Métiers

**Opening times:**  All day, every day

# Secret, Underground Paris Spots & Adventures

It's incredible what a little off-roading will do. Or, in some cases, a little off-cobblestoning. Some of the most trendy parts of Paris are the spots that weren't too beautiful until someone came along and saw its potential. Sometimes, it's taking something old and making it fashionable again, or turning it into something magical. Either way, there is more to discover in Paris than just what's in the tour guides, and here is a list for where to start.

## LA PETITE CEINTURE DE PARIS

 If you're down for a clandestine adventure that even many Parisians aren't aware of, this is for you. Finding an opening to this Little Belt railway is part of the experience, the other is going down and not getting caught sneaking onto the forbidden parts.

La Petite Ceinture is an abandoned railroad line, 32 kilometers in length (approx. 20 miles), that was built in 1862 encircling Paris' Boulevards des Maréchaux, but it closed in 1934 with the arrival of the Parisian metro. It used to connect the main train stations within Paris, but today is home to 70 unique animal species and 200 species of plants. Now, it sits below Paris, overgrown with wildlife, inviting the most daring to adventure down.

Over the years, the City of Paris has opened up the abandoned railway to the public. You can find different access points below, or venture to discover a secret **ouverture**.

- 16th arr. between the Porte d'Auteuil and the Gare de la Muette (accessible to physically disabled people, who possess an adapted wheelchair for the terrain)
- 12th arr., with a 200-metre-long nature trail and a shared garden, is accessible from 21 Rue Rottembourg
- Opened in 2013, the railway in the 15th arrondissement opened to the public between the Place Balard and 99 Rue Olivier de Serres
- Access opened up two years later in the 13th arr. at 60 Rue Damesme and runs from the Charles Trenet garden to the Moulin de la Pointe garden
- In the 20th arr. the access at 11 Rue de la Mare is opened to the public
- The latest section was added in June 2020 in the 19th arr. It's a 230 meter long walk between Rue de Thionville and 2 bis Rue de l'Ourcq

## L'ENTRE POTES

 Hidden below, in the basement of this French dive bar, you can enjoy an **apéro** in a deserted metro station. The remaining relics of what used to be the Paris metro system are the *mise-en-scène* of L'Entre Potes' pub and local hangout. Impress your friends on an evening out by stopping in at this bar for cheap drinks and a rare backdrop.

## LE VILLAGE SAINT PAUL

 Through the secret passageways leading from either Rue Saint Paul or the back way Rue des Jardins Saint Paul, you will find the Village Saint Paul. It's home to antique shops, cafes, and art galleries. The square is true to its name as a village within the city as its charming cobblestones and overgrown vines invite you in for a Saturday afternoon of getting lost. You're a true Parisian if you know about this village that was recently renovated in 2020, breathing new life into the hidden square.

## ARÈNES DE LUTÈCES

 This is a surprising spot to find as you exit out of the Metro Place Monge (exit, or **sortie**, that leads to Rue Navarre). This ancient Roman amphitheater reminds you of a once prominent Roman Empire. This park in the center of the Latin Quarter is a hidden refuge for those wanting to take a stroll, read a book, or do some outdoor sports. It's a great spot to throw a frisbee or just sit back and take in the history of the place.

## LES ÉGOUTS DE PARIS (OR PARIS SEWER MUSEUM)

 This adventure is not one for the faint of heart. The Sewer Museum explores just that, **les égouts**, or bowels of the city. See Paris from the inside out and experience firsthand the extravagant tunnel system and underground canals that were put in place in the later half of the 19th Century. This one-of-a-kind tour will leave you seeing Paris and your toilet with a new appreciation.

## SECRET PHANTOM OF THE OPERA TOUR

 For a truly mystical experience, you'll want to book a secluded after-hours guided visit at the Palais Garnier. Explore the history and legend of the Phantom of the Opera. You'll be immersed in the grandeur of the Great Hall, decorated staircases, Fountain of Pythia, Grand Foyer, and finally the Lodge Number 5, home to the infamous Phantom of the Opera himself.

## LES ESPACES D'ABRAXAS & ARÈNES DE PICASSO

 These dystopian-style apartments inspired by Brutalist architecture is the setting of some famous films like **Brazil** and the **Hunger Games**. I helped film a music video here back in 2014 that you can check out here. For an exceptional experience that will take you to into the future, you won't want to miss out on this trip that's only 15 minutes away from Paris. You can easily hop on the RER inter cities railway line A to the Noisy-Le-Grand stop.

## SECRET PASSAGES TOUR OF VERSAILLES

 If you want to sneak into the secret bed chambres of French royalty of antiquity, this private tour is for you. I have a secret Versailles confidant who will invite you to accompany him through the intimate spaces and private apartments of Louis XIV and Louis XV. My friend is one of only a handful of experts who has exclusive access with the **Château** for this kind of restricted access. This is an experience you won't find anywhere online, but with a true Paris insider such as **moi-même** !

## SUMMER SAILING ON THE SEINE

 Want to escape the summer heat and take a boat cruise on the Seine? Why not sail through the heart of Paris on a luxury boat!? Wine and dine on a yacht-style boat as the city glistens before you and your every needs are catered to in full comfort and tranquility. Or, if you prefer an ultra-private experience, you can book a small luxury collection boat while you ride along to celebrate a milestone or simply enjoy an afternoon ride with that special someone. If you're no stranger to the luxury lifestyle, you will love this lavish experience aboard the Parisian vessel of your choice.

To book any of these off-the-radar experiences, contact me[9] directly for your next visit. I can also propose a plethora of secret and undisclosed tours and visits that are not published online nor in tour guides you'll find on the shelves. I would be thrilled to curate a personalized tour for you and your party, whether you're celebrating a special occasion or have an unusual request, nothing is ever too big an ask for me and my team at Céline Concierge!

9  www.celineconcierge.com/contact-us/

# Live Like a Local:
# The Best Things the Locals Do

Experience an authentic Paris (like the locals do)... Here are my top 10 ways to experience Paris like a local if you want to live, feel, and breathe like a true Parisian. Whether you're coming to the city with your soulmate, looking to spark up a French romance, or simply looking to take in all that the city has to offer, these ideas will undoubtedly help you appreciate an authentic Paris.

Once you get past the fame of the Eiffel Tower, the history of the Louvre, and the glam of the Champs-Élysées, you're bound to want to settle down into the iconic Parisian lifestyle: partake in picnics with wine and baguettes, read a novel on a café terrace, take leisurely walks through farmer's markets, etc.

The culture, lifestyle, and routine become the heartbeat of the Parisian cliché... and for good reason! Paris is a fascinating place. There is something magical about the cobblestone streets that truly transform your perspective into **la vie en rose**– trust me, I walk these streets every day. But you have to remember that there are many more gifts this city has to offer than just macarons, baguettes, and berets. Live the charm of the city by experiencing a different, more personal, Paris through these unforgettable adventures.

## Picnic à la Parisienne on the Canal Saint Martin

Upgrade your local **savoir faire** from the classic Seine scene and head north to the edgy Canal Saint Martin. Grab your baguette, wine, and favorite French cheeses and snag a spot along the edge of this vibrant canal.

This captivating, urban space is a colorful glimpse into contemporary Paris, and a neighborhood favorite. Leading south from La Villette and running primarily along the hip 10th and 11th arrondissements, the Canal Saint Martin is a favorite hangout spot for graffiti artists and friends looking for a fun way to catch up over store-bought wine and snacks, and a cigarette (or two, or three...). Therefore, it's the perfect backdrop to an authentic Parisian experience for you!

If you want to settle into green grass at a park for your picnic, head over to the recommended Parks and Jardins chapter.

## Open-Air Cinema at La Villette

To enjoy a real local experience of Paris during l'été, sit outside watching a film at La Villette (19th arr.) during its Cinéma en Plein Air, or open-air cinema evenings. As the cinema HQ of Europe, it's no wonder Paris offers free entrance to this event to support and appreciate the arts.

Throughout the course of the summer, this program boasts 25-30 curated films, showing from mid-July to mid-August . Films go on at sundown. Snacks and drinks (alcoholic or non-alcoholic) are authorized on the lawn and lounge chairs are available for hire for 7€. So, bring your own blankets and cuddle with your lover as you watch the stars under the stars.

 TIP:

My personal tip is to arrive early to stake out your ideal spot around 7 PM when the gates open to access the lawn.

 ## Sitting on a Terrace enjoying an Apéro

Part of what makes the French the "French" (and more specifically the Parisians "Parisians"), is that their culture encourages sitting and talking for long hours over an **apéritif**, or **apéro**, for short. But what is it, you ask? This tradition joins drinks and friends, usually combined with a small snack like peanuts, chips, or olives to essentially whet the appetite before the evening's dinner.

Take a seat at any terrace in Paris and order a Kir (white wine with a splash of black currant syrup) or a Ricard (an alcoholic drink made from anise) — two of the most traditional drinks of **apéro**. Voila! You have essentially partaken in the French tradition of the **apéritif**. But don't stop there! You can follow with any kind of drink, alcoholic or not, from 5 PM onward and sit contemplating **la raison d'être**.

## Do as the locals do & head to an Open-Air Market

You won't only feel like a local in Paris, but you will get to know the locals best by strolling through one of the myriads of open-air markets. Paris hosts over 80 local open-air markets all through the week, dispersed throughout the city. My favorites are the oldest covered market, Marché des Enfants Rouge and the open-late Marché Anvers (Fridays 3 PM-8:30 PM).

## Enjoy a free museum or go to the museums outside of peak times

For a retreat in the midst of the city and a true experience of Paris like a local, stop by one of my favorite museums. The Musée de la Vie Romantique is a free museum in the 9th arr. that's all about art from the romantic period. This hidden treasure is nestled in the courtyard of two buildings through an alleyway. The museum is actually in a little house; it's the old atelier/living quarters of the late painter Ary Scheffer.

An alternative and my all-time favorite is the Musée de l'Orangerie located in the southwest corner of the Jardin des Tuileries. This short and sweet museum houses the renowned **Les Nymphéas** (Water Lilies Series) by Claude Monet.

**TIP:**

Most museums in Paris host free days or discount hours! Make sure to look them up before planning your trip... or reach out to me and save yourself the coordinating! For L'Orangerie, entrance is free 1 hour before closing time— plus you only need about an hour to see everything.

### Read a book or jog in Parc Monceau

How do the French always have so much to talk about over their **apéritifs**? They read! Escape to Parc Monceau for a relaxing retreat like a local. This ever-lovely little **jardin** park in the 8th arr. makes the perfect getaway spot for a picnic as well. It's populated with Parisian joggers, older folks perched on green benches for hours, and kids chasing the ducks and climbing on the playgrounds. This charming park will surely make you want to live as a full-time Parisian. Between the trees and weathered statues, the alluring walkways and tiny ponds, the options for you— the new Parisian— are endless!

### Ride around Paris on a bike like a native

Riding through the streets of Paris is probably my favorite way of getting around. Don't get me wrong, taxis are classic and effortless. And the Parisian metro is efficient (usually) and easy to navigate.

But riding around on a Vélib (city bike) or on your own bike is absolute bliss! You get to see Paris at your own pace and it's a typical experience of Paris as a local. You get to smell the bakeries as you pass by, see the light hit the baroque architecture, and feel the breeze on your skin as you cruise past chic looking Parisians walking their dog.

## Authentic French Food at a bistro or 5-star restaurant

This one might be too on-the-nose, but I always love to mention food when I can. My absolute favorite French brasserie is Le Comptoir de Relais, part of the Hôtel de Relais, in the 6th arr. I was brought here once by a Parisian man, and it was as close to classic French cuisine as it comes.

Anything that feels like grandma's cooking gets me— this place definitely has that taste and feel! Though not technically a Michelin-star restaurant, it's considered **une cuisine de qualité,** or quality cuisine, by Michelin, which is saying a lot. If you want my personal recommendation, try the **cuisse d'agneau au couscous,** or lamb leg over couscous.

For more French restaurant recommendations and reservations, contact me[10] to get you all set up for your next trip. I'm pretty good at getting my clients into those high-end 5-star Michelin restaurants.

## Flower Market at Île de la Cité or the Sunday Bird Market

The locals love dropping into this wonderland with its vivid array of flowers, bird houses, pots and plants. It's also a fantastic place to escape the crowds of Notre Dame. Right on the Île de la Cité, this little oasis of flowers will submerge you into Paris. This activity will make you just a little envious of the

---

[10]  www.celineconcierge.com/contact-us/

Parisians as you amble through the flower market wishing you had a Parisian apartment to fill with all those lovely flowers and plants.

Take a peaceful walk through the market whether or not you consider yourself a gardener. The market may even offer up a unique souvenir you can take back home for yourself or a loved one.

Although the flower market is closed on Sundays, another fun and original way to spend the afternoon is by visiting the Sunday Bird Market, which takes place in the same location.

## TIP:

If you're apartment hunting, let's talk. I partner with local luxury real estate companies and other property management companies that can help you find and manage your dream vacation home or second home in Paris. Are you making the move to Paris? I also provide various services to help make the transition a no-stress ordeal.

 **Coulée Verte (Promenade Plantée)**

Parisians love to take a stroll along the Coulée Verte, or their version of the New York City High Line. It's the urban sidewalk above the city that was once a railway line that runs along most of the 12th arr. Trees and greenery are scattered throughout this walkway, adding to the blissful experience.

Wandering along this 4.5 kilometers (2.80 mi) stretch of green walkway is a great way to spend the afternoon to gain inspiration for your next project, walk and chat with a friend, or just stretch your legs and feel like you aren't really in a big city.

Speaking of the city, along certain stretches of the promenade, you can get a spectacular rooftop view; you will undoubtedly be experiencing Paris like a local!

# Spas in Paris

Health and beauty are very much a part of a Parisian luxury lifestyle. You are sure to find a top-notch spa and wellness center in any 5-star hotel, but that's not to say that there aren't plenty of independent spas sprinkled throughout the city where you can go for care ranging from hair and nails to skin and health.

Pamper yourself with these recommended beauty salons and spas that are sure to take your breath away for an exceptionally relaxing time.

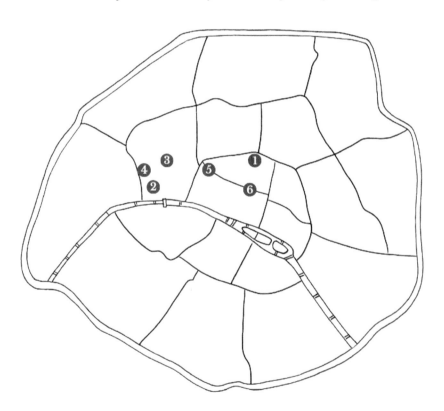

## 1 LES BAINS DU MARAIS

14 Rue Saint-Fiacre, 75002 Paris

01 48 87 20 20

This restaurant and spa in the trendy neighborhood of the Marais draws you in with its hammam (Turkish Bath), sauna, and its enticing array of well-being services. It has a hair salon, facial treatments, massages, and exfoliation treatments. The spa offers various membership plans or services **à la carte** to meet your personal needs. I highly recommend this spa for a girls day out where you can choose from their wide range of affordable services. This place is complete with everything— you can top off an appointment with brunch at the restaurant or drinks at the bar for an early evening **apéro**.

## 2 DIOR INSTITUTE AT THE PLAZA ATHÉNÉE

25 Av. Montaigne, 75008 Paris

01 53 67 65 35

The Dior Institute is everything you would expect a spa for a king or queen to look like— detailed care and insightful expertise! They embody opulence and serenity in their spa, providing various facial treatments, microabrasion treatments for revitalized and re-energized skin, as well as indulging body treatments for each client's needs and wishes. The institute prides itself on its sophisticated protocols exclusive to the industry standard.

###  LE BRISTOL PARIS
112 Rue du Faubourg Saint-Honoré, 75008 Paris

01 53 43 43 00

Hailing from Switzerland, La Prairie skincare collection leads the pack in luxury wellbeing at Le Bristol Hôtel. The airy and luminous spa sets the atmosphere of comfort and relaxation, overlooking the stunning French garden and private terrace. The menu extends its services of facials, body massages, and wellness rituals to include mother and child treatments as well as packages for a more versatile visit. You can stop in for a quick visit to the hand and nail beauty salon, get a wax or eyelash tinting, even enjoy a makeover at the hair salon. Or, you can get fit in the pool and fitness area offering personal coaches as you wish. The spa offers special packages for mothers to be, too. This spa and wellness center truly has something for everyone to enjoy!

### 4 FOUR SEASONS HOTEL GEORGE V, PARIS
31 Av. George V, 75008 Paris

01 49 52 70 00

The famous spa at the Four Seasons is nothing short of a five-star experience. Their luxury signature treatments offer an escape from the world into a deep relaxation and recharge. From the beautiful mosaic-tiled hamman and vitality pool, to its myriad of carefully curated treatments, the spa and wellness center knows how to present rest and relaxation to its patrons. Its services include restful massages, skin care, hair care, and treatments for men. If you're in need of revitalization, try their Japanese Kobido facelift. You'll leave this place feeling like a million bucks.

## 5 THE RITZ CLUB

17 Pl. Vendôme, 75001 Paris

01 43 16 30 60

This spa and salon, which serves the rich and famous, is an exclusive oasis perfectly providing an escape from the outside world. The facilities are open to hotel guests and club members, but a day pass is also available to outside patrons from 150 €. Its sublime indoor swimming pool, decorated with Greek and Roman style frescoes, is the perfect setting for a day of rest and relaxation at its finest. The health and fitness club include indoor squash courts, tanning beds, Jacuzzis, a Hammam, saunas, and various fitness rooms for when you're in the mood for yoga, Pilates, or group exercise classes.

## 6 SPA NUXE

32-34 Rue Montorgueil, 75001 Paris

01 42 36 65 65

Born from its French beauty brand of the same name, the Nuxe Spa is where luxury skincare and beauty merge for an ultimate spa experience. The spa is known most famously for its *Massage Sérénité*, a Korean and Shitstu duo massage technique and its exceptional facial *Soin Aromo-lacté aux 8 Laits Végétaux*, an extremely hydrating facial using eight types of plant milks.

The Montergueil location is its most spacious and prominent locale in Paris, inviting guests for a full day of R&R. Its other 4 locations in Paris welcome guests with a splendid array of hand and nail care, a myriad of massage and facial services, as well as beauty products to compliment the care.

# Best Day Trips from Paris

O ne of the reasons I love France is for its vast geographical diversity and landscape. You definitely want to get out of Paris if you have enough time to explore the surrounding regions. Exploration outside of the city allows visitors to delve deeper into the French culture, the language, and the locals.

Paris does not make up **La France** and when you're out of the capital, you will discover that France has much more to offer than just its Parisian streets, cafes, and monuments. You will soon uncover the extraordinary and diverse people and landscape whether you head north, south, east, or west.

Keep reading to discover the top places I recommend for simple day trips or weekend trips around the surrounding Paris area, known as Île-de-France. Further below, I briefly explain the top regions to explore by car or train.

Check out Transilien[11] for more information on how to explore Paris and the Île- de-France region via public transport.

## ① Château de Vincennes | Vincennes

**Distance:** 10 ki | 6 mi

14 mins by car from the center of Paris or 19 mins by train (RER) from Châtelet-Les Halles station

**Public Transportation Ticket Costs:** Metro line 1, 1.90 €, via the RER A, 2.85 €

**Mode of transportation:** Car, taxi, RER A train from Châtelet-Les Halles station

**Why visit:** The **château** was the home of Louis XIV before he settled at Versailles. The **château** exemplifies the diverse and tumultuous French history and is just a few minutes train ride from the center. Its position is a gatekeeper guarding the city center.

**Tickets:** 9.50 € for adults, free for EU residents 25 years and younger, and all children 18 years and younger. To purchase tickets ahead of time, visit this site[12].

---

[11]  www.transilien.com/en/page-tourisme/visit-the-paris-region
[12]  https://tickets.monuments-nationaux.fr/fr-FR/produits.

**Opening Hours:**

**Low Season**: From September 22nd to May 18th, open daily from 10 AM to 5 PM

**High Season**: From May 19th to September 21st, open daily from 10 AM to 6 PM

**Lunch options:** Located in the Parc Floral, Le Bosquet offers jazz on Saturdays in season, a brasserie menu and a green setting in a restaurant that can be privatized with a terrace.

## ② Château/Parc de Sceaux | Sceaux

**Distance:** 12 ki | 7.5 mi

24 mins to 1 hour by car from the center of Paris or 30 mins by train (RER) from Saint Michel station

**Public Transportation Ticket Costs:** RER B 2.80 €, RER B + Bus 192 4.70 €

**Mode of transportation:** Car, taxi, RER B train from Saint Michel station, getting off at Sceaux or Parc de Sceaux Stations. Both of these stops are at the steps of the park entrance.

**Why visit:** Just a stone's throw away from Paris, you can experience the lesser-known mini Versailles. The **Château de Sceaux** was built in the mid-19th century for the Duke and Duchess of Trévise. The pristine grounds and park are exquisite, especially in the springtime during the cherry blossoms (early April).

**Tickets:** 4 € for adults for the permanent collection, 5 € for the temporary collection.

**Opening Hours:** Open every day except Monday.

**Low Season:** From November 1st to February 28th, Mondays closed, Tuesday-Sunday 1 PM to 5 PM

**High Season:** March 1st to October 31st, Mondays closed, open Tuesday to Sunday 2 PM to 6:30 PM

**Lunch options:** Dine in at Le Trévise restaurant, or Le Kiosque du Château (the grounds kiosk) with its ice cream shop (to the left of the **château** from the esplanade). A third option is to picnic on the grounds.

## ③ Château de Versailles | Versailles

**Distance:** 21 ki | 13 mi

30 mins to 1 hour by car from the center of Paris or 49 mins to 1 hr 5 mins by train (RER) from Saint Michel station

**Public Transportation Ticket Costs:** 3.65 € one way via RER C

**Mode of transportation:** Car, taxi, RER C train from Saint Michel station

**Why visit:** Get a taste of the royal life from the 17th century to the late 18th century with a half-day or full-day trip to Château de Versailles. I can connect you up with a private secret passages tour with one of my touring partners who can grant you exclusive access to the private bed chambers of the royal family with this immersive experience.

If you decide to do it alone, you won't doubt that a visit to this famous castle is totally worth the trip out.

**Tickets:** 20 € with a passport pass with timed entry (Access to the whole Estate), 27 € with a passport pass with timed entry and access to Fountains Show or Musical Gardens (available in the high season). Private tour options available as well as access to the areas of the **château** not open to the public, contact me[13] for a quote.

**Opening Hours:** Open every day except Monday.

**Low Season:** From November 1st to March 31st, Mondays closed, Tuesday to Sunday 9 AM to 6:30 PM

**High Season:** From April 1st to October 31st, Mondays closed, Tuesday to Sunday 9 AM to 5:30 PM

**Lunch options:** Why not splurge on your next Versailles visit and dine in at Ore, an Alain Ducasse restaurant? La Veranda, or the terrace of the Bar Galerie at the Hotel Waldorf Astoria are both great alternatives for lunch or dinner.

 **Meaux**

**Distance:** 55 ki | 34 mi

45 mins to 1 hour by car from the center of Paris or 25 - 39 mins by train, Transilien P line from Gare de L'Est.

**Public Transportation Ticket Costs:** 8 € one way via Transilien P train line

**Mode of transportation:** Car, taxi, Transilien P line from Gare de L'Est

**Why visit:** Meaux is home to the famous Brie de Meaux with its picturesque Medieval streets and World War I Museum, Musée de la Grande Guerre. The city, pronounced "mo", is easily accessible by train from Paris' center. You will have plenty to visit for a half day trip, including the Saint Étienne de Meaux Cathedral, the city's rampart walls and Roman ruins, the lovely Garden Bossuet as well as the spacious Parc Naturel du Patis. You will have plenty to eat if you visit the open-air market on a Saturday, including the local Brie and mustard.

---

[13]  www.celineconcierge.com/contact-us/

**Lunch options:** L'Artiste de Meaux is a traditional French restaurant featuring Auvergne region specialties. Enjoy delicious home style cooking in a traditional French atmosphere.

## ⑤ Château de Fontainebleau | Fontainebleau

**Distance:** 69 ki | 43 mi

55 mins to 1 hr 20 mins by car from the center of Paris or 1 hour and 15 mins by train from Châtelet-Les Halles station via train (RER A) to Gare de Lyon, then board the TER train line R in the direction Fontainebleau-Avon, walk 36 mins to the **château**, or board the 10 minute shuttle bus 1 to the **château**.

**Public Transportation Ticket Costs:** 10.19 € one way via public transportation

**Mode of transportation:** Car, taxi, train and shuttle bus.

**Why visit:** Located about one hour from Paris, this royal home dates back to the 12th century and features four museums, three chapels, and expansive grounds. The **château** is even a UNESCO World Heritage Site. If you've been to Versailles already and want to skip it on your next trip, Fontainebleau is an off-the-radar location worth checking out— plus you'll escape the crazy tourist queues. Besides the **château**, you can explore the terrain of the surrounding forest with its many hiking trails.

**Tickets:** 13 € for adult general admission plus exhibition with timed entry, free for EU residents 25 years and younger, and all children 18 years and younger.

Tickets are half-price from 5 PM onwards in the high season. To purchase tickets ahead of time, visit this site[14].

---

[14] https://chateaudefontainebleau.tickeasy.com/en-US/home

Private tour options are available as well as access to the areas of the **château** not open to the public, contact me[15] for a quote.

**Opening Hours:** Open every day except Tuesday.

**Low Season:** From October to March, Tuesday closed, Wednesday to Monday 9:30 AM to 5:00 PM (last access at 4:15 PM)

**High Season:** From April to September, Tuesday closed, Wednesday to Monday 9:30 AM to 6:00 PM (last access at 5:15 PM)

**Lunch options:** L'Atelier Du Goût is located in the city center of Fontainebleau, a stone's throw from the **château**. Here you will experience traditional French semi-gastronomic cuisine in its air-conditioned vaulted cellar that can accommodate up to 50 guests.

## ⑥ Giverny

**Distance:** 73 ki | 46.6 mi

1 hr 24 mins by car from the center of Paris or by train from Gare Saint Lazare Station to the Vernon-Giverny Station (the train usually takes either 52 mins or 1 hr 30 mins, depending on the train).

**Public Transportation Ticket Costs:** 9 € to 16 € one way via train

**Mode of transportation:** Car, taxi, bus, TER train from Saint Lazare station, you also have the option to take a Transilien train to Vernon Station and can take a bus shuttle or taxi to Giverny.

**Why visit:** Either going on your own or with a knowledgeable guide, you will love exploring Claude Monet's heavenly garden oasis just one hour outside Paris. I cannot recommend Giverny, the Monet Gardens and home enough!

---

[15] www.celineconcierge.com/contact-us/

Pay a visit to the Museé des Impressionnismes then enter the fantastical world of Monet's gardens— it was the inspiration of so many exquisite paintings like the sublime **Les Nymphéas**, which can be appreciated at the Musée de l'Orangerie in Paris.

This experience is best appreciated with a private guide. I am always here to reserve your private visit with a licensed tour guide.

**Tickets to Claude Monet's house and garden:** Adult tickets: 12 €, tickets sold only online. To purchase tickets ahead of time, visit this site[16].

**Opening Hours:** Open every day from 9:30 AM to 5:30 PM, last admission 5:00 PM.

**Lunch options:** In Monet's time, Restaurant Baudy, a former inn, was frequented by many artists such as Renoir, Cézanne and even Rodin. Today, it serves traditional French cuisine. The dining room has its own charm with 1900s **décor**, as does the tree-shaded terrace. Do not forget to visit the garden at the rear of the restaurant— here you will find a hidden painter's studio. Note that on Mondays the restaurant is closed!

## HONORABLE MENTIONS:

Auvers-sur-Oise

Bordeaux

Chartres

Châteaux de Chambord

Saint Malo

Strasbourg, Colmar and its surrounding areas

---

[16] https://fondation-monet.com/en/practical-informations/#billetterie

# Must-See Regions

If you get a chance to explore other parts of France outside of Paris and Île-de-France, there is a beautiful country filled with stunning landscapes and rich history awaiting you. If you have the time, and transportation, I highly recommended you visit France outside of the capital, because true to what they say, "Paris is not France, and France is not Paris".

Discovering France will only help you to understand the people, the language, and its culture all the more when you start delving deep into other parts of the country.

Even Parisians crave getting outside the city on weekends and any chance they get to take some **vacances** for a change of pace or a new adventure, these regions provide just that!

###  Reims, Épernay, and the Champagne Region

**Distance:** 143 ki | 89 mi

1 hour 40 mins to 2 hours by car from the center of Paris or 1 hour 20 mins by train (TER) from Gare de l'Est station (tickets start as low as 10 € in low-peak seasons).

**Mode of transportation:** Car, private chauffeur, TER train from Gare de l'Est station

**Why visit:** Sprinkled throughout the region of Champagne are various **maisons de champagne** (champagne producers) where you can "taste the stars". From l'Abbaye d'Hautvillers, where the Benedictine Monk invented the bubbly delight marking the birthplace of Dom Pérignon to small and family-owned producers like Champagne Météyer Père et Fils[17] and Champagne Le Gallais[18], the Champagne region is the ideal place to savor French tradition.

The two main cities in the Champagne region are Reims and Épernay. Whether you decide to plan your trip on your own or choose to enjoy a private chauffeur for a high-end experience, the best is to visit the area by car. Either way, you are sure to appreciate your day trip or weekend trip in the region!

**Tickets:** Champagne tastings, wine cellar (**cave**) tours, and vineyard visits vary from vineyard to vineyard, but I recommend

---

[17] www.champagne-meteyer.com
[18] www.champagnelegallais.com

clicking the links I've recommended above for tastings on the vineyard. If you're in Épernay, you can taste or enjoy **une dégustation**, one of the sweetest bubbly in town at the cave and boutique Les Grands Vins de France for as little as 15 € for 5 glasses.

If you want a private tasting with the producers directly, contact me[19] to set up your exclusive tasting and experience. We can plan for an afternoon or weekend experience for a party of two or more.

## Ⓑ Region of Normandy

**Distance:** 367 ki | 228 mi

It takes 4 hours by car from the center of Paris to Mont-Saint-Michel and the Normandy region's western most point. If going by train, the most direct way is to board from Gare Montparnasse Station via TER train to the station Pontorson Mont-Saint-Michel; you will then board a free non-stop shuttle bus ("Passeur") for 25 minutes to take up to the Mont-Saint-Michel. The whole journey takes about 4 hours and 35 mins, so if you plan to go for the day, I would start early to enjoy the most of your day.

**Mode of transportation:** Car, private chauffeur, or optional TER train from Paris Saint Lazare to Caen then to Pontorson, then shuttle to Mont-Saint-Michel. If going by car, you must park on the mainland and shuttle in; visitors cannot drive to the island.

**Why visit:** This historical region welcomes you to take in the stunning Mont-Saint-Michel Abbey situated on the island that is a UNESCO World Heritage Site. Further north, you

---

[19]  www.celineconcierge.com/contact-us/

can likewise visit the D-Day Normandy Beaches and the picturesque cliffs of Étretat.

**Tickets:** 11 € for adults, free for EU residents 25 years and younger, and all children 18 years and younger. To purchase tickets ahead of time, visit this site[20].

**Opening Hours for the Mont-Saint-Michel:**

**Low Season**: From September 1 to April 30: Open daily from 9:30 AM to 6:00 PM

**High Season**: From May 2 to August 31: Open daily from 9:30 AM to 6:30 PM

The last entry is one hour before closing (last slot: 4:45 PM in the low season, and 5:30 PM in the high season).

## Region of Provence

**Distance:** 760 ki | 472 mi Paris to Aix-en-Provence

7 hours 15 mins by car from the center of Paris or 3 hours to 3 ½ hours by TGV train

**Mode of transportation:** Car or TGV train from Gare de Lyon

**Why visit:** It's the southeast region of France bordering Italy and the Côte d'Azur, or the French Riviera. The region is known for its extraordinary lavender fields, hilly landscape, charming southern villages, **rosé** wine, picturesque olive groves and vineyards and of course, the stunning coastline adjacent to the Mediterranean Sea. You can either go by car, stopping along the small country towns, or hit the main coastal cities— or appreciate a mix of both. Either way, traveling by car or train opens up the possibilities that allow you to profoundly explore the region.

---

[20] https://tickets.monuments-nationaux.fr/fr-FR/produits-seances

# Towns to visit in Provence:

## ① Avignon

It's a lovely and historic city with an annual theatre festival held in the summer. It was once a medieval town where the Pope resided.

## ② Gordes

This rustic mountainous city upon a hill is gorgeous, idyllic and surrounded by lavender fields.

## ③ Cassis

If you're aching for a swim in the Mediterranean, a scenic spot not to miss on your itinerary is Cassis with its beautiful white inlet beaches (**calanques**) surrounded by gigantesque cliffs (**falaises**).

## ④ Cannes

This luxurious vacation spot is a must if you want to savor some shopping and the glamorous life. Annually, every May, the town turns into a cinema city, hosting the International Festival of Cannes. (Remember it's pronounced "can", like "I **can** do it.")

## ⑤ St. Tropez

Another glamorous but pricey resort town welcomes you for a lavish time with its many 5-star resorts and gastronomy restaurants. Enjoy luxury at its finest!

## ⑥ Nice

This sophisticated city welcomes you for an ideal getaway that includes both a marina, city vibes, a glamorous beach front and a promenade. It has both the charm of a far-off getaway while having the pleasures of the city nearby.

# Interview with
# **Hope Curran**,
# a student at La Sorbonne, working on a Masters in Fine Arts

Hope

Hope moved to Paris after graduating with her undergrad in art and global studies in 2016 to do an art internship with Agape Art. She applied to do a Masters in Fine Arts at La Sorbonne two years later.

Hope is now a student at La Sorbonne, working on a Masters in Fine Arts who's originally from the Bay Area, California. She first visited Paris when she was 12 years old for a family vacation and fell in love with everything French. She is a self-proclaimed artist, poet, and dreamer.

Like many of my friends, Hope and I also met through our church. I have always loved Hope's contagious positive energy and bright attitude even in the face of difficult challenges.

I wanted to interview Hope because her journey to France is unique; she came originally as a volunteer and transitioned into a student. She renewed her visa in an unprecedented way that even the French administration didn't have a recognized path for this kind of transition. Hope faced a lot of uncertainty with the visa process but persevered and succeeded in staying two more years than planned and achieved her Masters degree.

Here is Hope's story of discovery and diligence in France as a young adult.

## Why did you move to Paris?

I came back when I was 16 to be a nanny for 3 weeks. I studied abroad with UC Berkeley in 2014 and that's when I decided I wanted to be in Paris.

I wasn't running away, but I was running towards a freedom here that I don't experience in America, specifically, because of the culture of "go-get-it-ness" that's like "oh, you should get a job and get married and buy a house".

And I think in Paris there's not that timeline here. Things just happen later in life for people here or there's accessibility to education so you're not in student debt.

I think I really did come because I felt God calling me here. And I have a heart for artists and I am an artist. And this is a place where artists gathered throughout history.

Paris is a place for artists to seek freedom, and acceptance, and belonging.

## What was your first impression of Paris?

When I was 12 years old, I came for a family vacation. We flew into Paris, and I fell in love with everything French. I loved art and fashion and it left a lasting impression.

And when we went back home, I told my mom I wanted to learn French, so I did because I was homeschooled.

What shocked me the most when I came here as a 22-year-old to live here was winter. I came with the emoji heart eyes, the "Ah, Paris!", and it was January. Winter.

Winter is really hard for me as a Californian because of the lack of sunlight. Paris is hard in the winter.

**What do you love about Paris?**

I came up with the term "gold dipping". I love gold dipping in Paris. You'll be walking, even at night, and the streets are gold. You're just walking and drinking in this magic feeling of the city... There's just gold everywhere and you can kind of dip your fingers in it.

Not every day is like that, but there are just moments like that where you can find it.

As an artist, I wanna be surrounded by beauty. And Paris is the place that I feel the most surrounded by beauty other than nature.

**Did you know French? If yes, where did you learn the language? If not, how did you learn?**

So, I have quite a history with Paris before and I started learning French throughout middle school, high school, and college.

**What challenges did you face with moving to Paris?**

Transition is challenging for me.

I came with two suitcases of my life. Transitioning my whole home and life and way of being into a new culture was hard. I was suddenly an **étrangère**.

I probably did a lot of things wrong, honestly, to try to be here— that wasn't culturally sensitive.

Something else that I learned last year after a really hard season of feeling like I wanted to leave was that I do belong. When I came out of that and finally got my resident permit renewal, I felt like I belonged. And then suddenly, I needed to start playing the American card a bit more.

Like having that excuse, almost for being different. I can play the American card now and I'm not ashamed of it because that's who I am.

A lot of me growing up was in Paris.

## What kind of visas/resident permits did you have to be able to stay in France?

There's an internship for people that have just finished university and love God. It's called STINT and they offer 9-month internships all around the world. So, I had applied through CRU (or Campus Crusade for Christ) in the US.

I came with AGAPE, which is a non-profit with a visitor's visa. AGAPE gave me the paperwork that I needed to apply. It's like I was a volunteer in France, because I was getting my salary from the US.

The first two years I had this resident permit, then when I started my Masters, which was a year and a half in. My position with CRU changed and I became part-time with AGAPE.

I was a part-time worker with a non-profit, not an intern anymore, so I had a student residence permit, and I could work, and my work was through the French organization of AGAPE.

My student card was for a year, and I had to renew it. My program was 2 years but after you get your Masters at a French institution, you could still be in the country with something called APS. It's a temporary resident permit that you apply for to request to stay in France when you are waiting to get a job.

So, I can have at least one more year to do whatever I want or work with AGAPE; the idea is to get a contract job to be able to work in France.

## What is your biggest frustration with Paris?

The prefecture! I think you know this well, don't you? But I spent nine months trying to change the status of my resident permit to a student permit.

Because I had already lived here, I applied to La Sorbonne as a French resident (not as an international student) with a French address, and I applied as a regular student. So, then my case became a **cas particulier**, or a special case.

In anyone's case that is a little different, you usually need an extra signature (from a higher up in my school) and you need to be persistent with people.

But I brought cookies and shared them with the people in the prefecture and I think that's why they also listened to me because I was nice, and I had cookies. That's terrible, but it's true. Sometimes, the prefecture means being patient.

**What is a lesson you have learned from living in Paris?**

I've learned to keep my eyes on things that matter and let go of the things that don't.

Just by moving apartments, I've learned that you can't hold onto a lot here that doesn't matter.

And in relationships, I've learned as an expat that Paris is a revolving door. That was really hard. I've learned a lot about relationships being kind of "seasonal" for a lack of a better term. I've found that the longer I stay, the more people leave.

But always keeping my eyes on the things above and not focusing on the hard things.

**What would you tell someone who is like you and wants to move to Paris?**

Right now, I would say if you really want to do it, then do it. You'll find a way even though there aren't always answers.

Anyone can come to Paris for three weeks and enjoy it, but don't feel like you have to move here. I would also say take a vision trip for two weeks to see what Paris is like.

A lot of people can have rose-colored glasses in Paris, so I would tell them to dream big but take your time.

I think so many people buy the one-way ticket, and they don't have a plan and end up leaving.

It's not for everyone to live here long-term, sorry to say it...

**What does living in France mean to you?**

If I'm on the train, I get to see the world. Every day, you get to experience culture in a new way— have a global perspective— I love the beauty of that.

People are the landscape here!

**If you had known about a lifestyle service like Céline Concierge, would you consider using our services, why or why not?**

If I had known before I came, I would have loved your help with housing, especially moving to Paris and finding an apartment. I would have used your service for housing and the visa process.

But having contact with someone in the country is super important coming in and I think that would be the most valuable thing. Just knowing there's someone here if you have questions and not being alone and finding out about different communities that exist.

**Would you recommend Céline Concierge services?**

Well Céline, I have recommended you before. I love recommending Céline Concierge— so you can take my word for it!

There are so many people who have asked me questions that I don't have the capacity to answer or it's a question that you need a professional for.

Your services are really tailored to people who want to do Paris well.

**Do you have a favorite book, film, or song about Paris?**

A cliché is **A Moveable Feasts** by Ernest Hemingway and my favorite spot in Paris is at 27 Rue Fleurus where Gertrude Stein lived and welcomed artists.

I also love the film Julie and Julia! It's about Julia Child because she's in Paris and is an American and is cooking up a storm at the Cordon Bleu.

*Hope was a student at the time of this interview and has since graduated with her Masters at La Sorbonne in 2020 and although she loved her time in Paris and tried to stay another year, she felt like it was time for her to moved back to California.*

*She is now married to her sweetheart and fellow Californian, Peter.*

# FOOD PARADISE

# An Introduction to French Gastronomy

French cuisine and the experience of enjoying a gastronomic meal is such a cornerstone of French pleasure, history, society, and culture that in 2010, UNESCO took notice and listed the gastronomic meal of the French as an Intangible Cultural Heritage of Humanity.

> *The gastronomic meal emphasizes togetherness, the pleasure of taste, and the balance between human beings and the products of nature. Important elements include the careful selection of dishes from a constantly growing repertoire of recipes; the purchase of good, preferably local products whose flavours go well together; the pairing of food with wine; the setting of a beautiful table; and specific actions during consumption, such as smelling and tasting items at the table. The gastronomic meal should respect a fixed structure, commencing with an apéritif (drinks before the meal) and ending with liqueurs, containing in between at least four successive courses, namely a starter, fish and/or meat with vegetables, cheese and dessert.*
>
> *-UNESCO*

Having meals at home with French people, albeit pleasant and cheerful, can differ from the restaurant experience entirely. One of the topics that seem to carry some confusion is the subject of gratuity.

Tipping isn't really part of the lifestyle in France like it is in the US, although in French, there is a word for tipping: **pourboire**. It literally translates as 'to drink' and may have originated from the old days of canteens and old bistros when people would leave a **pourboire**, or tip, for waiters to enjoy a drink after hours.

Today, restaurant servers are usually paid a decent wage and therefore do not depend on tips, although tipping is much appreciated. So don't feel obligated to tip at cafes, restaurants, and bars, unless the service was exceptional, and you want to show your appreciation through a tip.

As you know, Paris is iconic for its cafe culture and terraces, but another point of confusion is knowing the difference between the different kind of establishments. For example, when you walk down the streets and see a place labeled bar/brasserie or a cafe/bistro and yet another bar/restaurant, you may package them all together as the same. But don't! They aren't the same and these subtle differences will help you to know what kind of service to expect. Paris is filled with cafes, bars, brasseries, bistros, and restaurants, and every hybrid in between. So, what distinguishes one label from another and is it really that important?

In fact, these places are so synonymous with Paris' soul that without them, Paris wouldn't be what it is today. Keep reading for a breakdown of the different kinds of restaurants.

## CAFES

It has been said that the French revolution was started in Parisian cafes. Cafes back in the day, used to be known for serving up quick, snack-like food (like sandwiches and the famous **croque monsieurs** accompanied with a cafe or two) on tiny tables and chairs. They were hubs where writers would camp out to write entire novels. It was also and still is a place where intellectuals or **intelos**, as we say in French, gather to discuss any subject under the sun but most notably philosophy, art, culture and society's problems with a friend and a drink in hand. Today, they are still very present in French culture as places to grab a quick bite, meet your friends, and hang out on the terrace for hours on end.

## BISTROS

You can't understand what a bistro is without first looking back at the etymology, or history of the word. As my friend Olivier explained to me over a meal at the well-known bistro La Fontaine de Mars, bistro comes from the Russian word **bystro.** Apparently back in the early 19th century, when Russian soldiers occupied Paris, they would shout "Bystro!", meaning fast, to what they thought was slow wait staff in order to get quicker service. The term stuck and the Bistro was born. A bistro is particular in that it's like a quick service restaurant and usually has **le service continu**, or continuous service all day, unlike some restaurants that close after lunch and before the dinner rush.

## BAR / BRASSERIES

Unlike a bar, a brasserie is open all day and has **le service continu**, serving up meals at all hours of the day. Traditionally, a brasserie, meaning brewery, was a place to enjoy beer brewed on site, hence the need to serve food continuously like a restaurant. Back in the 19th century, many Alsaciens with the annexation of Alsace (region in eastern France), went west, opening up brasseries in Paris. Many restaurants and other establishments serve up alcohol in the form of beer, wine and cocktails, so it's no surprise to find the bar/brasserie labels attached to the establishments.

Furthermore, bars are abundant in Paris and in the last decade, specialty cocktail bars have become posh places to spend your evenings out. You can be a bar without being a restaurant, and many don't serve up food but will offer snacks or **les petit trucs à grignoter**, small things to nibble on as you enjoy your alcoholic beverages.

## RESTAURANTS
(the French say **resto** for short)

Finally, we arrive at the unequaled restaurant. Restaurant comes from the word "restauration" meaning to restore or refresh and was traditionally a place to eat food that restores or heals and was meat-based to give strength. If you are in a restaurant, you are likely to get a hardy, worthwhile meal that is refined and delicious. This is the reason only restaurants can receive Michelin Stars— because they're of higher quality and prestige.

# A LITTLE ENCYCLOPEDIA OF FRENCH TERMS RELATED TO FOOD TO KNOW:

**à emporter / pour emporter** | takeaway

**alimentation generale** | general store

**amuse-gueules** | appetizer, bite-sized snack meant to amuse the mouth and get the appetite started

**AOC (vin appellation d'origine contrôlée)** | Protected Designation of Origin for wine (is a geographical indication protecting the origin and quality of wine)

**AOP (appellation d'origine protégée)** | Protected Designation of Origin (is a geographical indication protecting the origin and quality of food products other than wine)

**apéritif / apéro for short** | apéritif, pre-dinner drinks

**boucher** | butcher (place)

**boucher (m), Bouchère (f)** | butcher (person)

**boulangerie** | bakery

**boulanger (m), boulangère (f)** | baker

**bouillon** | broth, stock

**buvette** | refreshment bar (think of it as a cuter name for a bar)

**charcuterie** | cold meats, deli meats, cold cuts

**comptoir** | counter, bar

**déguster** | taste, savor, eat, enjoy

**digestif** | digestive, after-dinner liqueur

**épicerie** | greengrocer

**fromager (m), fromagère (f)** | cheesemonger/ cheese seller

**fromagerie** | cheesemonger/cheese shop

**grignoter** | snack, nibble on

**papilles** | taste buds

**pâtisserie** | pastry/pastry shop

**petits-four** | appetizer, bite-sized snack either sweet or savory, usually cooked in an oven

**poissonnier (m), poissonnière (f)** | fish seller

**poissonnerie** | fishmonger/fish shop

**sur place** | eat-in

**une planche** | plank, board (As in a cheese or deli board.)

**viennoiserie** | sweet pastry, sweet bread and pastry traditionally from Vienna

For a Lexicon of Wine Terms in French, check out this list* by Elle Magazine:

Voilà— with that understanding, let us move onto my top picks for places you need to know and try in Paris for an authentic culinary experience for all my foodies out there.

* https://www.elle.fr/Elle-a-Table/Cote-cave/Lexique

# Where to Eat & Drink: Tried and True Best French Restaurants

Recommended by the Locals (left bank)

I f the left bank is known for anything, it's for the cozy, old-fashion mom and pop bistros and restaurants that maintain French tradition.

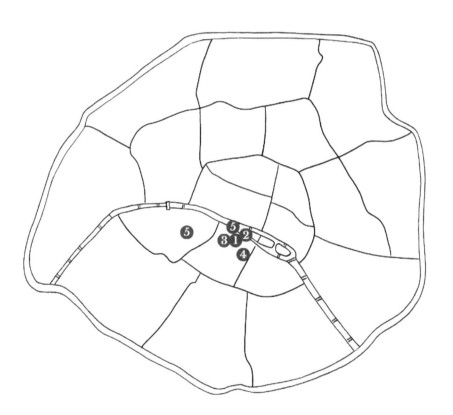

Here are my recommendations for restaurants that will fill up your stomach without emptying your pockets— the ones where the owners and waiters are larger than life and where you're sure to immerse yourself in the culture and cuisine **des français** as if you were a local yourself.

**Bon appétit !**

 **LE COMPTOIR DU RELAIS**

9 Carr de l'Odéon,
75006 Paris
01 44 27 07 97

Le Comptoir du Relais is my ultimate favorite restaurant for authentic French cooking. It's centered in the heart of Paris' left bank and at the footsteps of the pretty and idyllic four-star Hôtel Le Relais Saint-Germain. I recommend the duck confit dish with couscous.

Ask the server for his suggestion of a wine pairing. Its little brother, L'Avant Comptoir de la Mer, is next door and offers a more fast-paced atmosphere as patrons meet up to taste the delectable sea-inspired tapas before hopping next door to Le Comptoir for the elaborate gastronomical experience provided by the famous Yves Camdeborde.

## 2 ALLARD

41 Rue Saint-André des Arts,
75006 Paris
01 43 26 48 23

This old-school French Bistro was recomended to me by my friend and fellow Parisian, Basile, who swears by this place as one of the best bistros in the city. You will find the quaint decor charming as you eat your way through French history. The food is traditionally French comfort-food— uncomplicated, hardy and delicious— while the place brings you back to the 30s when the restaurant was founded (1932). Nothing much has changed since then, making this place a tried-and-true gem of French bistros, sticking to what is good, simple, and savory.

## 3 CHEZ GEORGE

11 Rue des Canettes,
75006 Paris
01 43 26 79 15

Since 1952, this French **épicerie et buvette**, otherwise known as a local hangout and wine bar, has been serving up glass after glass of **vin rouge** to its patrons. It's one of the few wine cellars left standing today that can show you a good time. For a solid French meal, endless bottles of wine and an atmosphere that hasn't left the 50s, paying a visit to Chez George will, no doubt, transport you to another time!

## 4  LE POULIDOR

41 Rue Monsieur le Prince,
75006 Paris
01 43 26 95 34

Since the mid-1800s, the Poulidor has been serving up French meals epitomizing a French grandma's cooking. You'll feel like you're in her kitchen— the meals are simple and affordable, yet hardy and savory. Le Poulidor renovated its historical bistro in the summer of 2020, for a facelift on its charming and iconic locale. The restaurant is known for welcoming among its patrons the likes of Paul Valéry, James Joyce and Hemingway just to name a few. It's even the setting of a scene where the characters meet in Woody Allen's **Midnight in Paris.**

## 5  AU PIED AU FOUET

### Location 1

3 Rue Saint-Benoît,
75006 Paris
01 42 96 59 10

### Location 2

45 Rue de Babylone,
75007 Paris
01 47 05 12 27

If you're not hungry, don't think about stepping foot in Au Pied! They serve up large portion dishes you'll feel are coming straight from mom and pop. They offer an affordable set menu that allows you to order a no-frills three course meal served with the recommended French wines. You may have to unbutton a button or two of your jeans on your way out. Their other enterprises worth checking out include a **bar à vin** in the 5th (Les Pipos), a brasserie with the same name in the 4th, and a more laid-back restaurant called L'Atelier au Pied de Fouet in the 7th.

# Traditional French Restaurants & Bistros to Take You Back in Time

France has a rich history and culture that spans centuries, and you can still explore some of that through not only the cuisine, but also the setting of where you enjoy those meals. Where is that better spent than at a restaurant with vivid architecture and feel?

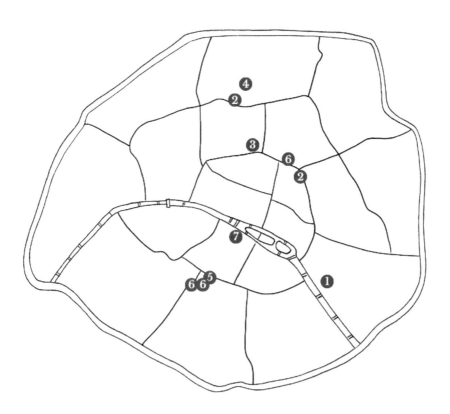

This chapter is all about transporting you through Paris' history through the food and ambience of the restaurants. You'll get a bite-size taste of where you must go to find beautifully designed restaurant interiors that are just as delicious to the eyes as the food is to the tastebuds!

 **LE TRAIN BLEU**
Pl. Louis-Armand,
75012 Paris
01 43 43 09 06

Le Train Bleu is equally majestic and opulent as it transports you to another time and place—the place of your fantasies! The lush setting combined with the decadent French cuisine of nourishing meats bathed in sauces and stews blows every patron away. This one-of-a-kind dining experience set in the rare backdrop of the train station is sure to blow you away. You can check out the assassin Nikita on assignment in the restaurant in an intense scene in the film **Nikita** by film auteur Luc Besson.

## 2 BOUILLON PIGALLE & BOUILLON PIGALLE RÉPUBLIQUE

**Location 1**

22 Bd de Clichy,
75018 Paris
01 42 59 69 31

**Location 2**

39 boulevard du
Temple
+33 01 42 59 69 31

I can only describe Bouillon as a meat-lover's dream to indulge in low-cost simple French food for the masses. Most of the French dishes steeped in tradition that are cooked at Bouillon involve meat and loads of sauce and **bouillon**, or broth. You can expect classic French dishes like a hard-boiled egg with mayonnaise, foie gras accompanied with onion confiture for the starter, beef bourguignon, Basque Boudin and **tête de veau** (or veal head!). All this accompanied with a nice glass or pitcher of red wine, of course.

## 3 BOUILLON CHARTIER

7 Rue du Faubourg Montmartre,
75009 Paris
01 47 70 86 29

Much like in the style of Bouillon Pigalle, Chartier is another brand cooking up French-style comfort food at inexpensive prices. Self-proclaimed the authentic Parisian Brasserie, Chartier is synonymous with Parisian style, prestige, and mysticism as it rides on the history of yesteryear. It welcomed the likes of Picasso, Modigliani, Fitzgerald, and now **you** to its two locations with its design inspired by art nouveau. Get ready to satiate your appetite with sumptuous French cooking!

## 4 LE REFUGE DES FONDUE

17 Rue des Trois Frères, 75018 Paris

01 42 55 22 65

At this one-of-a-kind restaurant, you'll sip wine served in baby bottles and participate in minor acrobatics as you climb over the dining tables to be seated. The waiters here are larger than life, too. Le Refuge is one for the adventurous and if you're in the mood to be entertained in a quirky setting that feels a little like you're in a carnival tent, this place is for you! Leave talks of a diet at the door and enjoy the satiable fondue that will leave your stomach satisfied— though you may have to loosen the belt by the time you stumble out of there.

## 5 LES FONDUS DE LA RACLETTE

209 Bd Raspail,

75014 Paris

01 43 27 00 13

Les Fondus specializes in meals from Savoie, the French region housing the French Alps. You can expect rich savory fondues and raclettes, a Swiss-inspired dish where the semi-hard cheese is melted on a special non-stick plate accompanied with heated potatoes, pickles, and cured meats. You'll feel like you're cocooning for the winter in a cozy ski resort when you step into the rustic cabin-esc restaurant. You can be sure to enjoy a hardy, cheesy meal at an affordable price. Reservations ahead of time are recommended as it's a popular winter eatery.

##  6  LE PLOMB DU CANTAL

**Location 1**

3 Rue de la Gaité,
75014 Paris
01 43 35 16 92

**Location 2**

5 Rue du Maine,
75014 Paris
01 42 79 89 79

**Location 3**

4 Boulevard St Denis, 75010 Paris
01 42 08 01 11

Specializing in cuisine from the Auvergne region, Le Plomb's three restaurants invite you to relax and indulge in cheesy meals accompanied with a refreshing glass of wine or a pint of beer. The Aligot dish, a home-made specialty of the house, consists of gooey melted cheese from the Massif Central region of France blended with mashed potatoes, garlic, butter and cream. The cozy, rustic cabin-like setting and comfort food are ideally to be enjoyed in the cooler months of the year. The servers add to the festive experience by entertaining guests with giant pepper grinders for a laugh or two!

## 7  ROGER LA GRENOUILLE

28 Rue des Grands Augustins, 75006 Paris
01 56 24 24 34

Looking for an audacious evening full of French influence? Try Roger La Grenouille that lives up to its froggy name. From the fresh and flavorful menu with frog cooked any way imaginable— from frog legs to a frog burger to homemade raviolis enveloping frog meat— Roger La Grenouille is more than a restaurant; it's a dining establishment for the most adventurous foodie! The restaurant is steeped in history and invites you to participate in its unique dining experience from the moment you step inside.

# Contemporary French Restaurants & Neo-Bistros to Try

**W**hat's a contemporary French Restaurant or Neo-Bistro? In the last decade, France has undergone a rebirth in the restaurant business by stripping off the traditional black and white bow ties. Instead, young restaurant owners opt for a more down-to-earth vibe by wearing jeans and casual sweaters.

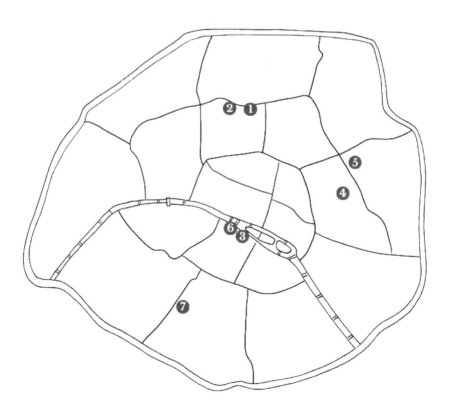

The meals cooked use seasonal and fresh local products instead of the heavier meals like beef bourguignon and duck confit. They endeavor to provide vegetarian and even gluten-free options to keep up with client needs and changing trends.

The decor in these neo-bistros and modern restaurants is usually minimalist— exposed stripped walls, many plants to add fresh greenery, stylish lighting and cooler colors like whites, soft green, blues and yellow tones instead of the reds and dark-colored woods of the older generation restaurants. You'll know you've walked into a contemporary French restaurant when you sit down, and it feels fresh and lively.

Here are my picks for the top contemporary restaurants worth checking out on your trip to Paris— eat your little heart out!

 ## MARCEL ET CLÉMENTINE

74 Rue de Dunkerque,
75009 Paris
01 40 37 91 60

Pay a visit to Marcel et Clémentine if you want a nice French meal with no frills and good friendly service. The young owners know what their patrons want and have aced everything from the charming decor to the colorful meals to the welcoming staff.

They serve up the classics— steak frites, burgers, homemade foie gras— as well as some inventive plates like veggie lasagna and their version of fish and chips. You won't be disappointed when you stop by.

## 2 BUVETTE PARIS

28 Rue Henry Monnier,
75009 Paris
01 44 63 41 71

You can enjoy a French bistro-style meal complemented with a curated wine pairing from their server-sommelier for any dish. Think traditional bistro meets modern French dining in a New York-style setting. Buvette serves up a variety of flavors and dishes from sweet and savory homemade waffles, eggs and bacon, to your classic **croque monsieurs**. Prices are reasonable and the service is fast and friendly. I've never been disappointed, and neither will you!

## 3 LE COLVERT

54 Rue Saint-André des Arts,
75006 Paris
01 42 03 73 67

You'll be pleasantly surprised to experience traditional French fare with an original spark. The young owners aim to bring you colorful classic French meals accompanied with exquisite wine choices at affordable prices. They will usually feature a special menu on occasions like Valentine's Day, so I recommend reserving if you are celebrating a holiday or special event. The servers are attentive, and the decor is picturesque, inspired by hunting, yet modern and pleasing.

**4** **LE SERVAN**

32 Rue Saint-Maur,

75011 Paris

01 55 28 51 82

This no-frills French restaurant was started by two sisters, Katia and Tatia Levha, who serve up your classic French cuisine with a modern twist by complementing the meals with unique flavors and unusual ingredients and sauces. The dishes will titillate your taste buds while the easy-going atmosphere and friendly staff brighten your day. The fusion of unexpected ingredients makes for a unique but satisfying approach to French cuisine. A visit will leave you delightfully surprised!

**5** **LE GRAND BAIN**

14 Rue Denoyez,

75020 Paris

09 83 02 72 02

This fool-proof restaurant will leave you coming back again and again. The trendy Grand Bain really does everything right, from the delectable high-quality dishes, the excellent and attentive service, to the clean and rustic decor. The setting is casual, but the meals are to die for! Every dish they create is with attention— always with the clients' enjoyment at the forefront of what they do. Although the meals and wine choices will run you a pretty penny, you won't be disappointed to try any of their wide selection of dishes from the meats to the seafood and the tapa-style finger foods.

## 6  ALCAZAR

62 Rue Mazarine,
75006 Paris
01 53 10 19 99

A visit to Alcazar is like stepping into a luxurious restaurant with a secret interior garden. The setting will blow you away and the traditional French food will dance on your tastebuds. The place is both romantic and stylish, lending itself as an ideal place to take a date for specialty cocktails, or to celebrate a special occasion. The vast space feels airy and light, so you won't feel crowded as you enjoy your visit either from the balcony bar or in the center of the restaurant. In the evenings, the place transforms into a lounge bar with music jamming, perfect for keeping the party going.

## 7  LA VERRIÈRE

4 Rue Niépce,
75014 Paris
01 83 75 69 21

La Verrière, which means the canopy in French, is truly a gem among the contemporary gastronomical restaurants in the city. Japanese chef, Kayori Hirano, serves up French-Japanese fusion dishes that are as pleasing to the eyes as to the taste buds. The **lieu** is stunning, starting with its sunroof that light pours through, the gold and bronze pendant lights, comfy chairs and wall lined with wine bottles. The prices are on the high end, but it's well worth it for this rare gastronomical experience.

# All Things French Wine

As you may have already guessed, wine is a big deal in France. In fact, if you were to try a new glass of French wine every night, it would take you eight years to try them all!

The country boasts over 27,000 wineries and is one of the largest wine-producing countries in the world, tied for the top spot with neighboring Italy. Not only that, France has the highest level of wine consumption per capita in the world. As a result, wine is ingrained into the French culture, to the point where a lot of what we would consider fairly specialized knowledge about wine is considered general knowledge over here. But don't worry! I'll teach you all you need to know to go from **quoi?** (what?) to **santé!** (cheers!).

Let's start with the grapes. Or not! Unlike wine from other countries, French wines rarely have the name of the specific grapes on the bottle. Instead, French wine is identified through its place of origin. You will see **AOC** (or the European AOP) on labels, which stands for **Appellation d'Origine Contrôlée** or Protected Designation of Origin. This certification ensures that winemakers are following that specific region's grape growing and wine-making methods that take into account things such as the climate, soil type, vineyard elevation and slope, plant genetics, and a whole host of other things. In short, they make sure that the wine you're getting is a true representation of that region.

The next word you need to know is **terroir**. We don't use **terroir** as much in English, but it's the idea that local produce embodies its place of origin. This is how the French see wine, and each **terroir** or **AOC** includes multiple types of wine, as well as different classifications and ways to know which wine is the best.

Here are a few of the main French wine regions and the wines they produce to get you started:

### 🅐 Burgundy

**Where:** East-central France

**Wine-growing areas:** Chablis, Côte d'Or, Côte Chalonnaise, Mâcon, and Beaujolais.

**Main varieties:** Pinot noir (red) and Chardonnay (white)

**Local facts:** Burgundy wines are classed by place of origin, not producer. The more specific the location is on the bottle, the better the wine will be! One wine from this area you must know is Beaujolais, which are wines made from the **gamay** grape. Watch out for the Beaujolais Nouveau that comes out once a year on the third Thursday in November to celebrate that year's harvest.

## Bordeaux

**Where:** Southwestern France

**Wine-growing areas:** Left Bank, Right Bank, "**Entre deux mers**"

**Main varieties:** Cabernet Sauvignon, Cabernet Franc, Merlot, Sauvignon Blanc, Sémillon, and Muscadelle

**Local facts:** Bordeaux wines are almost always a mix of several different grapes. The area is divided by the Gironde River into an upside-down Y shape, creating the three Bordeaux regions. Red wine from the Left Bank will usually be drier, with predominantly Cabernet, Sauvignon and Merlot in the blend. Red wine from the Right Bank will be softer, with a mix of Merlot and Cabernet Franc. White Bordeaux wines will be zesty due to their mix of Sauvignon Blanc and Sémillon. And lastly, Sauternais wines are sweet and are usually paired with dessert or **foie gras**.

## Loire Valley

**Where:** Central France

**Wine-growing areas:** The Pays Nantais, Anjou-Saumur, Touraine, and the Central Vineyards.

**Main varieties:** Muscadet, Chenin Blanc, Cabernet Franc, Sauvignon Blanc

**Local facts:** The Loire Valley is not too far from Paris, and it's a great idea for a day trip! Many vineyards give tours to visitors with a wine tasting session at the end. If you have time, try to check out multiple vineyards in different regions as each of their wines differ: The Pays Nantais, towards the coast, specializes in very dry Muscadets; in the middle, Anjou-Saumur and the Touraine have a wide variety of dry, sweet, still, and sparkling wines; and the Central Vineyards are known for their tart Sauvignon Blancs, the most famous of which is Sancerre.

## Ⓓ Champagne

**Where:** Northeast France

**Wine-growing areas:** Champagne

**Main varieties:** Chardonnay, Pinot Meunier, and Pinot Noir

**Local facts:** You must have heard that Champagne is only really Champagne if it comes from the region of Champagne! But do you know why? It's because of the **champenoise** method, the very complicated way in which the winemakers of Champagne make the bubbly that we know and love. The two main types of Champagne you will come across are the Sparkling **Blanc de Blancs** ("white of whites") and the Sparkling **Blanc de Noirs** ("white of blacks"). **Blanc des Blancs** are made with only locally-grown Chardonnay grapes and produce a crisper wine. **Blanc des Noirs** are made from two red grapes, pinot meunier and pinot noir, which give a richer, more full-bodied wine.

There are many other regions for you to explore, including Alsace, Rhône, Languedoc and Roussillon, Provence... and many more!

Now that you know a bit more about where French wine comes from and how it is classified, how do you choose what to order in a restaurant? Well, my friend, it all depends on what you're going to eat. A French person would never pick a bottle of wine just like that! **Ooh là là!** Wine must complement the food you're eating, and it goes a lot further than just red wine with red meat and white wine with seafood! Here is a cheat sheet to get you started:

Dry white wine pairs well with vegetables, starches, and fish.

Sweet white wine pairs well with cheese, cured meats, and desserts.

Rich white wine pairs well with cheese, starches, fish, and white meat.

Sparkling white wine pairs well with vegetables, cheese, starches, and fish.

Light red wine pairs well with vegetables, cheese, starches, white meat, and cured meats.

Medium red wine pairs well with vegetables, cheese, starches, white meat, red meat, and cured meats.

Bold red wine pairs well with cheese, starches, red meat, and cured meats.

If you are unsure of what to order in a restaurant, ask the server! They will always be able to recommend something, and more often than not, they love explaining the different wine options for the dishes on their menu. The same goes for taking wine to a party. If there is going to be a sit-down meal, it is always best to ask your host what the main dish will be and then bring a wine that goes with it. Or, if not, bring a dessert wine for the end of the meal to be on the safe side.

Buying a bottle of wine in France is as easy as going to your local supermarket. Even the smallest ones have a good selection! Prices range from around 2 € a bottle, which I don't recommend, to the more expensive wines at 20 € and more. In between, you will find some great choices for around 6 € to 10 €. My recommendation is to pick one that has won an award and has a gold or silver sticker on it. It has never let me down! I also had a French friend tell me to never buy a screw-top, only a corked bottle, and to never buy one with a flat-bottomed bottle. Follow these tips and the wine will always be good!

Another option for more special occasions is to go to a wine shop (Nicolas is a well-known chain in France) or find your local **cave à vin**. More info on this in the next chapter!

# Caves à Vin

What's a **cave à vin** ? **Cave à vin** literally translates in English as "wine cave" and is synonymous with the wine cellars used to store wine. **Caves à vin** as we know them today in Paris were born from this concept of storing, selling, and serving up good wine accompanied usually with tasty cold-cut meats and cheeses on a board called **une planche**. In short, they are wine bars and shops specialized in first-rate wine and delectable snack-like foods to go with.

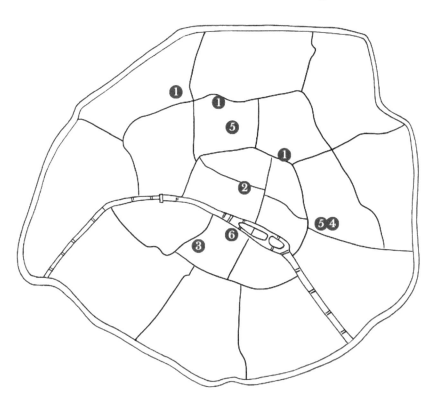

You can usually pop into one to purchase a nice bottle of wine or enjoy a glass **sur place** (on the spot).

**Caves à vin** that serve up the famous French **planche** are endless in Paris. They usually consist of small rustic restaurants with small tables, and even smaller chairs. Some are hybrid **épicieries,** or small grocers, selling wine and food products revolving around wine culture. Wine bottles stretch the length of their walls and are run by wine connoisseurs; often, sommeliers are ready and willing to explain the subtleties of the wine notes and to help you choose the best one for your mood and meal. You can encounter a few great wine caves in each arrondissement but here are my top picks, chosen and vetted for you!

 **LE 17.45**

**Location 1**

45 Rue des Dames, 75017 Paris
09 86 40 25 75

**Location 2**

49 Rue Jean-Baptiste Pigalle, 75009 Paris
09 88 30 32 46

**Location 3**

7 Rue René Boulanger, 75010 Paris
09 83 82 14 28

The bar, self-proclaimed as the **temple of the apéro,** is ready to serve you one of their choice cheeses or fine cured meat **planches** that are 100% original. Open every day except Sundays, the bar invites visitors to come sharp at 17h45, or 5:45 PM. They encourage patrons to curate their own **planche** from their selection of 40 local products. Don't forget the very important wine pairing, which the bar staff is happy to suggest and pair with your meal. They have 3 locations in Paris— one in the 17th arr. in the Batignolles; in the 9th arr. at Pigalle, and in the 10th arr. near Republique.

## 2  Ô CHÂTEAU

68 Rue Jean-Jacques Rousseau,
75001 Paris
01 44 73 97 80

Savor the **mélange** of fine cheese accompanied by the best wine selections you can find in Paris. You can participate in a wine tasting of various degrees, they offer a Tour de France tasting with 5 French boutique wines and 1 Champagne with an optional cheese or **charcuterie** board. Likewise they serve up a Champagne flight and various seasonal tastings from spirited English-speaking sommeliers. Definitely check out their website for more details and book ahead of time to reserve your spot. They can also privatize one of their wine cellars if you're going to one of their masterclasses with a large group.

## 3  LE VIN EN BOUCHE

27 Rue de l'Abbé Grégoire,
75006 Paris
01 42 22 02 07

This modest wine bar whose name literally translates in English as "the wine in the mouth", was proudly started by two wine sommeliers, Jonathan Jean and Vincent Martin, who want you to experience just that, lovely wine in your mouth! They have a knack for selling only the top wine choices and local food products for their **planches**. Check them out in the 6th arr. for a festive evening surrounded by wine experts and foodies!

### 4  SEPTIME LA CAVE

3 Rue Basfroi,
75011 Paris
01 43 67 14 87

This is the little brother of the restaurant Septime (see the Michelin-star Restaurants chapter), and is a modest wine bar with rich flavors, which the friendly wait staff effortlessly pairs with your meat and cheese choices. It's a rare gem where you'll find natural wines as well. It's also an ideal place to take a date as the cozy and intimate, yet vibrant, setting breathes a romantic and down-to-earth vibe.

### 5  L'ATELIER SAISONNIER

**Location 1**

58 Rue La Fayette
75009 Paris
09 73 18 48 75

**Location 2**

15 Rue de Charonne
75011 Paris
09 73 18 48 75

This modest French restaurant features all things local, fresh, homemade, and organic. Their **planches** are their golden child, named one of the best in France by Le Bon Bon and showing off a tour of France in its presentation.

This unassuming, yet delicious bistro invites you to visit and cherish all things good when it comes to eating French food! They have two locations, one in the 9th arr. and a second in the 11th arr.

## 6  BAR ETNA

33 Rue Mazarine,
75006 Paris
06 13 88 57 16

Bar Etna presents natural and organic wine choices along with seasonal food to whet your appetite or have a full dinner. The atmosphere is warm and inviting. It's the perfect place for drinks with colleagues after work or with friends to catch up. The servers are what you would expect— friendly and knowledgeable in their recommendations. A glass of wine starts at 5 €.

# Tapas in Paris

Tapas, if you aren't familiar with the term, are small appetizers that hail from Spain which have turned into a favored way to dine in France, too. Their cousin, the pincho, or **pintxo**, a native of the northwest Basque Country of Spain are similarly prepared— hot or cold— and eaten in bars or taverns.

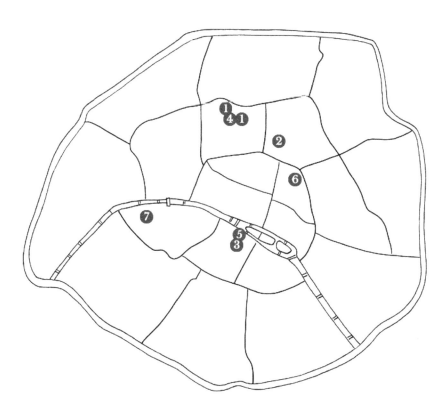

Both encourage socializing and are a cornerstone of the Spanish culture, where bars won't serve you drinks unless you're simultaneously snacking on food. Usually accompanied by a cold alcoholic drink, these sumptuous Spanish-influenced meals are a wonderful way to enjoy a night out with friends or sit in an intimate bar snacking on finger food with a date. I would argue that the Spanish tapa inspires a similar style of eating as say the French **planche**, or meat and cheese boards; **bocas** in Central American countries; **mezzes** in Mediterranean cuisine, or even izakaya-style Japanese tapas.

Perfect for grabbing a quick lunch with a couple of bite-sized snacks or for a more drawn-out dinner in France, tapas have gained a steady growth in popularity with the opening of a plethora of tapas-inspired bars and cantines. Many of which are branching out from its Spanish roots and inspiring Asian fusion, Persian cuisine, as well as South American cuisine. Continue reading for my top picks you'll be thirsting to try on your next visit to Paris!

## 1 LE BARBICHE

**Location 1 & 2**

11 & 12 Rue Pierre
Fontaine, 75009 Paris
01 42 85 21 90

**Location 3**

3 Rue Rodier
(Le Cerf-Volant)

This **cave à vin**/tapas bar hybrid is known for its selection of basque products from the **pintxos** (Basque-style tapas) to the wine and to their **planches** that are delicately created and presented. The bar has three locations in the 9th arr., two on the Rue Pierre Fontaine facing each other near Pigalle; the third is on Rue Rodier, ready to serve you. They pride themselves on serving the finest food products and partner with vineyards to ensure the highest quality wine.

## 2 FARAGO PINTXO CLUB

11 Cr des Petites Écuries,
75010 Paris

This place has the creative genius of chef Fernando Canales, bringing his roots of Spanish Basque country to Paris through lovely pintxos. You can visit for pre-dinner drinks and appetizers or dine in for the whole gastronomical experience of colorful flavors on your tastebuds. You won't eat at Farago without raving about their tantalizing **Œuf Incroyable** (incredible egg and truffle) dish. They are also known for delicious Spanish sangria and giant gin cocktails.

### 3 THE COD HOUSE

1 Rue de Condé, 7
5006 Paris
01 42 49 35 59

This spacious and airy place is a nice change to the often tiny restaurants of Paris. It goes one further by featuring Japanese-French fusion tapas in this Izakaya-style bar and restaurant. They have a selection of specialty cocktails made with yuzu and matcha that are **fait maison**, or homemade; their house specialty Black cod melts in your mouth, and their vegetarian tapas are packed with flavors. The Cod House goes above and beyond to leave a lasting impression on your tastebuds as well as your experience.

### 4 LA ABUELA

43 Rue Notre Dame de Lorette,
75009 Paris
06 59 12 20 40

Escape to Barcelona for a night while eating grandma's home cooking! That's exactly what La Abuela does— transports you to another place through the flavors in the warm and cold tapa dishes, authentic Spanish sangria, and colorful seafood fare. The owner promises good food and a friendly experience, so don't wait to stop by La Abuela for a lively and delicious experience the next time you're in the 9th arrondissement!

## 5 L'AVANT COMPTOIR DE LA MER / L'AVANT COMPTOIR DE LA TERRE

3 Carr de l'Odéon,
75006 Paris
01 42 38 47 55

From reputable French chef Yves Camdeborde, come two worthy wine bars bringing Paris two distinct tapas bars. The first, focused on the sea, L'Avant Comptoir de la Mer , serves up tempting sea-inspired fare. L'Avant Comptoir de la Terre, its neighboring wine bar, two doors over, offers up sharable mini-dishes inspired by the land (meats, poultry, breads and cheeses) for patrons waiting to be served at the Avant Comptoir next door. The fun part is a glass of wine starts at only 3.50 €.

## 6 CLANDESTINO

6 Rue Charles-François Dupuis,
75003 Paris
01 43 48 54 25

Clandestino mixes unexpected flavors and food combinations, bringing a fresh and contemporary angle on the Spanish tapas concepts. They serve up, for example, grilled octopus over fresh grilled veggies, fried calamari accompanied with a homemade tartar sauce, and your classic patatas bravas with homemade aioli sauce. Whether you opt for a cold beer or specialty cocktail to accompany your meals, you'll feel right at home in the warm atmosphere. Plus, the highlight of the evening (beside the delicious food) is a stop in the discrete speakeasy bar hidden within the establishment.

## 7 LIBRA

27 Rue Augereau,
75007 Paris
01 47 05 51 22

If you're in an adventurous mood, you should check out Libra, the French-Iranian fusion tapas bar in the 7th arr. Their intimate and colorful setting will transport you to Persia while you enjoy succulent flavors on your pallet from a cognac-flambéed chorizo served under a saffron sauce to the cod bathed in orange and caramelized-honey sauce. Its homemade desserts, infused with flavor such as the delectable chocolate mousse and saffron rose ice cream are a winner. A visit to Libra will take you on an aromatic journey as the spices tell a story through each dish.

## HONORABLE MENTIONS:

A. Noste

Boca Dos

L'Avant Comptoir du Marché

Le P'tit Barcelone

Le Petit Pan

Osaba

# Hip Bars & Restaurants to See and Be Seen in

(right bank)

**P**aris is frequented by the rich and famous, and many people come to Paris for a taste of that lifestyle. If one of your goals in the City of Light is to experience this, look no further than the following bars and restaurants.

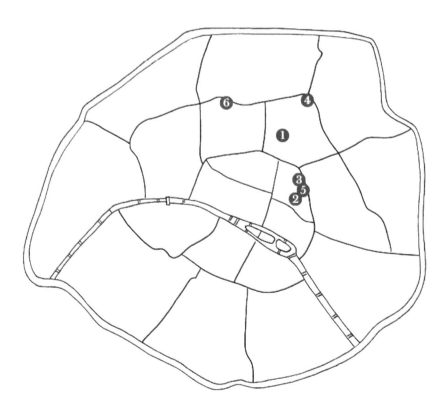

## 1 CHEZ JEANETTE

47 Rue du Faubourg Saint-Denis,
75010 Paris
01 47 70 30 89

This trendy Parisian bistro serves up your classic French fare with low-cost drinks and friendly staff who will take care of you with a smile! With the bustling Rue du Faubourg Saint-Denis, it's never a dull moment. The locals will tell you they love it and it's a fun spot to find yourself on a Monday afternoon, not unlike a Friday evening.

## 2 LA PERLE

78 Rue Vieille du Temple,
75003 Paris
01 42 72 69 93

This cafe is known as the place to be, especially during Fashion Week and is reputed for being the afterparty, after the party. It's perfectly situated in the Marais neighborhood (3rd and 4th arr.) on the Rue de la Perle. You can go there any day of the week to enjoy a drink as well as delicious homemade lunch and dinner options.

### 3 CAFÉ CRÈME
4 Rue Dupetit-Thouars,
75003 Paris

This is one of my favorite cafes in Paris and one of my go-to brunch places for a hangover cure. It's the weekend hotspot where you can spend a long lunch on the terrace with a plate of sweet pancakes or a salty burger and **frites**. And of course, a visit to Café Crème is not complete without a delicious **café crème** or two!

### 4 POINT ÉPHÉMÈRE
200 Quai de Valmy,
75010 Paris
01 40 34 02 48

This versatile space situated along the Canal Saint Martin is established as an art center, restaurant and bar that transforms into a club on nights and weekends. There is something for everyone in this popular local hangout at all hours of the day, but it's most notably the place to be into the late hours of the night with various DJ sets to keep your groove flowing!

## 5 LE MARY CELESTE

1 Rue Commines,
75003 Paris
09 50 84 19 67

This high-end hipster bar and restaurant has beautiful nautical-inspired decor, delicious specialty cocktails and delectable dishes. I recommend reserving a table and stopping by for special occasions— you won't be disappointed to spend an evening indulging in all that this bar has to offer.

## 6 PINK MAMMA

20bis Rue de Douai,
75009 Paris

Pink Mamma is best known for its heavenly Italian cuisine served in its beautifully designed three-story building. Each floor is thoughtfully designed with florals and bright colors, plus you're sure to snap some pictures that are Instagram-worthy. Every item on the menu is sure to temp you, from the truffle pasta to the oven-baked pizzas and cocktail creations.

# Michelin-Star Restaurants

In the early 1900s, The Michelin Tyre (tire) Company in France decided that it needed a way for drivers to find excellent service on their travels— be it mechanics, hotels, or food. Their goal was to increase the demand for cars, and therefore tires, by encouraging people to travel and to explore.

The company started publishing free city guides in the early 1910s— the Red Guides for restaurants and the Green guides for cities, regions, and countries. After World War I, they started charging a small price for the guide, adding value to it and they started to notice the increasing popularity of the restaurant section and decided to send a team of anonymous critics, or "inspectors" to review the restaurants.

It wasn't until 1931 that the ranking system of zero, one, two, and three stars was introduced and published in the guide for the first time five years later. Michelin also features restaurants that offer "exceptionally good food at moderate prices", an honor known as "Bib Gourmand" (an homage to the company's mascot the Michelin Man nicknamed Bib, short for Bibendum).

The Plate, a new Michelin symbol was introduced in 2016 to recognize restaurants that "simply serve good food". Then again in 2020, Michelin initiated a green star to symbolize "excellence in sustainable gastronomy".

Today, a restaurant receiving a Michelin star is a high honor, and usually makes these places more exclusive, high-end, and harder to get into. One star means "a very good restaurant in its category," two stars mean "excellent cooking, worth a detour," and three stars mean "exceptional cuisine, worth a special journey."

Before booking, you must know that a visit to a Michelin-worthy restaurant will be a memorable experience, no matter which one you choose— you can't go wrong! It will be an experience like none other and if you've never been to a place of such caliber, you should expect it to be an expensive fine dining experience, and one that I highly recommend making reservations for.

With 129 Michelin-star restaurants in Paris (as of summer 2021), how are you to filter through and decide which to try? To help you decide, let me walk you through the top choices my clients always book so you can experience one of the most remarkable meals of your life!

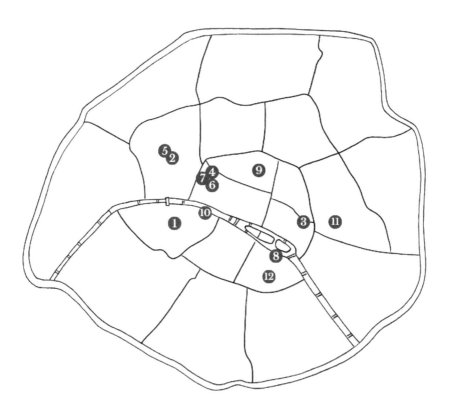

Without further ado, below are my top picks for the restaurants **étoilés** worth checking out in Paris.

## 3 Michelin Stars

As of writing this book, there are currently nine 3 Michelin-star restaurants in Paris. Voilà, my top three picks you should try out for yourself!

### ① ARPÈGE

84 Rue de Varenne,
75007 Paris
01 47 05 09 06

Alain Passard, noteworthy chef of the 3 Michelin-star restaurant Arpège, brings us class to the highest degree and cuisine that takes you to the moon. Passard was the youngest chef at 26 years old to receive two Michelin stars; the restaurant earned three stars in 1996 and since then maintained the three with their high-quality ingredients, fascinating flavors, and fine dining with sustainability at the forefront. Arpège also holds the rare "**étoile verte**" distinction for gastronomy and sustainability.

## 2 ÉPICURE

112 Rue du Faubourg Saint-Honoré,
75008 Paris
01 53 43 43 40

Le Bristol Hotel features its 3 Michelin-star restaurant led by the acclaimed chef, Eric Frechon, who is considered chef royalty. Not only does he hold 4 Michelin stars, the 4th for his luxury French brasserie 114 Faubourg, also present at Le Bristol, the chef earned the **Meilleur Ouvrier de France**, France's highest award for craftsmanship. With so much praise, you know that any restaurant of Frechon is bound to be wonderful. Épicure's exceptional stuffed truffle macaroni with foie gras and aged Parmesan are a must-try! Don't leave without tasting their heavenly cacao bean with smocked vanilla milk emulsion specialty dessert, as they also proudly carry Michelin Guide's **"Passion Dessert"** accolade.

## 3 L'AMBROISIE

9 Pl. des Vosges,
75004 Paris
01 42 78 51 45

Nestled on a corner of the Place des Vosges, L'Ambroisie presents an exceptional fine-dining experience. Notable chef, Bernard Pacaud, features carefully calculated dishes bursting with flavor. The ambience in the restaurant will make you feel like a king or queen in your own palace. Visit the three-star restaurant for an extraordinary experience and if you're a lobster lover, order the lobster **feuillantines**, or lobster puff pastry embellished with sesame seeds and a succulent curry sauce.

## MORE 3 MICHELIN-STAR RESTAURANTS

Alléno Paris au Pavillon Ledoyen

Arpège

Épicure

Guy Savoy

Kei

L'Ambroisie

Le Cinq

Le Pré Catelan

Pierre Gagnaire

# 2 Michelin Stars

There are currently 12 restaurants in Paris that boast 2 Michelin stars. Here are a handful of my picks worth trying.

### LA TABLE DE L'ESPADON

15 Pl. Vendôme, 75001 Paris

01 43 16 33 74

Dining in at La Table de l'Espadon, the Ritz's in house restaurant, is all that you can expect for a fine-dining experience: each plate is worthy to be put on display as art at MOMA, not to mention the succulent flavors that are packed into each bite. La Table is definitely **worth the detour** as Michelin Guide proudly awards it 2 Michelin Stars and the exceptional standing award, or **nos plus belles adresses** (our most beautiful addresses), for being one of the most beautiful places to dine in France.

##  5 LA SCÈNE

32 Av. Matignon, 75008 Paris
01 42 65 05 61

This beautifully designed restaurant from visionary chef, Stéphanie Le Quellec, is thought out to the T. Their bistro is traditional yet contemporary and the terrace is the perfect spot to visit for lunch or dinner in the warmer seasons. From the lovely, warm, diffused lighting, the comfy banquette-style seating, to the way the food garnish is delicately placed on the plate, every detail is carefully considered and executed at La Scène. In 2021, Michelin Guide acclaimed the restaurant's patisserie chef, Pierre Chirac, with "**Passion Dessert**" that honors talented patisserie chefs.

## 6 LE MEURICE ALAIN DUCASSE

228 Rue de Rivoli, 75001 Paris
01 44 58 10 55

No guidebook on Paris is complete without mentioning Alain Ducasse and his empire of restaurants, including the one in Le Meurice which carries his name. Dining at Le Meurice is like stepping into a time capsule as the well-preserved decor inspired by the Château de Versailles' Salon de la Paix, takes you back to another era. You almost expect for the late king to walk in as you're biting into your crispy roasted lamb. Every detail about Alain Ducasse is methodically calculated and executed with excellence and sustainability with the leading of executive chef, Amaury Bouhours.

## ⑦ SUR MESURE PAR THIERRY MARX

251 Rue St Honoré, 75001 Paris

01 70 98 73 00

Walk into a surrealist dream as internationally renowned chef, Thierry Marx, takes you on a sensory journey of experimental, vibrant dishes contrasted with the blank canvas walls and white interior design of the Mandarin Oriental Hotel that leads the imagination to wander. The concept is simple: a modern, minimalist setting where the food speaks for itself, invoking goodness in every bite.

## MORE 2 MICHELIN-STAR RESTAURANTS

David Toutain

L'Abysse au Pavillon Ledoyen

La Table de l'Espadon

La Scène

Le Clarence

Le Gabriel

Le Grand Restaurant - Jean-François Piège

Le Meurice Alain Ducasse

Le Taillevent

Maison Rostang

Marsan par Hélène Darroze

Sur Mesure par Thierry Marx

# 1 Michelin Star

And last but not least, here are the 1 Michelin-star restaurants. There are currently 91 in Paris. It would take you a month and a half to check them all out if you decided to try one every day for lunch and dinner. Of course, if you don't have that kind of time, at least check out my favorites.

**Bon appétit !**

 **TOUR D'ARGENT**

15-17 Quai de la Tournelle, 75005 Paris

01 43 54 23 31

A visit to Tour d'Argent is one for the ages— it will delight all your senses! Its interior design will make you feel like you've just landed the leading role in a French film. As you look out the window, you'll realize that the restaurant sits a few hundred meters behind Notre Dame cathedral. Everything is magical in this place— the beautifully presented dishes, the beck-and-call service, and the explosion of flavors that hit your tongue. The well-known chef, Yannick Franques, who leads the restaurant, won a **Meilleur Ouvrier de France** in 2004 and continues to impress today.

## 9 FRENCHIE

5 Rue du Nil,
75002 Paris
01 40 39 96 19

Nestled in the Sentier neighborhood in Paris, Frenchie, decorated with 1 Michelin star, serves up modern French cuisine for its hungry patrons. The prominent restaurant focuses on fresh and seasonal products for their homemade cooking, blending original flavors into the innovative quality dishes. Reserving a table at Frenchie can be tricky, but well worth the wait if you book in advance.

## 10 LES CLIMATS

41 Rue de Lille,
75007 Paris
01 58 62 10 08

This restaurant, known as the paradise of wine from the region of Bourgogne, or Burgundy, is renowned in the English-speaking community as a go-to for high-dining. Les Climats opened in 2013, and just two short years later, received its first Michelin star. Beyond the beautifully designed decor and terrace, which is open seasonally during the summer months, this establishment is granted awards every year for excellence in wine and gastronomy.

## 11 SEPTIME

80 Rue de Charonne,
75011 Paris
01 43 67 38 29

The young and inspiring chef, Bertrand Grébaut, champions for market-fresh produce, no-waste cuisine and sustainability. The high quality of the produce, meats and fish is evident in the creative cooking and rich pallet that is served up in the restaurant, earning itself a 1 Michelin star. The meals served up with precision and thoughtfulness are going to satisfy and inspire any foodie who dines in, beckoning you back again and again.

## 12 LE MAVROMMATIS

42 Rue Daubenton,
75005 Paris
01 43 31 17 17

Treat yourself and your loved ones to a high-end Greek night at Le Mavrommatis. It's Mediterranean inspired with a gourmet spin. Andréas Mavrommatis, the celebrated chef hailing from Cyprus, knows how to blend French and Greek flavors to create fresh dishes like the stuffed squid with candied fennel and hints of rusted tumeric as a starter or the grilled red mullet bursting with coconut and saffron notes as your main. The 1 Michelin star restaurant provides reliable service while simultaneously serving up succulent dishes that will take you on a flavorful voyage.

## MORE 1 MICHELIN-STAR RESTAURANTS

114, Faubourg
Abri
Accents Table Bourse
Agapé
Aida
Akrame
Alan Geaam
Alliance
Anne
Apicius
Armani Ristorante
Aspic
Auguste
Automne
Baieta
Benoit
Comice
Copenhague
Divellec
Dominique Bouchet
ERH
ES
Étude

Fleur de Pavé
Frédéric Simonin
Frenchie
Gaya par Pierre Gagnaire
Helen
Ken Kawaski
Jacques Faussat
Jin
La Condesa
La Dame de Pic
La Grande Cascade
L'Arcane
L'Arôme
La Scène Thélème
Lasserre
L'Archeste
L'Atelier de Joël Robuchon - Étoile
L'Atelier de Joël Robuchon - St-Germain
Le Baudelaire

Le Chiberta

L'Écrin

Le Faham by Kelly
Rangama

Le George

Le Jules Verne

Le Rigmarole

Le Sergent Recruteur

Les Climats

Le Violon d'Ingres

L'Innocence

L'Oiseau Blanc

Loiseau Rive Gauche

L'Orangerie

Louis

Lucas Carton

Marcore

Mavrommatis

MoSuke

Nakatani

NESO

Niege d'Été

Nomicos

Oka

Oxte

Pages

Pantagruel

Pavyllon

Pertinence

Pilgrim

Pur' - Jean-François
Rouquette

Quinsou

Qui Plume la Lune

Relais Louis XIII

Restaurant du
Palais Royal

Restaurant H

Septime

Shabour

Shang Palace

Sola

Solstice

Sushi B

Table - Bruno Verjus

Tomy & co

Tour d'Argent

Trentre-Trois

Virtus

Yam'Tcha

Yoshinori

Ze Kitchen Galerie

# Best Food in Paris that Isn't French

Paris has so much more to offer than just French food, as savory and diverse as it can be. One of the things that I love about France, and Paris specifically, is that it's a melting pot of ethnic diversity and nationalities. You can expect to see people, cultures, and cuisine of various kinds that can carry you away to different cities and countries through the food and flavors.

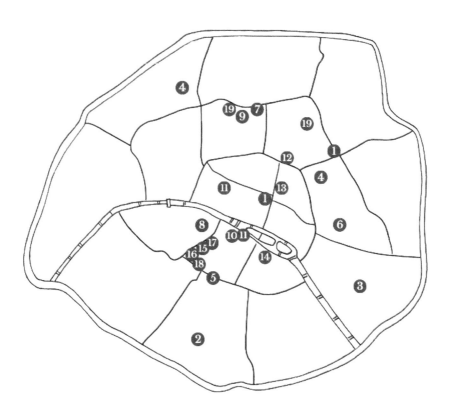

From the Indian curries of Passage Bradley, known for its Indian community and restaurants, the famous noodle houses springing up in the new "Chinatown" of Arts et Métiers neighborhood, to Italian bodegas and pizzerias sprinkled throughout the city, you are sure to go on a culinary journey to different countries through the diverse range of dishes served up in these restaurants. My only disclaimer is that this list is not at all exhaustive of the abundant choice of restaurants serving up non-French fare.

## Chinese

 **RAVIOLIS DU NORD**

| **Location 1** | **Location 2** |
|---|---|
| 115 Rue Saint-Denis, | 11 Rue Civiale, |
| 75001 Paris | 75010 Paris |
| 09 81 17 19 08 | 01 75 50 88 03 |

This place has Asian dumplings to die for— but not literally, we still want you alive! Their two locations— Belleville and Les Halles— invite you to devour these delicious, dough stuffed goodness consisting of veggie, pork, beef, chicken or shrimp. They are savory and full of flavor.

Each little dumpling is handmade and filled. Their soups and side dishes are similarly tasty. This is a great spot to have a generous meal without breaking the bank. The best part is, you can order 100 frozen dumplings to enjoy at home.

## Moroccan

 **LE GOURBI**

54 Rue des Plantes,
75014 Paris
01 45 45 58 98

You're bound to satisfy your taste buds with its Moroccan flavors and friendly service. Whether you're out on the town with a significant other or celebrating a special occasion, Le Gourbi is a lovely spot to commemorate the festivities. I highly recommend the pear and roasted almond lamb tajine— my favorite— but frankly, none of their dishes will disappoint! So, invite your friends and dig into some couscous!

## Turkish

 **LE JANISSAIRE**

22/24 All. Vivaldi,
75012 Paris
01 43 40 37 37

In the mood for some authentic Turkish cuisine? Tucked away in the 12th arr., Le Janissaire has the answer for a table full of delicious, sweet and savory Mediterranean inspired dishes. From the lamb chops to the homemade hummus, every meal is delicately prepared for your tasting pleasure. Enjoy every dish packed with flavor and fragrance. You'll want to top off your meal with a classic Turkish tea or dark Turkish coffee and traditional sweet Baklava.

## BBQ

 **MELT**

| **Location 1** | **Location 2** |
| --- | --- |
| 74 Rue de la Folie | 83 Rue Legendre, |
| Méricourt, 75011 Paris | 75017 Paris |
| 09 81 36 42 76 | 09 87 09 99 25 |

Melt is your one-stop shop for authentic Texas barbecue. As a true Texan myself, I can feel at home knowing that I can always stop into Melt for a taste of real slow-cooked brisket, smokey ribs, or tender pulled pork with spicy, mouthwatering bbq sauce.

The Pit Master, Jeffrey Howard, hails from Dallas' Pecan Lodge, so you know it has to be great! Their two locations welcome you with Lone Star beers, homemade coleslaws, and potato salad like we do in the Lone Star State.

## Seafood

 **LA COUPOLE**

102 Bd du Montparnasse, 75014 Paris

01 43 20 14 20

La Coupole is a classic French restaurant, serving up fresh seafood and oysters from their oyster bar. This is where I tried my first oyster ever and I'm glad I did because I've loved them ever since. La Coupole's art deco themed interior will transport you in time to the days of Hemingway as you enjoy their crustacean platters, whether for two or a multitude. The **Bar Americain** serves up cocktail creations as well as a lengthy wine selection to pair with any dish you order. This remains one of my favorite restaurants in Paris and is not to be missed on your next trip!

## 6  CLAMATO

80 Rue de Charonne,
75011 Paris
01 43 72 74 53

Calling all seafood lovers! Clamato is Septime's maritime sibling, offering shellfish dishes revamped with high-dining standards while remaining relatively affordable for a night out on the town. They serve up caviar and tartar dishes, not to mention delicious oysters, which are named some of the best in town. You won't dine at Clamato without expecting good food, good people, and good feels!

**Oyster Bar**

## 7  LA DOUZAINE

12 Rue Gérando,
75009 Paris
01 48 74 41 36

La Douzaine is a little shop in the 9th arr. that has a subtle hole-in-the-wall feel whose specialty is none other than oysters. This tiny oyster bar delivers big flavor with their seafood and oyster platters. They promise to deliver the sea to you, and they don't fail to do just that! The fresh seafood is served with house specialty wines at local prices. You can eat in house or take a basket to go to enjoy **chez toi.**

## Peruvian

 **COYA**

83-85 Rue du Bac,
75007 Paris
01 43 22 00 65

For a Central American-inspired evening, Coya is your Peruvian stop, perfectly and discreetly nestled in the Beaupassage near Rue du Bac. From the cocktails, the appetizers to the main courses, every dish is infused with flavor and is a delightful surprise for your tastebuds. The restaurant's warm and vibrant vibes will provide a fantastic setting for your Instagram feed, too!

## Thai

 **THAI HOUSE**

42 Rue Rodier,
75009 Paris
01 42 80 11 83

This family-owned Thai restaurant serves up authentic Thai food packed with flavor. Every little detail will transport you to Thailand, from the live fish tank full of exotic fish, the colorful dishes that come out of the kitchen, to the warm and friendly staff. You can eat generously here without a heavy price tag. I recommend the red coconut curry. They also have one of the best Pad Thai dishes in the city— it's well-worth a visit! They offer meals to eat in as well as to go.

## Sushi

 **BLUEBERRY MAKI BAR**
6 Rue du Sabot, 75006 Paris
01 42 22 21 56

For a taste of Japan, stop by none other than Blueberry for authentic, fresh, delicious and multicolored delights. Blueberry serves up the best maki— but you'll feel like you're actually tasting these bites in Tokyo. The restaurant presents original and tasty treats rolled up, marinated in sauces, and featured across plates as if the meals were modern art paintings at the Pompidou. Blueberry's specialties include: izakayas, chirashis, sushis and sashimis. The specialty cocktails with a Japanese twist are also a lovely treat.

## Ramen

 **KODAWARI RAMEN (YOKOCHŌ)**

| **Location 1** | **Location 2** |
| --- | --- |
| 29 Rue Mazarine, | 12 Rue de Richelieu, |
| 75006 Paris | 75001 Paris |
| 09 70 91 12 41 | 09 84 30 99 26 |

If you're craving a warm ramen, look no further than Kodawari Ramen for your fix. The crew serves up homemade artisan ramen that is created before your eyes. Every ingredient is carefully curated, from the free-range chicken stock to the self-grown wheat produced for the flour in the noodles. Additionally, the ramen toppings are high-quality and various to heighten the aromas of the dish on the tongue as for the nose. The establishment was awarded a Palme d'or in 2017 and Palme d'argent in 2018 for their excellent menu from Michelin Guide.

## Indian

 **BARANAAN STREET FOOD & COCKTAIL BAR**

7 Rue du Faubourg Saint-Martin,
75010 Paris
01 40 38 97 57

Who knew you could get spicy Indian street food presented with colorful ingredients against the backdrop of a train in Mumbai without leaving Paris? You can get all of this at BaraNaan and more! Their delectable menu of contemporary Indian food takes the center stage. While a visit will satisfy your tastebuds and fill your belly, the restaurant does this without emptying your wallet. A pleasant surprise awaits any willing guest to check out their speakeasy bar at the back of the restaurant for cocktails and drinks.

## Lebanese

 **QASTI**

205 Rue Saint-Martin,
75003 Paris
01 42 76 04 32

Qasti takes the traditional Lebanese cuisine and steps up the flavors to bring you a gastronomic journey worthy of kings and queens. The Michelin-Star chef, Alan Geaam, created Qasti as a personal homage to his homeland, bringing contemporary Lebanese food with a seasonal menu to Paris. He entices you with pops of color, aromas and textures of Beirut— it's a must if you love Lebanese!

## Ethipoian

 **RESTAURANT GODJO**

8 Rue de l'Ecole Polytechnique,
75005 Paris
01 40 46 82 21

For a taste of Africa, you've got to try the savory dishes of Godjo. The restaurant is run by a couple of Ethiopian women who deliver authentic and tasty plates that will fill up your tummy at an affordable price. They have vegetarian options as well as meat, poultry, and fish dishes bathed in spices and sauces. These rich flavors are like none other that you will taste in Paris. The warm welcome and African-inspired setting will make you feel right at home, as if you were directly in an Ethiopian's kitchen.

## Italian/Pizza

 **ANIMA**

78 Rue du Recherches-Midi,
75006 Paris
01 40 47 90 41

If you're craving fine, oven-baked pizza with respect to Italia, I've got just the place for you! Anima creates simple, rustic and above all, delicious oven-baked pizzas. The high-quality and fresh ingredients are served over light and fluffy dough. They also serve up a small selection of antipasti and desserts, keeping the menu small while maintaining quality. The servers are attentive, funny, and kind. I highly recommend paying a visit to cure that pizza craving.

## Gluten-Free Italian

 **MIMI**
105 Rue du Cherche-Midi,
75006 Paris
01 83 89 52 85

If you or someone you're with is gluten-intolerant or gluten-sensitive, this is definitely the place to invite them. Mimi Cave à Manger serves up innovative meal creations that are all 100% gluten-free. Their cuisine is Neapolitan-inspired, colorful and delicious; plus, you'll never know you're eating gluten-free! They also have a lovely selection of Italian and French wines.

## Vegan

 **APETI**
72 Rue du Cherche-Midi,
75006 Paris
01 43 22 17 98

Apeti is your one-stop shop for vegan, healthy, organic, and even gluten-free and lactose-free options. They champion healthy and natural foods with loads of color, packed with flavor. The dining room is enchanting, modern and calm. You'll really enjoy everything about this restaurant, including the attentive service.

## Vietnamean

 **THUY LONG**

111 Rue de Vaugirard, 75006 Paris

01 45 49 26 01

An old colleague introduced me to this humble family owned and operated restaurant. A meal here, whether for lunch or dinner is definitely a treat. To begin with, you need a long lunch to fully enjoy the setting, entrées and mains. They take their time cooking up the meal in the tiny kitchen, but it's well worth it. Next time you have a craving for good old-fashioned Vietnamese food, stop in.

## Mexican

 **EL NOPAL**

| **Location 1** | **Location 2** |
| --- | --- |
| 3 Rue Eugene Varlin | El Nopal Taqueria |
| 75010 Paris | 5 Rue Dupérre, |
| 07 86 39 63 46 | 75009 Paris |

Having Mexican grandparents, Mexican cuisine is vital in my family. I cannot recommend El Nopal Taqueria more for authentic, spicy, and tasty Mexican food. They do tacos **al carbon** and **barbacoa** (my favorites), as well as burritos, and chips and salsa. The salsas, guacamoles, and bean dip are all worthy of grandma's cooking. They have two locations; the one at Canal St Martin is takeaway only, but I recommend stopping by for pick up and walking over to eat along the banks of the canal in the warmer summer months.

# Best Burgers in Paris

How could I go on our culinary roadmap without shouting out a few of my favorite burger joints— after all, I am American and from Texas and I **love** my burgers. And so do the French— so much so that you are likely to see a cheeseburger on the menu of any Parisian cafe's menu!

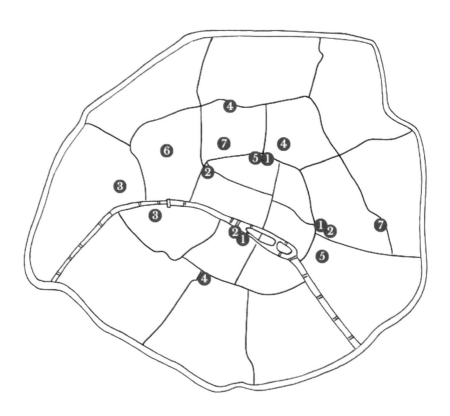

Unlike in the States, in France, you will most likely be asked how you want your meat patty cooked: **bleue** (rare), **saignante** (medium rare), **à point** (medium), **cuite** (medium well), or **bien cuite** (well done).

I apologize in advance to my veggie or vegan friends, but a few of these places do offer veg options and would be worth checking out if you're down for a good burger every now and again.

So, without further ado, here are some noteworthy specialty burger places to bite into a mouthwatering, cheesy burger in Paris, possibly accompanied with some **frites**.

**Bon appétit !**

### BURGER & FRIES
**Location 1**

1 Bd de Bonne
Nouvelle, 75002 Paris
01 42 36 22 79

**Lacation 2**

95 boulevard Saint
Germain, 75006 Paris
01 71 93 39 83

**Location 3**

5 Rue de la Roquette,
75011 Paris
01 48 07 16 46

If you're looking for a sure win, you cannot go wrong with Burger & Fries. Most of their **menus,** or meal combos, are under 10 €. Their burger buns are homemade, and they have gluten-free options. This no-frills option is just simple, tasty food.

## 2  BLEND

**Location 1**

15 Rue de Charonne,
75011 Paris
01 48 07 10 78

**Location 2**

4 Rue de l'Ancienne
Comédie,
75006 Paris
01 42 49 28 35

**Location 3**

18 Rue Duphot,
75001 Paris
01 40 15 06 69

If you have ever wanted to order your hamburger by pictogram, Blend is for you! As well as being super hip (#BURGERNESS), they are open and transparent about their ingredients and production methods. They also have good veggie options and limited edition recipes.

## 3  BIRDY

**Location 1**

49 Av. Bosquet,
75007 Paris
01 84 25 09 88

**Location 2**

69 Av. Kléber,
75116 Paris
01 47 04 16 67

Birdy is a family business with two locations in the West of Paris. True to their name, each burger is represented by its own bird and there is enough choice that you will never get bored! They also have a burger of the month, and each location has its own exclusive burgers for you to try.

## 4 PNY

**Loaction 1**

50 Rue du Faubourg
Saint-Denis,
75010 Paris
01 42 47 06 59

**Location 2**

24 Rue Pierre
Fontaine, 75009 Paris
01 42 47 06 59

**Location 3**

15 Rue de la Gaite,
75014 Paris
01 42 47 06 59

PNY has some of the fanciest burger restaurants I have ever seen! PNY stands for Paris New York and they definitely add a classy Parisian spin to the classic American burger. I have never seen a restaurant put so much effort into making the perfect burger: everything is made with the utmost precision, from the grinding of the meat to the recipe for their bread. Go for the decor, come back for the delicious food!

## 5 KING MARCEL

**Location 1**

166 Rue Montmartre,
75002 Paris
01 42 36 42 85

**Location 2**

30 Bd Diderot,
75012 Paris
01 45 83 82 38

Does eating American food while visiting France make you feel like you're missing something? King Marcel has the answer! Founded by two Frenchies with a love for American food, King Marcel combines the great American burger with French cuisine, creating **My Burger is French**— perfect for when you want some comfort food, but you're still an adventurer!

## 6 BURGER & FILS

9 Rue du
Commandant Rivière,
75008 Paris
01 45 61 15 05

At Burger & Fils, the menu is simple: you can order whatever you want! Home of the "**Smashburger sur mesure**" (customizable Smashburger), the options are almost endless, and they bring together the best of the USA and France. I'm not joking, the buns are imported directly from the USA and their French beef patties are freshly ground every morning. All that's left is to choose your toppings!

## 7 MANGEZ ET CASSEZ-VOUS

### Location 1

39 Rue Taitbout,
75009 Paris
01 49 70 66 88

### Location 2

64 Rue Alexandre
Dumas, 75011 Paris
09 82 40 92 06

Mangez et Cassez-Vous has been causing a stir in Paris since they opened a couple of years ago. Their name literally means Eat and Go Away, so if you are looking for a restaurant in which to enjoy a two-hour lunch, this is not your place! You will, however, find a burger and fries for under 3 €. Yes, you read that right! Be careful though, these restaurants are in high demand and queues may be long.

# Best Brunch Restaurants in Paris

One thing that Paris does not have a shortage of are great brunch places. So, obviously, I can name a few for you, but this list is definitely not exhaustive. You can almost write a whole book on all the incredible cafes in Paris with a brunch theme. Here are my tried-and-true brunch spots.

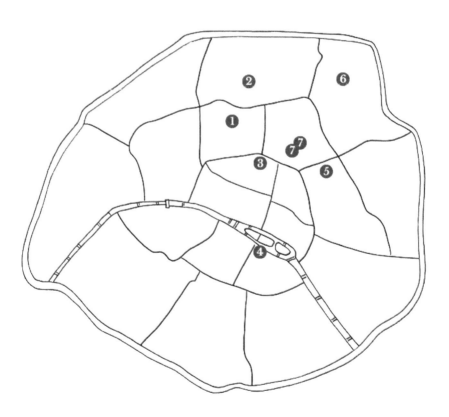

## ① LA COMPAGNIE DU CAFÉ

19 Rue Notre Dame de Lorette,
75009 Paris
09 81 25 74 16

This place is not only one of my favorite coffee shops, but the brunch is extraordinary too. The chef knows how to pair the right **mélange** of items on the dish to get the most colorful dishes. The coffee is to die for, and they bake their own pies and cakes. My go-to is the banoffee (banana pudding/coffee) cake with a cortado.

## ② THE HARDWARE SOCIÉTÉ

10 Rue Lamarck,
75018 Paris
01 42 51 69 03

I sent my Parisian friends here for an Australian-influenced brunch and even they were impressed. They have the classic brunch items like eggs benedict, but also some unexpected dishes like melt-in-your-mouth duck confit. They go one step further as they are a bakery too and bake all their cakes and pâtisseries **sur place**. If you go, go early or expect to wait in line to get a table as they don't take reservations. They have both sweet and savory options if you go here with foodies who love both!

### ③ SALATIM

15 Rue des Jeuneurs,
75002 Paris
01 42 36 30 03

You will delight in delicious Israeli-inspired dishes for this brunch. You can taste the Mediterranean colors through the yummy food. The Shakshuka egg dish is a must order! They feature a brunch with a starter (Shakshuka), main, Israelian bread, juice, coffee and dessert for only 23 €. It's a lot of food and your belly will be satisfied by the end. As the place is tiny, you may have to wait for a seat, but trust me, it's well worth it.

### ④ LOU LOU CAFÉ

90 Bd Saint-Germain,
75005 Paris
01 46 34 86 64

If you're staying on the left bank near the Saint Michel area, this place is a must for your weekend coffee and brunch. The coffee is exquisite and perfectly brewed; they present various fresh squeezed juices, and healthy options for the health-conscious eater. Try their traditional brunch options of savory poached eggs benny, hearty burgers, or one of their fresh salads for something on the lighter side. And what is brunch without a nice, sweet ending? Lou Lou has light and fluffy cheesecakes and yogurt bowls to wrap up your weekend brunch, too.

## 5 THE HOOD

80 Rue Jean-Pierre Timbaud,
75011 Paris
07 80 97 54 38

This lively cafe offers up delicious grub and coffee in a beautiful coffee shop. The Asian (Vietnamese and Singaporean heritage) brunch menu compliments the French pastries, cakes, and coffee drinks perfectly. They have a mean banh mi as well as chicken rice and laksa that patrons love. But don't let me convince you— check out their colorful Instagram for more food envie and go there when you're in Paris!

## 6 LE PAVILLON DES CANAUX

39 Quai de la Loire,
75019 Paris
01 73 71 82 90

If you want a flawless brunch experience with a lovely sun-kissed terrace with a perfect view of the Canal, visit Le Pavillon des Canaux. It's the most adorable coffee shop/restaurant. Located in an old house— work on your laptop in a bathtub or lounge with a book and coffee in hand — this is the place to check out. Le Pavillon is a rare gem in Paris, serving up a brunch menu where they encourage conversation and community. They will certainly make you feel **chez toi** in this cozy home turned coffee shop.

## 7  HOLLYBELLY 5 & HOLLYBELLY 19

**Location 1**

5 Rue Lucien
Sampaix, 75010 Paris
01 82 28 00 80

**Location 2**

19 Rue Lucien
Sampaix,
75010 Paris

Both of their locations are 200 meters away on the same street and serve up mouthwatering everything: specialty brunch cocktails to help with that morning hangover, coffee to get your day going, brunch items that include a buttermilk chicken biscuit, poached eggs, hashbrowns, bacon and everything in between. Their chefs take food seriously and present everything so beautifully, but the true test is when you bite into your meal and your tastebuds come alive!

# Best Coffee Shops on Both Sides of the River

L anding my first apartment with roommates in Le Marais district (3rd arr.) when I first settled in Paris, I naturally gravitated to the shops, bars, restaurants and cafes in the right bank. My new place at the time was on Rue Chapon, upstairs from Le Taxi Jaune (Yellow Taxi) restaurant, which sadly doesn't exist anymore.

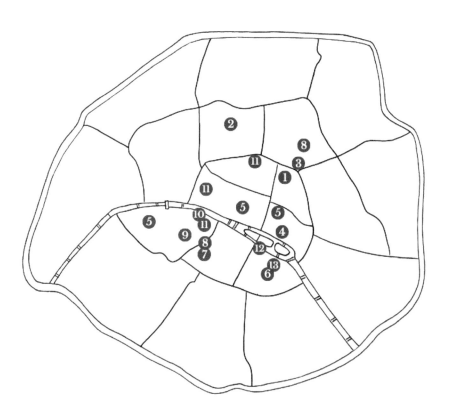

An iconic turquoise blue door welcomes you at the entrance then leads to a curving staircase worthy of Audrey Hepburn. The 5th floor apartment with its creaking but oh-so-charming wood floors, white walls and ceilings with lush crown moulding, and a **vis-à-vis** that revealed the neighbors' kitchen, gave way to half the rooftops of Paris. Yes, this was the charmed life of tiny bathrooms and kitchens.

In that same tiny kitchen, my roommates had an Italian coffee maker. We would have to brew two rounds of coffee just to get enough for an Americano— after all, I was **l'Américaine** of the household and not used to my pint-size cups of strong coffee. Although I loved that little Italian **cafetière** that poured out hot steaming black gold coffee, it didn't stop me from venturing out to some of the local coffee shops every now and again to get my fix of a great cup 'o Joe in the form of a piccolo, cortado, latte or mocha.

As a coffee connoisseur, I love scouting out new coffee shops in Paris. If you're reading this, it's probably because you want to know where to find good coffee in Paris.

Here are my picks for the most noteworthy coffee shops on both sides of the Seine River.

# Coffee Shops on the Rive Droite

## ① CAFÉ LOUSTIC
40 Rue Chapon,
75003 Paris
09 80 31 07 06

- proud espresso bar, offering up a new espresso of the week
- also features a weekly "Coffee of the Moment"
- homemade cakes, pastries, sandwiches
- quiet place, good for reading
- coffee to go
- cozy and laid-back vibe
- wifi only on weekdays

This place was definitely my first taste of real coffee in the city that doesn't really know how to make good coffee. It's true that Paris is known for its **cafés** and bars, but it isn't known for great coffee. The extent of what Parisians know of coffee is pitch black espresso that comes out of Cafe Richard or Lavazza machines— it's so bitter that most Parisians have to add a full tablespoon of sugar to get it down the esophagus and then chase it with a cup of water.

Café Loustic understood the concept and need for great coffee in Paris. Owner, Channa Galhenage, opened up this cozy coffee shop in March 2013 and he opened up his second shop of the same name in Marseille, France in 2018. If you're in the Arts et Métiers area, definitely come check out this spot for that afternoon coffee craving.

## 2 LA COMPAGNIE DU CAFÉ

19 Rue Notre Dame de Lorette, 75009 Paris

09 81 25 74 16

- ▸ roast their own coffee
- ▸ great for bunch/lunch
- ▸ homemade pies and pastries
- ▸ wifi, laptop friendly
- ▸ friendly staff
- ▸ coffee to go
- ▸ good for social meetings
- ▸ welcoming ambience that is spacious with good lighting

Love this place! Only a few meters from the lovely Saint George metro stop, it became one of my local coffee joints when I moved to the 9th arrondissement back in 2015. So, yes, I'm a bit biased, but the best places are always the local hang outs.

Owner, Romain Fabry, roasts his own coffee grains in house. We became acquainted when I started frequenting the coffee shop weekly for my afternoon coffee fix and would end up staying for hours working away on my laptop. My favorite drink at La Compagnie du Cafe is the cortado they do for me—that, with a side of Banoffee tart made from scratch. You'll never want to leave this place with the invigorating smell of freshly roasted coffee, good java, sky lighting, and the tranquil, open space!

### ③ REPUBLIQUE OF COFFEE

2 Bd Saint-Martin,
75010 Paris
09 83 35 38 13

- ▸ colorful sweet & savory food options
- ▸ Mexican-Cali style food
- ▸ delicious coffee
- ▸ unique coffee options
- ▸ vegan options

Situated near Place de la République, this coffee shop serves up colorful Mexican-Californian inspired grub along with delicious coffee beverages. Their unique charcoal latte is a must try! The coffee shop has a lovely terrace facing the bustling boulevard as well as a beautifully designed interior with exposed brick and mirrored ceiling. You're going to enjoy every part of your experience here!

### ④ LE PELOTON CAFE

17 Rue du Pont Louis-Philippe,
75004 Paris
06 18 80 84 92

- ▸ homemade waffels
- ▸ friendly, English-speaking staff
- ▸ showcase beautiful latte art
- ▸ strong community of cycling-lovers
- ▸ rental bike and bike tour resources

Community is at the heart of Le Peloton Cafe, located in the Marais neighborhood. Besides taking coffee seriously, they champion bringing people together— namely the English-speaking expat community— through cycling and the cycling culture. The cafe was opened in 2015 by the same guys, Christian and Paul, who run Bike About Tours, a bike tour company in Paris. The coffee shop serves up specialty coffee and their famous homemade waffles for a little slice of home abroad. When you stop into Le Peloton, you won't expect anything less than a good cup of coffee and a friendly community of people around you who love life. Who wouldn't want a piece of that?

 **5 TERRES DE CAFÉ**

### Location 1

36 Rue des Blancs Manteaux, 75004 Paris

09 87 02 51 76

### Location 2

150 Rue St Honoré, 75001 Paris

09 86 51 02 00

### Location 3

67 Av. de la Bourdonnais, 75007 Paris

01 45 50 37 39

- ▶ sustainably produced coffee
- ▶ 100% roasted in France
- ▶ cute, cozy, modern coffee shops
- ▶ coffee discovery subscription available
- ▶ selection of teas and chocolate drinks
- ▶ wide selection of merchandise available in their shops

Terres' distinguished, cute, and peaceful coffee shops welcome you to taste a cup of coffee however you prefer. They advocate for sustainably produced coffee beans, knowledge of the **terroirs**, or territories, as well as respect for its producers— the nature producing it, and the consumers drinking it. They work with a network of farms and cooperatives in Latin America and Africa to bring you the highest quality beans that are 100% roasted in France while honoring the land and communities that are producing them. You will love the coffee as well as their values!

# Coffee Shops on the Rive Gauche

Here are my picks for the best coffee shops in Paris on the left bank plus some honorable mentions below.

 **DOSE, COFFEE DEALER**

73 Rue Mouffetard, 75005 Paris

01 43 36 65 03

- ▸ sell coffee grains
- ▸ freshly prepared food options
- ▸ vegan and vegetarian options
- ▸ take away options
- ▸ juice bar

Tucked away on a corner of the famous Rue Mouffetard is Dose Cafe. You'll find bookshelves covered in books among an intimate and cozy setting.

The staff is friendly and attentive to clients' needs. It's the perfect spot, either indoors or outdoors under the covered walkway, to sit for a coffee break in the Latin Quarter.

 **COLOROVA**

47 Rue de l'Abbé Grégoire, 75006 Paris

01 45 44 67 56

- ▸ colorful displace of homemade pastries
- ▸ great place for weekend brunch
- ▸ quiet, cozy atmosphere
- ▸ natural lighting and colorful decor
- ▸ friendly staff that welcomes you with a smile

This place not only has great coffee, but they have delicious, beautifully crafted pastries to complement your coffee drink. Their brunch is a must on the weekends, too.

The natural light welcomes you and you'll love the cozy bohemian vibes. It's a very Instagrammable spot that will add color to your day.

I highly recommend taking a coffee break here before heading over for a short walk in the neighborhood of the historic Saint Sulpice Church.

### 8 TEN BELLES

**Location 1**

10 Rue de la Grange aux Belles, 75010 Paris

09 83 08 86 69

**Location 2**

53 Rue du Cherche-Midi, 75006 Paris

09 83 34 33 65

- ▸ delectable scones and jam
- ▸ offer take-away options
- ▸ cozy and lively ambience, good for people watching
- ▸ lunch options
- ▸ offer vegan lunch options

This tiny cafe is nicely situated on the bustling Rue du Cherche-Midi. It is the sister cafe of the Ten Belles on the **rive droite,** near the Canal Saint Martin.

The scones and homemade baked goods complement their coffee selection that is locally sourced from Téléscope Cafe. Head on over to this inviting coffee bar for your favorite kind of cup o' Joe. You won't be disappointed!

## 9 COUTUME CAFE

47 Rue de Babylone,
75007 Paris

09 88 40 47 99

- ▸ have a wide array of coffee beans and preparation methods
- ▸ large & spacious cafe
- ▸ lunch and brunch options
- ▸ knowledgeable baristas

This place is perfect for a lunch and after lunch coffee break. This spacious place makes it an ideal place to meet up for a lunch date.

They also have their own coffee brew on tap. Their large selection of coffee preparation methods makes this place ideal for discovering the many ways to drink coffee.

Their staff is very knowledgeable about the grains, and you can learn a lot from just striking up a conversation with any of the baristas.

## 10 CUPPA CAFÉ

86 Rue de l'Université,
75007 Paris

- ▸ lovely, peaceful & modern decor
- ▸ friendly staff
- ▸ coffee sourced from Drop Coffee, changes every 3 weeks
- ▸ homemade food
- ▸ veggie options
- ▸ sells coffee grains
- ▸ take-off away option available

The first thing you'll notice is the friendly smiles of the staff as you step into Cuppa. The whole ambience of this place is top notch, from the divine smell of the freshly brewed coffee to the well thought out decor. Its lovely dark marble tables and artwork from local artists make you feel at peace.

Every detail of this place, from its decor to the coffee presentation is 5 stars. They source their coffee from Drop coffee in Sweden and the selection changes about every 3 weeks. I tried the piccolo, one of my favs, and it was probably one of the best I've had in my life!

 **ARABICA**
**Location 1**
83P Rue du Bac,
75007 Paris
01 43 21 13 41

**Location 2**
44-47 Pass. des
Panoramas, 75002
Paris
01 43 21 13 41

**Location 3**
8 Rue de Castiglione,
75001 Paris
01 42 36 12 89

▸ fun experience to find this hidden gem
▸ matcha latte option
▸ sells its own grains
▸ take-away available
▸ only outdoor seating available
▸ no wifi here, but this is the perfect chance to unplug from the computer for five minutes

You'll have to do a little scouring to find this place, but it's well worth it. Their left bank location is hidden in a building courtyard through the Beaupassage on the notable Rue Du Bac. Their right bank locale is also hidden, but this time, in the Passage des Panoramas.

Their specialty coffee is a must try! It's as much an experience to find this place as it is to drink the black gold from their brewers. Their philosophy is simple, see the world through coffee— they definitely don't fail to bring that experience to your cup of Joe.

## 12  SHAKESPEARE & COMPANY

35 Rue de la Bûcherie, 75005 Paris

01 43 25 40 93

- ▸ bookstore and coffee shop
- ▸ expat staff and community
- ▸ take away available
- ▸ healthy meal options
- ▸ outdoor seating

This is your perfect spot to get great books and a little taste of home if you miss speaking English. Shakespeare is most famous for its English book shop, but the coffee shop is a great extension to the bookstore next door. Perfect for making an afternoon of it, the coffee and healthy meal options go great together with a book in hand.

This place does get really busy during the lunch hour, but they also have big benches and tables outside with one of the best views in Paris of her highness— Notre Dame de Paris.

## 13 STRADA

24 Rue Monge,
75005 Paris

- ▸ big open coffee shop
- ▸ healthy food options, brunch options available
- ▸ unique coffee brewing options
- ▸ great locale for brief meetings
- ▸ friendly staff
- ▸ wifi available

Strada has two cafes, one on each side of the river, serving up freshly brewed coffee and healthy meals. Strada on the left bank is a bright and open coffee shop contrasted with the right bank's intimate smaller cafe. The left bank's location is a spacious and luminous cafe, perfect for short work meetings over a good cup of caffeine. They also have a full lunch menu that is worth trying out as they serve healthy food options for the health-conscious patron.

## HONORABLE MENTIONS:

Coffee Spoune

Eggs & Co.

KB coffee

La Cafeotheque

Le Loulou

Noir Coffeeshop

# Best Tea Houses

Un salon du thé, or a tea house or tearoom as we know them in English, are akin to coffee shops, but specialize in tea drinks and other refreshments as well as desserts and baked goods that compliment your tea experience. Tea houses are social settings, much like coffee shops or cafés, where you can enjoy afternoon tea from their selection of house blend teas accompanied with small cakes.

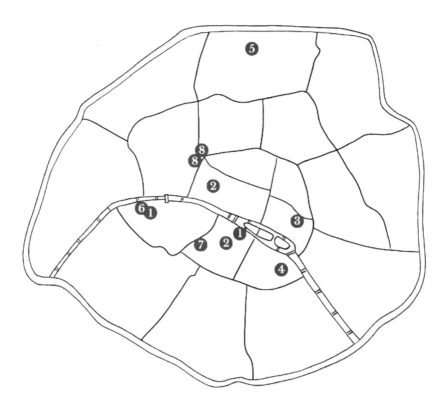

Tearooms and tea houses, which are popular in Britain because of the tea culture, are gaining popularity in France and many hotels now present a luxury afternoon tea service with a selection of specialty teas.

However, you don't have to spend a lot of money to still enjoy an afternoon tea experience in Paris. Continue reading for my top tea houses to check out in order to relax, sip on delicious tea, and enjoy a sophisticated afternoon tea like our reputed British compatriots.

## 1 MARIAGE FRÈRES

| Location 1 | Location 2 |
|---|---|
| 13 Rue des Grands Augustins, 75006 Paris 01 40 51 82 50 | 129 Rue de Grenelle, 75007 Paris 01 44 42 38 77 |

Mariage Frère has several locations in Paris to sip on tea, but I recommend you go to the one near Odéon because it's three in one: tearoom, tea shop, and museum. The pastries are to die for, and the tea options are enormous. You can visit for a few cups while indulging in their delicate, homemade pastries. Pop into the tiny museum downstairs, then buy yourself some tea to take home. You'll get a well-rounded experience here!

## 2 ANGELINA

**Location 1**

226 Rue de Rivoli,
75001 Paris
01 42 60 82 00

**Location 2**

19 Rue de Vaugirard,
75006 Paris
01 46 34 31 19

This tearoom, inspired by the **belle-epoque,** serves up delicious tea options but Angelina is most known for its thick, homemade hot chocolate called "**L'Africain**". Founded by the Austrien confectioner, Anton Rumpelmayer, in 1903, Angelina has become a staple in **pâtisseries** (pastries). The tearoom has been known for welcoming guests such as Prost, Coco Chanel and many others in the art and design world. I recommend visiting the original tearoom on Rue Rivoli or the one in the Luxembourg Gardens if you're on the left bank.

## 3 LE LOIR DANS LA THÉIÈRE

3 Rue des Rosiers,
75004 Paris
01 42 72 90 61

Le Loir, whose name in English means the dormouse in a teapot, is an eclectic tearoom wonderland. The vibe feels like Alice in Wonderland stepped into Bohemia with great tea, pastries, and lunch options. The tearoom in the Marais doesn't pretend to be anything it isn't other than a quirky but cozy place to meet friends for tea and where you can eat fresh delicious meals and their signature lemon meringue pie. This place fills up quickly and provokes a queue outside, mostly on weekends, so you know it's got to be good!

## 4. GRANDE MOSQUÉE DE PARIS

2bis Pl. du Puits de l'Ermite,
75005 Paris
01 45 35 97 33

The tearoom and restaurant of La Grande Mosquée welcomes guests to enjoy tea at 3 € a pop, in the company of a few Arab pastries from the patisserie shop. It's a fun spot to change worlds as you enter a secret garden of sorts within the courtyard. The Grande Mosquée, France's largest mosque, has a gift shop and offers guided tours every day, check the website for more details.

## 5. CHEZ HÉLÈNE

89 Rue Duhesme,
75018 Paris
01 42 64 49 04

Chez Hélène is an **épicerie** (little grocery shop), tearoom, and charming boutique that invites you into its tiny space, serving up meals and desserts with enormous flavors. Every dish is homemade and delicately created for impactful flavor. They serve **un thé du jour**, or a tea of the day, to help you discover new flavors. I recommend a visit to this tearoom if you're looking for a quiet and cozy cityscape with delicious food and warm teas.

## 6  LES DEUX ABEILLES

189 Rue de l'Université,
75007 Paris
01 45 55 64 04

Les Deux Abeilles is discreetly nestled on the Rue de l'Université but is a stone throw away from the Eiffel Tower. Les Deux Abeilles, or the two bees, is a dainty little cafe and tearoom that serves homemade pies and desserts with teas and hot chocolate on tables with white lush tablecloths under a skylight that fills the entire inner room. I definitely recommend taking a pause here after a busy day of visiting the Eiffel Tower nearby.

## 7  MAMIE GÂTEAUX

66 Rue du Cherche-Midi,
75006 Paris
01 42 22 32 15

Stepping into Mamie Gâteaux is like walking into your grandmother's dining room, which is no surprise as the cafe is named after **mamie**, or granny herself! The tearoom does an excellent job of invoking the nostalgia of childhood with its family recipes of sweet pies and savory comfort meals, teas, and warm drinks. You will definitely feel like you're back in your childhood when you stop in.

## 8 CAFÉ POUCHKINE

**Location 1**

16 Pl. de la Madeleine,
75008 Paris
01 53 43 81 60

**Location 2**

64 Bd Haussmann,
75008 Paris

Step into a fancy, palatial-style tearoom inspired by Russian aristocracy and excellence. The menu of savory dishes and sweet pastries is a marriage of Franco-Russian ties. The tea options are abundant and the desserts embody an array of color and flavor infused delicacies. Indulge in an afternoon at their grandiose **salon du thé** while you take in Paris!

# Best French Bakeries & Patisserie Shops

We simply cannot move on and continue talking about food without discussing all things **sucrée** (sweet)! The French **love** their sweet treats, **pain**, and **gâteaux** as much as they love their cultural experiences, wine and cheese.

The French bakery, or **boulangerie**, as it's known in French, is as much a part of the French identity as the gastronomical meal is. The French **baguette** is a daily staple and couldn't make the adage of 'daily bread' ring truer. If people carrying baguettes in the streets is a cliché of French society, it's an arguably accurate depiction of it— in the best way possible!

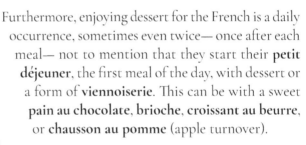

Furthermore, enjoying dessert for the French is a daily occurrence, sometimes even twice— once after each meal— not to mention that they start their **petit déjeuner**, the first meal of the day, with dessert or a form of **viennoiserie**. This can be with a sweet **pain au chocolate**, **brioche**, **croissant au beurre**, or **chausson au pomme** (apple turnover).

In France, you must distinguish the **boulangerie** apart from the **pâtisserie** shop. **La boulangerie** is a bakery that sells mainly baked goods: bread items, baguettes, and baked cakes (**gâteau**). Whereas **la pâtisserie** specializes in sweeter items like desserts and colorful pastries: macarons, **éclairs**, and tarts. You will often times see hybrid **boulangerie-pâtisserie** shops as well as exclusive **pâtisserie** shops concentrating on the singular sweet treats.

Lastly, the French have a special time of day besides **le petit déj** and dessert after meals when they opt to enjoy a sweet delicacy, too. This is the **goûter,** or snack time, which is usually partaken of after school for school children, and in the late afternoon for adults with a coffee or as an afternoon break and opportunity to raise the blood sugar with something sumptuous.

If you appreciate sweet things and have a sweet tooth yourself, you're going to love this list of my favorite **boulangeries** and **pâtisserie** shops in town.

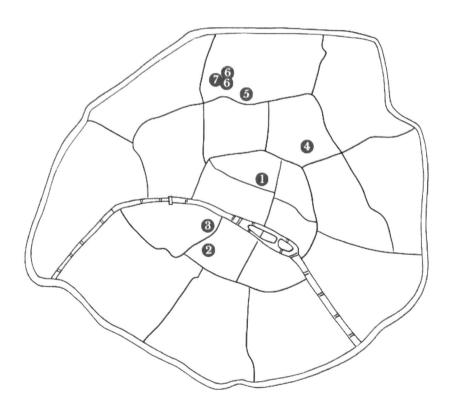

**1** **STOHRER**
51 Rue Montorgueil,
75002 Paris
01 42 33 38 20

*Oldest pâtisserie shop in Paris, founded in 1730*

Stohrer invented the savory rum baba pastry, which is a fluffy dough pastry soaked in rum and topped with candied fruit. The **pâtisserie** shop is perfectly located on the bustling Rue Montorgueil and is known for its elegant-looking delicacies. Your sweet tooth will thank you for tasting one or two of their sweet treats!

**2** **COLOROVA**
47 Rue de l'Abbé Grégoire,
75006 Paris
01 45 44 67 56

*Best pâtisserie bar with colorful pastries & desserts*

This place is king when it comes to delectable, sweet **pâtisseries**. Their brunch is also 5-star. They offer up a classic brunch menu, but their highlight is their pastry bar that you can pick and choose from among the day's homemade pastries. The treats pair well with their specialty coffee options, too. Try the mango cheesecake dessert if they have it when you go.

## ③ HUGO & VICTOR

40 Bd Raspail,
75007 Paris
01 44 39 97 73

*Carefully crafted French pâtisseries*

Pledging to use only the finest and freshest seasonal ingredients in their recipes, Hugo & Victor seals that promise with the high quality of their creations. Their counter serves not only some of the best pastries, but you may want to stop in for chocolates and one of the best **croissants** or **pain au chocolat** in Paris. They have gift sets ready to be created for take away in their signature black and white **petites boîtes**.

## ④ DU PAIN ET DES IDÉES

34 Rue Yves Toudic,
75010 Paris
01 42 40 44 52

Authentic French desserts

Stop into Du Pain et des Idées, translation: Of Bread and Ideas, for authentic French pastries coming straight from **Grandmère's** traditional family recipes. The recognizable building facade is enough to entice you to take a peek inside to discover all the wonderful **delices** (delicacies). Visitors rave about the **escargot chocolat pistache** that's not actually a snail, but a snail-shaped flakey bread with pistachio and chocolate filling. You won't be disappointed with a simple croissant, or **chausson au pomme** (apple turnover) either.

## 5 PAIN PAIN

88 Rue des Martyrs,
75018 Paris
01 42 23 62 81

*French desserts and pâtisserie*

Pain Pain isn't your typical French bakery. It's a contemporary take on bakeries, bringing you mouth-watering breads and pastries with carefully selected and high-quality raw ingredients. The pastry shop features unique flavors such as their mango/passion fruit **éclair** and the heavenly **speculoos éclair**. The shop is a local favorite with raving reviews, so if you're in the area, consider popping in for your baguette and daily dessert!

## 6 BORIS LUMÉ

**Location 1**

48 Rue Caulaincourt,
75018 Paris
01 46 06 96 71

**Location 2**

28 Rue Lepic,
75018 Paris

*Beautifully designed French pâtisserie*

This charming little bakery and pastry shop serves not only the neighborhood patrons but attracts international visitors as they tempt you to try their delectable treats! The selection of **viennoiserie** (breakfast pastries) and **pâtisserie** is small but intense.

The pastries are sublime and packed with flavor thanks to their carefully put together creations and fine-tuned selection of ingredients. Lumé founded the bakery with his Japanese wife, Mihona, also a baker, and the special marriage inspires exceptional unions of flavors reflected in the pastries.

**7**  **LA BOSSUE**

9 Rue Joseph de Maistre,
75018 Paris
09 81 72 65 59

Cafe, bakery, *épicière* (shop) and
*comptoir* (counter)

La Bossue is a cafe, bakery and
**épicerie**, or shop that bakes
delicious cakes and French
pastries. The adorable cafe is
cozy and welcomes you to enjoy
a sweet morning or afternoon
snuggled up with a coffee, baked
goodie, and a book. It's located
in a prime spot in the bustling
neighborhood of Montmartre,
yet this is a wonderful spot to
escape the city and just rest.
They have a great selection of
sweet and savory treats as well
as a splendid weekend brunch,
not to be missed!

# French Cheese Shops

camembert

brie

chevre

munster

comté

saint nectaire

tomme
de savoie

roquefort

emmental

bleu    raclette

No guidebook of Paris is complete without talking about French cheese. Cheese and wine are synonymous with French culture and is **un style de vivre,** or lifestyle, that the French embrace to the fullest. They love their wine and cheese pairings and usually enjoy a cheese plate before dessert but after a meal— that's how much they love, love, love **le fromage!**

Cheese has always been a source of pride as well as identity for the French. They don't take the art of making and eating cheese lightly.

Probably the biggest question surrounding French cheese is how many cheese varieties actually exist? The true answer is unknown, but we can guess that there are around 1200 French cheeses produced in France each year, according to the National Interprofessional Center for the Dairy Economy or CNIEL (**Centre national interprofessionnel de l'économie laitière**). This figure takes into account all cheese categories: raw, pasteurized, farmstead, industrial, matured or hard, and soft cheeses and spreads. It even has AOP label (**appellation d'origine protégée**) of which there are 45, according to Androuet's cheese guide[1]. This official label certifies and protects the cheese producers, recognizing their original products based on the local region they're produced as well as the process and geographical area.

But the four umbrella categories that cheese is organized in is raw (**lait cru**), pasteurized (**lait pasteurisé**), cheese from cow's milk (**fromage de vache**) and cheese from goat's milk (**fromage de chèvre**).

Below are a few cheese terms that will help enrich your cheese experience.

**Bonne dégustation !**

> Every cheese falls into these categories and it's useful to have in mind that cheeses can be from cow milk or goat milk and that raw milk cheeses are usually stronger and tastier than the ones made from pasteurized milk.

-Olivier Fourcade
*French-American cheese love*

---

[1] http://androuet.com/guide-fromage.html

# AFFINAGE DU FROMAGE CHEESE RIPENING

**AOP (appellation d'origine protégée)**
Protected Designation of Origin (PDO - is a geographical indication protecting the origin and quality of food products other than wine)

**Artisanal** Artisanal

**Cru** Raw

**Fermier** Farmstead

**Fromage** Cheese

**Fromage au lait cru** Unpasteurized cheese

**Fromager (m), Fromagère (f)** Cheesemonger, cheesemaker

**Fromagerie** Cheese shop, cheesemonger

**Fromage de chevre** Cheese produced from goat's milk

**Fromage de vache** Cheese produced from cow's milk

**Industrial** Industrial

**Intolérance au lactose** Lactose intolerance

**Lactose** Lactose

**Laiterie** Dairy

**Sans Lactose** Lactose-free

**Une planche de fromage** A cheese board

Watch a Cheese Pairings Video here:
www.youtube.com/watch?v=itD1FJQEaJc.

## TOP FRENCH CHEESES:

Bethmale (very good cheese from the Pyrenees)

Bleu d'Auvergne

Brie

Cantal

Camembert

Chaource

Chèvre (goat cheese)

Chabichou du poitou (type of goat cheese)

Crottin de Chavignol (type of goat cheese)

Ossau-iraty (type of sheep cheese)

Comté

Emmental

Morbier

Munster

Neuchâtel (heart-shaped cheese from Normandy made with cow's milk)

Raclette de savoie (original recipe is Swiss)

Reblochon

Roquefort

Saint-Nectaire

Tomme de Savoie

## FAMOUS CHEESE DISHES/MEALS:

Raclette

Fondu

Tartiflette

Cheese soufflé

La salade de chèvre

Gratin aux crozets (popular in Savoir region)

L'aligot (cheese blended with mashed potatoes and popular in L'Aubrac region)

La truffade d'auvergne

Here is a brief list of cheese shops I recommend among the endless list of notable cheese shops in Paris

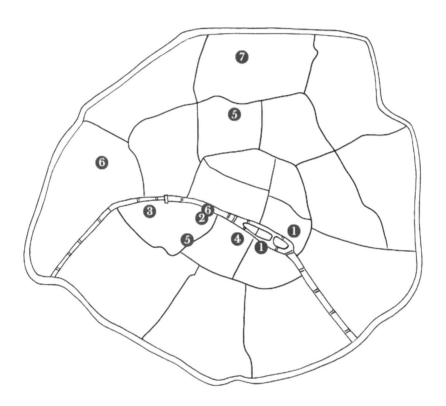

## 1 LAURENT DUBOIS

**Location 1**

47 Ter Bd Saint-
Germain,
75005 Paris
01 43 54 50 93

**Location 2**

97-99 Rue Saint
Antoine,
75004 Paris
+33 1 48 87 17 10

This cheesemonger has been awarded the **Meilleur Ouvrier de France**— the highest honor awarded by the French government for craftsmanship. Their philosophy is to tell the story behind each cheese while passing on the richness of their craft to each client they serve. Luckily, Laurent Dubois operates out of four locations in Paris, so you're bound to find one of their cheese shops close to you!

## 2 BARTHÉLÉMY

51 Rue de Grenelle,
75007 Paris
01 42 22 82 24

If you're looking for cheese for your picnic or dinner, search no further than the most iconic cheese shops on the left bank: Barthélémy, founded by Nicole Barthélémy. This cheese shop can be intimidating for the novice cheese shopper, but the reward is having hundreds of quality aged cheeses at your fingertips. If you're staying in Paris long-term, visit this shop regularly to become a recognizable face. In typical French manner, they treat their patrons more warmly than they would a one-time shopper.

## 3 FROMAGER MARIE-ANNE CANTIN

12 Rue du Champ de Mars,
75007 Paris
01 45 50 43 94

Situated just off of Rue Cler, this charming, tiny cheese shop is packed with a myriad of cheese choices. Their knowledgeable cheese experts can advise on cheese pairings based on meals and wine preferences. What's so great about this cheese shop is their close, well-established relationships (dating from 1950) with the dairy farmers that ensure quality in the products they sell. Don't hesitate to pay a visit if you want prepared cheese platters for special occasions and wine pairings as they sell wine from their cave directly to their customers, too.

## 4 LA COOP - COOPÉRATIVE LAITIÈRE DU BEAUFORTAIN

9 Rue Corneille,
75006 Paris
01 43 29 91 07

This cheese co-op specializes in wines, products, and cheeses from the Savoie region of France—think Beaufort, Tomme de Savoie, and fondue. The shop, located in the 6th arrondissement, welcomes you for wine and cheese tastings. And if you're in a large group, they invite you to privatize their venue for parties of at least 10 people.

## 5 QUATREHOMME

**Location 1**

62 Rue de Sèvres,
75007 Paris
01 47 34 33 45

**Location 2**

26 Rue des Martyrs,
75009 Paris
01 45 26 42 89

Operating since 1953, this prestigious **Maison du Fromage**, or house of cheese, has five shops in and around Paris. Several accolades extol the shop's reputation, including the head cheesemonger, Marie Quartrehomme, as the first woman awarded the **Meilleur Ouvriers de France** (Best Craftsman of France) in 2000. Later, in 2014, she was promoted to the highest honorary decoration in France, **Chevalier de la Légion d'honneur**. You will get expertise, quality, and variety when you visit the shop. They even provide tastings and masterclasses for the most enthusiastic cheese lovers.

## 6 ANDROUET

**Location 1**

37 Rue de Verneuil,
75007 Paris
01 42 61 97 55

**Location 2**

17 Rue des Belles
Feuilles, 75116 Paris
01 45 05 11 77

These master cheese makers who have been in the business since 1909, are a leader in the art of cheese in France. Recognizable by its bright red awning, the shops located throughout Paris and its surrounding area tempt cheese lovers to step into the aromatic and robust shops. Since 2018, Androuet trains and educates future cheesemongers in its Androuet Academy, created for educating the next generation of cheese lovers and small businesses to keep the art of cheese alive.

**7** **FROMAGERIE DE MONTMARTRE**

9 Rue du Poteau,

75018 Paris

06 98 29 88 09

If you're in Montmartre and you need cheese to complete your gastronomic meal, look no further than Fromagerie de Montmartre. At this humble cheese shop, you're sure to get first-class service with experienced and helpful cheesemongers who will recommend the best pairings for your wine and meal. They have a wide selection of cheeses from different regions, along with **accompagnements** (sides) to compliment your tastings, such as jams and preserves.

## HONORABLE MENTIONS:

Alléosse

Chez Virginie

Fromagerie Griffon

Fromagerie Jouannault

Fromagerie Saisons

Taka & Vermo

# Best Outdoor Markets

Have you visited the flower market, or **Marché aux fleurs** on the Île de la Cité? What about the **Marché des Enfants Rouges**? These are some of the covered markets that are open to the public most days of the week and a fun pastime that will help immerse you in the local vibes.

Paris has under 100 markets— whether outdoor food markets (**marchés alimentaires découverts**), flea markets (**marchés aux puces**), flower markets (**marchés aux fleurs**), and the distinct stamp market (**marché aux timbres**), the options are endless to what you can find at any one of its covered or open-air markets that take place every day throughout the city.

Whether you go for fresh-cut flowers, organic fruits and veggies, fish, meat, poultry, wine or chocolate, the outdoor markets in Paris will always be your one-stop-shop for anything you need for a well-rounded dinner at home. These **marchés parisiens** are the lifeblood of Paris and occur every day of the week in various neighborhoods.

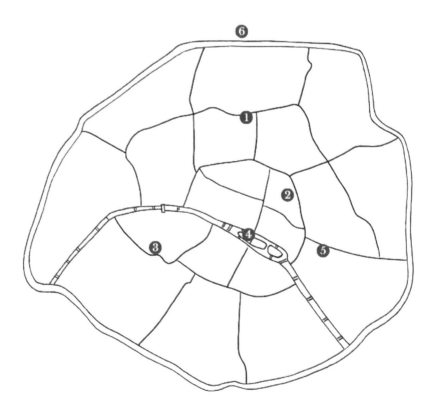

Check out the Antiques, Brocantes, Flea Markets and Shops chapter for specialty markets and the Paris.fr site (in French) for specific days of the week and operating hours for the markets in your neighborhood.

Let's journey on to my top picks of Paris' outdoor markets you must visit soon.

 **MARCHÉ ANVERS**

Place d'Anvers,
75009 Paris
01 45 11 71 11

This Friday afternoon open-air market is the perfect spot to grab your weekend groceries with a stunning view of Sacré Cœur from Square d'Anvers. They have everything from Moroccan stands, wine stands, to organic green grocers. This was my personal favorite when I lived in the 9th arr. and was traditionally my first stop to get the weekend started. The vendors are easy to talk to and usually let you taste the fruit if you ask nicely. If you live in the area, visit the same vendors each week to help you become a regular.

## 2  MARCHÉ DES ENFANTS ROUGES*

39 Rue de Bretagne, 75003 Paris

01 40 11 20 40

*Closed on Mondays

This **marché couvert**, or covered market, is Paris' oldest outdoor market and full of pleasant surprises. It opened in 1615 and is still running today. The site pays tribute to an orphanage of children who wore red clothes donated by Christian charities, hence the name "**les enfants rouges**". This market, located in the Haut Marais (3rd arr.), is a village within the city, featuring not only green grocers and flower stands, but also must-try mico-restaurants within its arches. A visit to this market makes for an afternoon adventure where you can stop in for a bite and go home with a bunch of goodies for the week. I recommend grabbing a mouthwatering **crêpe** or sandwich from Chez Alain Miam Miam **crêpe** stand.

## 3  MARCHÉ SAXE-BRETEUIL

Avenue de Saxe, 7

5007 Paris

01 40 11 20 40

Like the Marché Anvers, the Marché Saxe-Breteuil has a beautiful view displaying the most famous Parisian icon. So, while you shop and meander around this local open-air-market, you can enjoy the Eiffel Tower in the background. This market offers up an array of fruit and veggie stalls (some organic), meat and poultry, and wine stalls. You'll love getting to know the local merchants on the left bank while picking up some fresh produce from their stands.

## 4 FLOWER/ BIRD MARKET

Place Louis Lépine & Quai de la Corse, 75004 Paris

This flower market is open every day of the week, transforming into a hummingbird market exclusively on Sundays. I love that the covered market is adjacent to Notre Dame, perfect for an afternoon of wandering the big sites, then finding refuge among the myriad of plant and flower species. It's a great spot to find unique souvenirs for your friends and family members back home. And if you plan to stay in Paris for a while, you can find plants to spruce up your Parisian home.

## 5 LE MARCHÉ COUVERT BEAUVAU/ MARCHÉ D'ALIGRE

Rue d'Aligre et place d'Aligre
75012 Paris
01 45 11 71 11

This covered food market is a delightful place to visit and get a taste of authentic local life. The Beauvau market, also known as the Aligre Market because of its location on the Rue Aligre has a wide variety of food and veggie stalls, home and antique goods, as well as book stalls. This unique market features rare gems such as a vegetarian butcher stall and cheese shops selling hundreds of cheeses. You're going to want to pay a visit to this market to experience a genuine feel for the city and its inhabitants while taking away a few goodies to snack on, too!

## 6 LE MARCHÉ AUX PUCES DE PARIS SAINT-OUEN

110 Rue des Rosiers,
93400 Saint-Ouen
01 55 87 67 50

If you're feeling extra adventurous and want to get out of the city without going far, I recommend you check out Le Marché aux Puces de Paris Saint Ouen. The walkable marketplace on the edge of town is easily accessible from the metro line 4 up to the stop Port de Clignancourt. From there, it's an additional eight-minute walk north to reach the bustling village-like shops. Less of a food market than an antique market, you're sure to find priceless treasures, be it art, vintage designer goods, antiques, or knickknacks. A visit to this market won't disappoint. It's an immersive experience in the French language and the trade culture.

# Interview with
# **Eric Davis**,
# an architect who moved
# to Paris with a one-year
# visitor's Visa

Eric

**E**ric is an American architect who lived in Paris for a year and worked remotely for his company in the States. Growing up in Louisiana, Eric's interest in France began with his studies and later evolved into dreaming of living there.

His first visit to Paris was in 2013 on a trip to celebrate a friend's birthday. He recounts that on this trip, there was something about being here. He told himself, "I want more of this— the lifestyle, the people, the language, the surroundings." He visited three more times before moving to the French capital in 2019.

Eric and I met through church, but we became friends by attending the same weekly home group. He's the ultimate optimist and one of those guys that brings the life to the party. With his infectious smile and all-around good spirit, he inspired me and other friends with his drive to up and move to Paris despite the stable life he had built for himself.

Even though he was a successful architect and homeowner back in the States, he felt God calling him to the City of Light and took a risk and just went for it.

I wanted to interview Eric because he is someone who transplanted his life to France not at a young age, or as a student, but someone who was established with a successful career in his hometown. I wanted to know what inspired him to do this and how he followed through with it.

Read Eric's story on how he followed his heart and overcame challenges to live in France for a year.

### Why did you move to Paris?

I started to find myself daydreaming. I had a good job; I had good friends; I was a homeowner, and yet, I still felt dissatisfied.

I kept thinking, "This isn't exactly what life was supposed to look like. But if I want it to look different, no one is going to make that happen; it has to be me."

Allowing myself to think where I want to move to suddenly opened up the possibilities. If I can move across town or across the country, I can move across the world. I started realizing that the times that I felt the most at peace and the most at home was when I was in Paris.

It took a couple of years of soul searching and figuring out "what do I want to do, where do I want to be?" For me, it felt like a God thing to move to Paris. As a person of faith, I try to honor God with what I do, and so, over time, I felt like it was something I wanted to do and something that God wanted me to do.

### What was your first impression of Paris?

Paris was intimidating the first couple of days...but after my third or fourth day, the sun came out and I was able to walk around more and I thought "Ok, this is what I was expecting." Little by little, I relaxed and I started feeling more comfortable, truly absorbing where I am, what I was experiencing.

After a week, I didn't want to leave. It really grew on me. It felt like **possibility, opportunity**. Not feeling hemmed in by things that I had constructed for myself. What life is supposed to look like or what life is going to look like.

I kept saying to myself, "Oh wait, life can be different; it can feel different."

You can tell and feel it by the pace. It's not New York; it's not this hustle-bustle place.

### What do you love about Paris?

I loved that I didn't get in a car for a week. Within five minutes, I was at an incredible restaurant or historic site or a hidden little park. There's so much to see when you walk out your front door.

There is so much packed within one kilometer. There's not one grocery store, there's not one boulangerie or one cafe, there are dozens of them, and you experience so much within that little radius. It's almost overwhelming but in a good way...

Also, so much has happened here; there is so much history and I feel like I'm a part of that.

### How did you move to France when you had a full-time job in the US?

So I came on a one-year long-term visitor visa and there's a lot of stuff you have to prove. One of them is that you can live here without working here, so you have to show them that you have money and enough money to live on.

And so, I was going to look for work online. I tried quitting my job– that's how sure I was about moving to Paris.

And a few weeks after initially talking to my boss (after I told him I was moving to France), I thought that I would ask to stay on and work remotely. The owners of the firm considered it and ultimately said, "let's try it."

So, I became a consultant through my LLC as an independent contractor for the firm. It turns out that I was able to keep my job.

## As an LLC, can you technically work in France?

I had been told that French companies technically couldn't hire me as an independent, but they could hire me through a company. So, I set up an LLC in the US so that any French company could hire my company as a foreign consultant.

## Did you know French before moving to France?

I had studied French in school, so I have a basic knowledge of the language. After my first trip to France, I decided to continue studying French on Saturday mornings.

## How did you find housing?

When you apply for a French visa, one of the things is you have to tell them where you're going to be living, and I didn't have a lease set up yet.

I provided the name of my real estate agent who I had hired, and she actually allowed me to use her business address for my application. Then it allowed me to schedule a meeting through the French consulate.

But I ultimately worked with a real estate agent to find my apartment.

## What challenges did you face with moving to Paris?

The housing and the visa process were so intertwined. I wouldn't have been able to get it, the visa, without the housing. And on the housing side, I had to assume I was going to get the visa to move forward with my apartment.

I've learned that there are a lot of Catch-22s. You need A for B and you need B for A. And everybody has a different way of getting there.

## What is a lesson you've learned from living in Paris and the process of getting here?

France has a lot of red tape.

It has a lot of bureaucracy, and you really need to know that coming here.

If you don't know that, I think you're going to be miserable or feel defeated.

That's not to say that you can't do it, but it helps to know that.

Coming here, I've learned that that's very true. Even if you have all the documents, they ask you to have, still, something's gonna be wrong.

**What is your biggest frustration with Paris?**

The attitude of, "Oh, well, we do it this way because that's how we do it."

Kind of keeps them a little bit slow to adopt new ways. Some days, that's what's charming, and some days, that's what's frustrating.

**What is your biggest love about Paris?**

Knowing that I am so close to so many amazing things— museums, culture, art, community— and having easy access to that.

I feel like I'm in the center of what drives this world.

**What would you tell someone who is like you and wants to move to Paris?**

I would tell them if they are considering a move, go ahead and do it. Start the process, don't do it haphazardly. Don't be too intimidated by France or the move.

It is doable. I'm proof of that; you're proof of that. There are resources for people if they want to do it.

Don't be afraid to come here; come here to assimilate to fit in and not complain about the differences but be excited about the differences.

Do it when you still can, not one day when you retire. If you want to be here, why put it off?

For me, I thought, "If I don't do this, I'm gonna regret it." It would be hard for me to live with myself for not trying.

**If you had known about a lifestyle service like Céline Concierge, would you consider using my services, why or why not?**

One of the things that I have learned through this process is that to go through it alone, especially being overseas like I was— being American, not being fluent in French— it's a really tricky process, even when you get here.

You definitely need the help of somebody that can help you through that. Without help from others, I wouldn't have been able to come.

To know that you're working with an American who has been through that process, understands the normal fears, or experiences those differences is extremely valuable.

**Would you recommend Céline Concierge services?**

I highly recommend that people get in touch with you or someone like you who knows what they are doing and has been through that process. It helps you to relax and to put some of that worry and that burden on someone else.

**Do you have a favorite book, film, or song about Paris?**

**Amélie** and **Midnight in Paris** are both films that resonated with me. I also like the song La vie en Rose.

Eric wanted to stay in France and tried to renew his visitor visa for a second year but was denied at the end of 2020. Along with this setback and the challenges that Covid presented for Eric to stay, he decided to move back to Louisiana for the time being.

When he found out he couldn't make it back to France due to the complications with COVID at the time, he ended up hiring me to pack up his apartment and send back his personal effects when he couldn't travel to France. If it hadn't been for the borders being closed between the US and France, as well as the stricter administration rules at the time, Eric would have had an easier time renewing his visitor's visa to stay.

I will be here to welcome and assist Eric if and when he decides to come back to France to ensure his success.

# PARIS NIGHTLIFE

Paris at night glistens as you would expect it does— it truly is the City of Light. There's a certain magic that comes out at night over the city that you don't get to see during the day, whether that's from the sparkling Eiffel Tower, the way the gentle waves of the Seine shimmer, or the way the streets brighten under the incandescent lamp posts.

While New York may be the city that never sleeps, there is an inconspicuous nightlife waiting to be tapped into in Paris after the sun sets. From night club buses, walking the docks of the Seine, having a midnight snack at a cafe, to watching the sunrise at Sacré Cœur, you'll keep every night lively. Just remember to plan in some time to sleep so you're rested and energized for the next day... and for your next **nuit blanche**, or all-nighter!

Whether you want to have a nightly venture that is low-budget, but still amusing, or on the high-end side of things, in this section, I give you a jumping-off point for experiencing both during your nocturnal hours spent in the capital.

# Cheap Bars & Good Happy Hours

Whoever said Paris is expensive, hasn't spent enough time in the city to discover its cheap beers and generous happy hours. It's true that the cost of living can be on the pricier side of things, especially considering the unfavorable dollar to euro conversion. But let me assure you that in this chapter, you can find cheap drinks so you, too, can relish in Parisian cafes if you're on a tight budget.

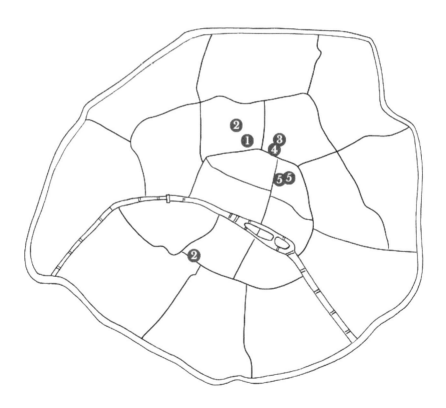

If you're serious about finding inexpensive beers, I recommend you download the MisterGoodBeer app; otherwise, here are some of my choice bars where you can enjoy yourself at bargain prices in Paris.

## 1 LA COMÈTE

19 Rue du Faubourg Montmartre,
75009 Paris
01 47 70 46 73

This is my bestie and I's favorite spot to go when she visits. The trendy Art Deco interior design makes this place a fun spot to be immersed in. We always start off with happy hour cocktails and with **une planche mixte**, or a spread of Italian deli meats and French cheeses. The inexpensive cocktails and food make it an evening well spent and one where we can start early and end late without fearing a large bill at the end of the night.

## 2 DREAM CAFÉ

**Location 1**

8 Rue des Martyrs,
75009 Paris
01 71 37 63 74

**Location 2**

39 Bd du Montparnasse,
75006 Paris
01 71 73 95 00

If you're down to have a great time, you can't go wrong with the Dream Café with its sun drenched terrace to its cheap beers at 3.90 € a pint. Its two locations are equally bustling, but the one in the 9th arr. has a cozier feel and slightly older crowd; the location in the 6th arr. is a hot spot for the student crowd. I would recommend both locations if you want to see **un match de foot** (soccer match).

### ③ AU FAUBOURG

92 Rue du Faubourg
Saint-Denis,
75010 Paris
01 42 29 75 53

At the footsteps of Gare de l'Est, you're gonna have a blast in this modern brasserie where you can find cheap drinks and delicious French food. The terrace is a perfect spot to people-watch over a coffee or beer, depending on what time of day you visit. The Pint of Stella runs at 3.90 €. I especially like this brasserie because it's fool-proof— you're sure to have good food and service every single time.

### ④ LE SULLY

13 Rue du Faubourg
Saint-Denis,
75010 Paris
01 77 10 74 70

From the outside, nothing seems special about this bar, but take a step inside and the original old-fashion decor of the 30s still exists. You'll feel welcomed with the friendly vibes in this old-timey dive bar that glows with neon florescent lights. This down-to-earth brasserie is not only a local hang for Parisians, but also a space for expats to meet up. Prices go as low as 3.50 € a pint.

## 5 L'ATTIRAIL

**Location 1**

9 Rue au Maire,
75003 Paris
01 42 72 44 42

**Location 2**

77 Rue des Gravilliers,
75003 Paris
06 81 09 15 93

I discovered this bar when I was living two streets down from it on the Rue Chapon. This eccentric bar, also known as the potato bar, serves up its pint of French beers paired with seasoned potatoes and a side of mayonnaise, on the house. Clients tag the wall with ID photos from top to bottom, providing an unconventional decorative style— so if you want to leave a memento for Paris, you can bring your own to blanket the wall. It's the ideal spot to unwind at the end of the day and grab your 3.50 € /pint of beer served all day. Its sister location is two stone's throws away at 77 Rue des Gravilliers and offers up a similar vibe, food, and drinks.

# Favorite Craft Beer Bars

Craft beers might be trending in the US, but they are few and far between in Paris. Slow to hop on the bandwagon, the French usually consume wine as their preferred libation. Despite this, there are ways to find craft beer in a country known for its wine. Not only have specialty beer bars jumped on the map, but a new generation of **brasseries**, or breweries, have also sprung up locally. These trailblazers are the ones introducing craft beer to the scene, such as the local La Parisienne, Maison BapBap, and Paname Brewing Co, which are creating demand and a new market for beverage lovers.

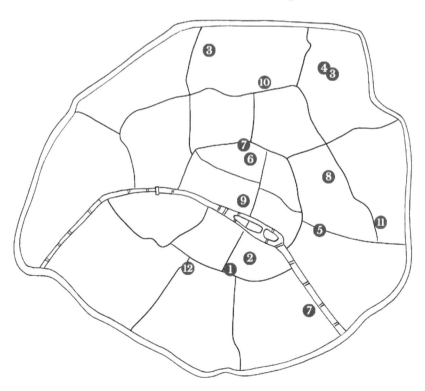

Within its wonderful and concentrated selection of bars, you can find refreshing craft beers and outdoor terraces to enjoy them on— an excellent way to pass a lovely summer evening.

Here are my picks for the best places to find craft beers in Paris.

## 1 ACADÉMIE DE LA BIÈRE

88Bis Bd de Port-Royal,
75005 Paris
01 43 54 66 65

This French bistro gives off a **dive-bar-à-la-français** kind of feel which suits the place recognized for serving up artisanal and Belgian beers. They also have comfy outdoor seating on the terrace. When I went here with a few girlfriends back in 2018, I was surprised to discover that on a Thursday night, the place was packed. It was not only the best proof of the popularity of the place, but also of the good beer selection and tasty food. Many folks go here for the decently priced **moules-frites**, or mussels and fries, which go hand-in-hand with a cold beer. If you aren't into seafood, I recommend trying the **planche,** or meat and cheese platter, they serve up to accompany your pint.

## 2 BREWBERRY

11 Rue du Pot de Fer,
75005 Paris
06 62 46 75 13

Situated right off of the bustling Rue Mouffetard, you'll be happy to find a spot that offers up a wide choice of quality craft beers. They have beers that range from your classic lagers, malts and IPAs, to a curated selection of flavors ranging from coffee, fruity, and seasonal flavors like a peanut butter beer. The bar is clean and modern, accompanied with exterior seating ideal for the summer months. One of my favorite features is their beer flights where you can sample different varieties.

## 3 KIEZ / KIEZ KANAL

**Location 1**

24 Rue Vauvenargues,
75018 Paris
01 46 27 78 46

**Location 2**

90 Quai de la Loire,
75019 Paris
01 42 02 33 94

This bar is a little slice of Germany right in our backyard, nestled in the 18th arr. This bar is known for its selection of German beers and food fare. Beside the beer (of course), one of the best features is their beer garden that's a perfect hang out in the warm months of the year. You can order a bratwurst and Bretzel while enjoying an inner Parisian courtyard with friends. As of 2017, they opened up the Kanal Kiez, which now provides a second lieu for great beer and a view of the artificial lake, Bassin de la Villette. They also do takeaway beers so you can conveniently sit along the docks by the basin.

##  PANAME BREWING COMPANY OR PBC

41 bis Quai de la Loire,
75019 Paris
01 40 36 43 55

Opening in 2015 along the Bassin de la Villette, in the 19th arr., this contemporary French brasserie is one of the better known artisanal micro-breweries in Paris. Their bar serves up a plethora of beer selections on draft and tasty food. They also provide beer tastings and tours for those looking for a unique experience in Paris.

## 5 TROLL CAFE

27 Rue de Cotte,
75012 Paris
01 43 42 10 75

For a lively and divey feel, go to none other than the Troll cafe. They showcase over a hundred beers, a few of those on tap, but the majority in cans or bottles. Visiting this **bar à biere** feels like taking a trip through history with its rural and garish feel. The happy hours are from 5 PM to 7 PM where you can find a pint for as little as 4 €. It's also the coziest of bars on this list—one where you're most likely to strike up a conversation and a friendship with the patrons if you're searching for a way to connect to the locals.

## 6 HOPPY CORNER

34 Rue des Petits Carreaux,
75002 Paris
09 83 06 90 39

Since 2016, this bar and **cave à bieres** has been serving up a line-up of 15 continually rotating artisanal beers for the hoppy enthusiast. Beside the large selection of draft beers, they have a supplementary selection in cans and bottles. One of my favorite features about this bar is that they serve up flights for the opportunity to travel through your taste buds. The bar is modern with a rustic feel—perfect for on a date if you want to impress him or her, or for a group of friends. Tapas and food are available upon request from their kitchen.

## 7 THE FROG PUBS

**Location 1**

176 Rue Montmartre,
75002 Paris
01 44 82 04 72

**Location 2**

114 Av. de France,
75013 Paris
01 44 82 04 72

Get your British on by stopping into one of their eight pubs around Paris for some British and Irish inspired brews. Started in 1993, and one of the oldest microbreweries in France, The FrogPubs now offer close to 40 recipes of beers served in their pubs and restaurants. You can also take away their selection of beers at any of their pubs or stop in for brunch, lunch, or dinner.

## 8 MAISON BAPBAP

79 Rue Saint-Maur,
75011 Paris
01 77 17 52 97

This two-in-one microbrewery/ modern bar is a perfect spot to do a tasting of 100% Parisian beers that are brewed on location. Besides the local fare, the bar presents you with a wide array of bottled local and artisanal beers to enjoy at the bar or takeaway for later. They offer tours and tastings at the brewery; sign up on their website, or **contact me**[1] for exclusive tours.

## 9 BIÈRE CULTES CHÂTELET

14 Rue des Halles,
75001 Paris
09 81 98 93 32

This hybrid beer cave/ bar is decked out with a terrace in the Châtelet neighborhood, in the heart of Paris. You can sit and enjoy on site or take away any of their abundant collection of international as well as local beers. The friendly and insightful staff will help you in choosing the perfect beer for your taste and mood.

---

[1] www.celineconcierge.com/contact-us/

## 10 LA GOUTTE D'OR

28 Rue de la Goutte d'Or,
75018 Paris
09 80 64 23 51

This microbrewery and tap room is rightly located on the street of its namesake "Rue de la Goutte d'Or" translated "street of the golden drop". This brasserie's pride is its pioneering start in craft beers in Paris back in 2012, before the movement took off in the city. The bar offers tapas and an array of over 30 home-brewed beers to savor as well as their beer of the moment. I encourage a visit to taste the local flavors of Paris.

## 11 LE BOUILLON BELGE

6 Rue Planchat,
75020 Paris
01 43 70 41 03

The bar that literally means Belgian broth is about all things Belgian beers and bites. Located in the underrated 20th arr., this bar offers some of the lowest prices for their pints at 3.50 €. To encourage camaraderie, they hold quiz nights as well as beer tastings curated by the knowledgeable bar staff. It's worth a visit if you want to indulge in Belgian fare and enjoy the nearly 30 beer options on tap for a very fair price.

## 12 KER BEER

10 Rue Vandamme,
75014 Paris
01 42 84 43 22

This craft beer cooperative specializes in artisanal Breton beers— beers brewed in the region of Bretagne (Brittany) in Northern France. It has something for everyone. You can select from their choice of 15 beers on tap or opt for a bottled beer— to enjoy **sur place**, or to take away. They have a Breton-inspired food menu as well as beer flights if you're feeling adventurous to try several beers.

Paris truly has a one-of-a-kind beer culture! You can find young microbreweries taking off with success in a city whose gastronomy is evolving to include more beer alongside its already strong wine culture. This is a very telling sign in the fact that wine caves like the franchise Nicolas are now expanding to sell more artisanal beers from local brewers.

Beer caves are popping up and they seem to be here to stay with the thriving artisanal craft beer movement that has struck Paname. Finally, beer subscriptions like the one Saveur Beer proposes is further proof of the expanding and successful beer culture that is here to stay in the City of Light.

## MICRO BREWERIES:

Bap Bap

Brasserie de la Goutte d'Or

Brasserie de l'Être

Brew Unique

La Parisienne

Paname Brewing Co

The Frog Pubs

# Favorite Speakeasies & Cocktail Bars

You may find yourself going through worlds— picture yourself transported from an actual Parisian laundromat or through a taco joint serving up Mexican street food, to reach a secret bar. If this sounds like your kind of venture where you'll be rewarded with a specialty cocktail at the end, don't come to Paris without checking out a few of the best speakeasy and specialty cocktail bars.

Whether your preferred libation is vodka, whisky, rum, or gin, each of these bars are going to have a special cocktail you're sure to savor.

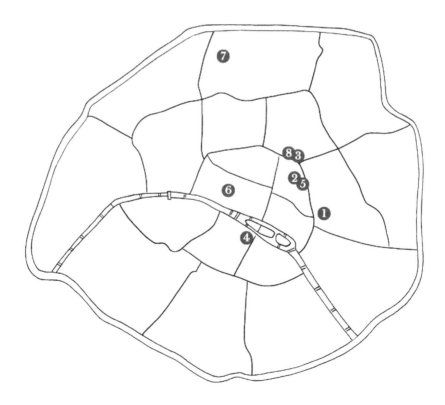

If you find that you can't read the menu because it's only in French, many of the bar men and women speak English and are more than willing to clarify and even experiment to give you a personal cocktail if you tell them what kind you fancy best. Below are my approved speakeasies and specialty cocktail bars you should check out every night of your stay!

 **MOONSHINER**
5 Rue Sedaine,
75011 Paris

This gem of a bar is literally hidden— the store front looks like any old Italian pizzeria in the Bastille neighborhood but take a step through the swinging doors and you're transported to a 1930s Paris during prohibition. This swanky little bar is equipped with a **fumoir,** or smoking room, that adds to the bar's authenticity. Don't leave here without having at least two different specialty cocktails. My favorite is their tasty Old Fashion, if whisky and bourbon are your thing.

 **LITTLE RED DOOR**
60 Rue Charlot,
75003 Paris

The mysterious little red door past the ordinary street door is where you'll find this place at 60 Rue Charlot in the 3rd arr. I know— that sounds very nondescript, but trust me, finding the place is half the adventure and you won't regret it once you're in! The modern design and sexy vibes make this a suitable spot for a date. The mezzanine is a coveted nook to feel like a VIP in Paris. Tell Daniel, the bar's CEO, that you know me for exclusive treatment!

### 3 LAVOMATIC

30 Rue René Boulanger,
75010 Paris

You'll be surprised to find this marvel through the hidden doorway behind the facade of stacked washing machines. Finding the **lavomat** is the easy part, but finding the secret passage door to the upstairs attic is the mysterious part. Pay a visit; you'll discover an array of exotic cocktails to whet your palette and indoor swings to relax in your hideaway.

### 4 CASTOR CLUB

14 Rue Hautefeuille,
75006 Paris
09 50 64 99 38

The discrete exterior with only a slip through an all-wood door is also a treasure hunt that, if you come upon, will be a titillating experience. The cocktails are carefully curated and if you want to take a chance on trying something original, ask the barman for what you desire. You'll end up with a signature cocktail they can name after you! The intimate space is suitable for a date or to appreciate an intimate evening with a friend. The bar is open late Thursday to Saturday where they play dance music in the basement until the early hour of 4 AM.

## 5 CANDELARIA

52 Rue de Saintonge,
75003 Paris
09 50 84 19 67

The misleading facade of this bar is a tasty Mexican taco joint. You won't be disappointed to venture deeper into the rabbit hole of this tiny restaurant— it leads to a limestone laden cellar of camaraderie and cocktails. The bar, only accessible through the taco restaurant, serves up Mexican-inspired cocktail creations. Its intimate setting is ideal for a girls' night out with your besties as much as for a romantic date.

## 6 REHAB

7 Rue de l'Échelle,
75001 Paris

If you don't drink alcohol or very little of it, this bar is for you! It's the first "spirit-free" cocktail bar in France, promoting alcohol-free, low alcohol and cannabinoid (a non-intoxication cannabis) cocktails. This speakeasy is discreetly tucked away in the restaurant Le Comptoir du Chantier of the Hotel Normandy on the Rue Saint-Honoré. Its winding staircase is found only once you skirt past the mirrored door, revealing an elegant boudoir inspired by the Belle-Epoque. Its intimacy and serenity provide a delightful spot to disconnect from the world and reconnect with a friend.

## 7 B.O.U.L.O.M

181 Rue Ordener,
75018 Paris
01 46 06 64 20

Besides its stellar brunch on weekends, hosted in their open dining area, and homemade baked goods, there's a special surprise awaiting you upstairs of this French bakery-restaurant. You may have to build up a little courage to trudge upstairs beyond the nautical-style wooden door unbeknownst to many of the other patrons to find yourself in a secluded bar. I encourage you to go to taste the food and the drinks that will have you coming back again and again because you'll find, you just can't get enough of the atmosphere and the perfectly mixed cocktails.

## 8 BARANAAN

7 Rue du Faubourg Saint-Martin,
75010 Paris
01 40 38 97 57

Baranaan is a modern take on Indian street food with a clandestine bar that will carry you away to Bombay. Like any curious traveler, you'll metaphorically board the bar that's set as an Indian prohibition train to fully experience the ride. This original concept will make you feel like you've left Paris for the evening as you sip on cocktails made from Indian inspired flavors and exotic ingredients. If you're hungry, I can't recommend the Indian street food enough. So, **hop on** as Baranaan immerses you in a unique experience full of tasty delights.

# Ritzy Hotel Bars

If you're anything like me and love dressing up a couple of nights a week— dabbing on that **rouge à lèvre**, slipping on some heels to go with a dressy outfit— to wind down your evening at a fancy hotel bar, then you're in the right place for my top recommendations!

I don't do this often, but when I do, I want to go all out and splurge on an extravagant locale where I'm going to be the star of the night.

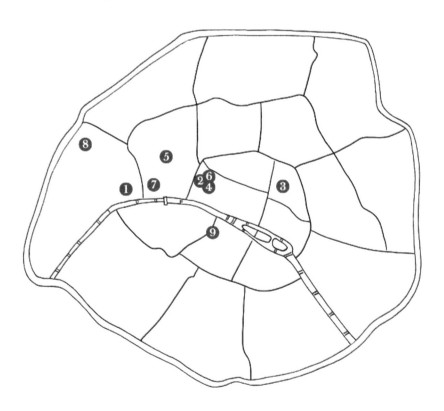

Here are my picks for the best hotel bars you must visit the next time that little black dress is calling you for a special evening out where you can celebrate **you** as you sip on drinks against a beautiful setting under the Parisian night.

 ## LE BAR BOTANISTE | HÔTEL SHANGRI LA

10 Av. d'Iéna,
75116 Paris
01 53 67 19 98

This warm and elegant bar features botanical inspired spirits and serves up absinthe fountains the old-fashion way for an authentic treat. If you're in the mood for a one-of-a-kind concoction, head barman, Clément Emery, invents personalized cocktail creations for every patron's specific **goût**. Don't be shy to ask the bar staff for a special drink that has your name on it!

 ## BAR 8 | THE MANDARINE ORIENTAL

251 Rue St Honoré,
75001 Paris
01 70 98 78 88

For an evening of haute sophistication and luxury, delight yourself in gourmet tapas and 8's signature cocktails with or **sans** alcohol. Its elegant and breathtaking marble bar at the center embodies sexy nights out of the utmost enjoyment. The dim lighting sets an intimate backdrop. Or escape Paris altogether in the garden haven found in the exterior courtyard. Everything is exceptional here— the service, the ambience, the drinks and cuisine.

### 3 JULES & JIM | HÔTEL JULES & JIM

11 Rue des Gravilliers,
75003 Paris
01 44 54 13 13

This sleek bar in the modest boutique hotel Jules & Jim is invisible to the outside world. You have to know that the hotel exists to know where to find its discreet address in the Marais. Just through the building courtyard of 11 Rue des Gravilliers, you'll stumble upon the modern, yet cozy hotel and bar. Fans of great cocktails can come here for a little break from the city. Cocktails start at 12 €.

### 4 BAR 228 | HÔTEL LE MEURICE

228 Rue de Rivoli,
75001 Paris
01 44 58 10 10

The Bar 228 is known for its evenings of live music and is worth a visit for all musicians and music lovers alike. Next to its signature live music nights, the bar prides itself on the artistry of mixology wherein every barman masters his craft to deliver its patrons a twist on the classics, or a personalized drink to indulge in. The bar is warm and welcoming and will inspire you to think, ponder and dream deep into the night. Drop in for a lounge setting, background music, and cocktails to satiate your taste buds.

**LE BAR GASPARD | HÔTEL LA RESERVE**
42 Av. Gabriel, 7
5008 Paris
01 58 36 60 50

Ideal for drinks with business partners or to celebrate a special occasion, Le Bar Gaspard invites you into a cozy atmosphere full of timeless sophistication, inspired by travel itself. Complimenting the bar, the restaurant, Le Gabriel, provides a delicate selection of tapas and **bouchés** created by 2 Michelin-star chef, Jérôme Banctel. Take a seat in the comfortable yet chic bar or sit outside on the terrace during the warmer months of the year.

## 6 BAR HEMINGWAY | THE RITZ HOTEL
15 Pl. Vendôme,
75001 Paris
01 43 16 33 74

The Bar Hemingway is like a time capsule for the present, offering a perception of the past through its walls peppered with photos and artifacts that hold the secrets of antiquity. For celestial cocktails from head barman, Colin Field, you must pay the bar a visit and order his famous **chef-d'oeuvre:** the Serendipity. He can also attest to the countless narratives of the famous figures passing through Paris that have sat in the same chairs as patrons of this prominent place.

## 7  LE BAR | HÔTEL PLAZA ATHÉNÉE

25 Av. Montaigne,
75008 Paris
01 53 67 66 00

For a modern and sleek atmosphere while you enjoy innovative cocktails, visit Le Bar at the Plaza Athénée. From the moment you step foot inside, you will be transported to a sublime space that prides itself in its savory and exclusive champagne selection. Every detail is thought out—from the transparent resin bar to the customized cocktails the barman is eager to create, inspired by your taste buds. So tell them what you're in the mood for to get a cocktail made to order.

## 8  THE LIBRARY | ST. JAMES PARIS

5 Pl. du Chancelier Adenauer,
75116 Paris
01 44 05 81 81

Akin to being in a university library, this bar inspires philosophy and intellect. It's the perfect setting for business meetings or just to unwind after a busy day in Paris. The head barman and his crew pride themselves on customized cocktail creations if you're daring enough to ask for one. The garden-terrace is open to non-hotel guests starting in the evenings; you can even enjoy a dinner from their restaurant (by reservation only) after or over drinks. Gastronomical chef, Adrien Brunet, indulges you with divine flavors and dishes, of which many of the fresh ingredients come from the hotel garden.

## 9 BAR JOSEPHINE | HÔTEL LUTETIA
45 Bd Raspail,
75006 Paris
01 49 54 46 00

In the heart of Rive Gauche, the Bar Jospehine is one-of-a-kind, offering a luminous space with gorgeous frescos inspired from the Art Nouveau **époc**. The bar exhibits live music on various nights along with cocktails delicately crafted for a heavenly getaway. Everything is precise and lovely here, from the details in the painted walls, to the bitters and accompaniments in the cocktails. Bar Lutetia is truly the place to be on any evening of the week or weekend if you happen to find yourself on the Rive Gauche.

# Rooftop Bars & Restaurants

I love getting up high and overlooking Paris from its iconic rooftops. There's some sort of magic that fills the sky when you see Paris from up high. Whether that's from the Tour Montparnasse or from the Iron lady, you're sure to feel inspired when you stand atop one of the peaks, getting a splendid bird's-eye-view.

And what better way to breath in Paris than from one of these great bars and restaurants. You don't have to be celebrating anything special for the experience to be a festive one.

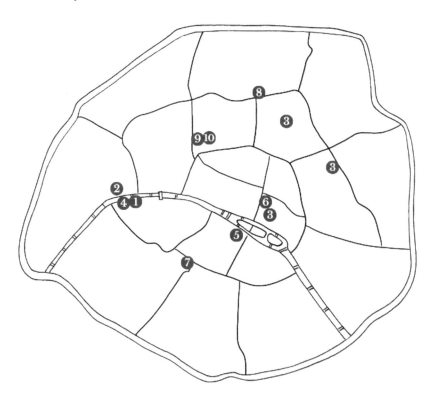

Check out these approved rooftop bars for your next evening out! Go for a drink, but stay for the view!

###  LES OMBRES

27 Quai Branly,
75007 Paris
01 47 53 68 00

Les Ombres is the rooftop terrace of the Musée du Quai Branly, conveniently overlooking the rooftops of Paris with the Eiffel Tower lingering in the near distance. Th+is is the kind of place you can go for a simple cocktail or two or make a full night of it with a five-course meal. Whatever you choose, you can expect a rich and refined experience accented with a beautiful view! I highly recommend making reservations online ahead of time as this place is popular year-round.

### ② GIRAFE

1 Pl. du Trocadéro et du 11 Novembre,
75016 Paris
01 40 62 70 61

What can't be said about this sublime restaurant, bar, and terrace overlooking the Esplanade du Trocadéro! Not technically a rooftop, but a terrace overlooking the Eiffel Tower, Girafe features one of the best views of the city at night. The sophisticated and inviting Art Deco design welcomes you for a treat. The fancy cocktails are just the beginning— its refined starters and cuisine serves up mostly succulent seafood dishes and even caviar for the cultivated. Go to Girafe for an escape to the 30s and dress up with your favorite heels and **rouge à levre** for your visit!

### 3 LE PERCHOIR - MENILMONTANT/ EAST / LE MARAIS

**Location 1**

14 Rue Crespin du
Gast, 75011 Paris

**Location 2**

33 Rue de la Verrerie,
75004 Paris

**Location 3**

10 Place du 11 Novembre 1918,
75010 Paris

This Parisian hideout is a fun spot to spend the long summer evenings escaping the heat. Whether you choose its unique location atop the Gare de l'Est train station, in the Marais or on the east side of Paris, each spot offers a contemporary hangout with a great mix of tourists and locals. This is an oasis that will make you feel like you're miles away from Paris. Its urban rooftop gardens invite, refresh, and relax as you blend into the contemporary Brooklyn vibes.

### 4 THE CHAMPAGNE BAR

5 Av. Anatole France,
75007 Paris

This magical spot is the summit bar on the Eiffel Tower. Its steep location is the highest in Paris and an ideal place to take your loved ones to clink glasses as you sip on bubbly champagne while taking in the bird's-eye-view of the city. You'll want to go at dusk as the tower begins to sparkle— it is one of the most magical moments you can experience in Paris. I can organize a private guided tour on the tower with a licensed tour guide who will take you on a historical journey if you want to dive deeper into the history of the monument and the city. Contact me[2] for more details and to book.

---

[2] www.celineconcierge.com/contact-us/

## 5 43 ROOF TOP

4 Rue Danton,
75006 Paris
01 81 69 00 60

The Holiday Inn's exclusive rooftop bar is worth a visit for an incredible 360 view of Paris from the heart of the left bank. With reasonable prices, friendly wait staff, and great cocktails, this place is perfect for impressing your date. I recommend calling to make reservations ahead of time, especially on busy evenings like Valentine's Day.

## 6 GEORGE, LE CENTRE POMPIDOU

Place Georges-Pompidou,
75004 Paris
01 44 78 47 99

You won't expect anything but **art moderne** from the restaurant/bar of the Pompidou modern art museum. For a great view of the city, go straight up to the restaurant George through the elevator entrance on the ground level of the building. Prices are on the pricier side, but the view is worth every bit of it. You'll see the Eiffel Tower in the distance along with other beautiful monuments including Notre Dame and Les Invalides.

## 7 LE CIEL DE PARIS ON MONTPARNASSE TOWER

Tour Maine Montparnasse, 56ème, Av. du Maine,
75015 Paris
01 40 64 77 64

Whether you want to enjoy a fine-dining experience, a gourmet Afternoon Tea, or evening drinks with dessert, this Parisian high-rise is the spot to get an intimate view of her majesty The Eiffel Tower. Its floor-to-ceiling windows help feature an incredible view of Paris. The tower offers the ideal location for a romantic night or just drinks with the girls with an incredible (and the second highest) view of the city.

## 8 BRASSERIE BARBÈS

2 Bd Barbès,
75018 Paris
01 42 64 52 23

This traditional French brasserie located in a bright multi-level building is modern with a vintage feel. The food is delicious, the ambience is inviting, and the rooftop is to die for— an ideal locale to sip on summer. Get exclusive access to the rooftop directly for an evening show or by reserving for a private event or birthday celebration. Its giant windows feel airy and open, giving you a high-end experience with affordable food and beverages prices. Additionally, their second-floor rotunda overlooking the aerial metro line 2 is the perfect spot to jam out to their showcase of live music every week. Check out the website for the monthly program where local artists frequently play.

## 9   PERRUCHE

Printemps de l'Homme, 2 Rue du Havre 9ème étage,
75009 Paris
01 40 34 01 23

Just a couple of rooftops down from Galeries Lafayette, you have Perruche atop the Printemps Haussman department store. The lovely terrace rooftop, with vibes from Provence with its bright yellow stripped seat cushions and neat, white table cloths, is a summer sanctuary in the city center. The lush setting further invites you in with local musicians and DJ sets playing throughout the day. The food is top-notch, offering summer flavors full of Provincial herbs and spices such as the Niçoise Salade, or summer prawns flambéed with pastis. Its ritzy bar is a great place to overlook Paris as you escape for an afternoon staycation before or after sunset.

## 10   CRÉATURES ON THE GALERIES LAFAYETTE PARIS HAUSSMANN

25 Rue de la Chaussée d'Antin, 8th Floor
75009 Paris

This luxurious ephemeral rooftop bar and restaurant with a panorama view of Paris is a must! It's an impressive place where **you** can impress, that's for sure. The specialty cocktails and its vegetarian-only meals are the perfect combination of an Instagram-worthy Parisian rooftop view. If you plan to go to Galeries Lafayette for some shopping anyway, you won't want to miss Créatures' rooftop. Stop in for a drink or two, or stay the whole day to enjoy the sun-glistening roofs of Paris. Check the website or call ahead for opening times outside of the summer because, although it's open 7 days a week for lunch and dinner, the place is open seasonally and when good weather permits.

# Jazz Bars and Live Music Venues

Jazz slowly made its way to France around the early 1920s by black American army musicians playing in cafes and underground bars after World War I. Spirits were high after the war and musicians like James Reese Europe, and later Louis Armstrong, brought jazz to the scene in Europe in the roaring 20s.

Soon after, other artists like Josephine Baker also helped to reinforce jazz and dance performance with her controversial show **Un vent de folie**.

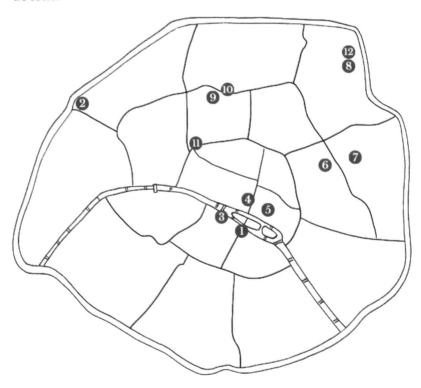

Paris experienced a live music boost in the 1920s and 30s, especially in the artist-centric quarters like in the Latin Quarter and Montmartre areas. Notably, the musical wonder, Édith Piaf was discovered in the clubs of Pigalle in the mid 1930s.

Before World War II, many bars and clubs opened to satiate the thirst for live music as political tensions were rising. Unfortunately, a few venues closed down due to the tumultuous situation in Europe, but one famous music venue got its start at the beginning of the war and still stands today: Le Caveau de la Huchette.

Paris' love for music spans from classical to opera, to Jazz, to dubstep. Today, it offers a low-key music scene that is abounding in limitless new artists and groups. Even if Paris isn't known for its music scene, don't let it fool you— the city hosts an immense number of bars, clubs, venues, amphitheatres, and concert halls where you can catch some tunes of your choice.

 **LE CAVEAU DE LA HUCHETTE**
5 Rue de la Huchette,
75005 Paris
01 43 26 65 05

Situated in Paris' Latin Quarter, across the river from Notre Dame, Le Caveau gives its patrons an immersive jazz experience— one that even Hollywood wants to exemplify! Le Caveau is briefly featured in the 2016 jazz spectacular **La La Land**. And since 1949, Le Caveau has been inviting spectators and legendary jazz musicians alike to participate in the show through the jazz and dancing atmosphere.

## 2 JAZZ CLUB ÉTOILE
81 Bd Gouvion-Saint-Cyr,
75017 Paris
01 40 68 30 42

The Jazz Club Étoile welcomes jazz lovers to enjoy a variety of tunes from jazz, funk, blues and soul every night in the newly renovated venue located in the posh Méridien Etoile Hotel. The club that once welcomed BB King now welcomes contemporary names like the famous jazz pianist, Diana Krall, among many others each night. You won't be disappointed to participate in a spectacular evening here; reserve ahead of time and arrive early to take in the full experience.

## 3 CHEZ PAPA JAZZ CLUB
3 Rue Saint-Benoît,
75006 Paris
01 42 86 99 63

This cozy restaurant with its grand piano in the front and center of the room invites hungry guests to enjoy a delectable meal while appreciating the rich jazz tunes. From Tuesday through Saturday, jazz enthusiasts can savor the live music and its eclectic musicians in this intimate and inconspicuous setting where the focus is having a good time!

## 4 LE DUC DES LOMBARDS

42 Rue des Lombards, 7
5001 Paris
01 42 33 22 88

Showcasing two live concerts a night, you know you are sure to have a wonderful time at Le Duc des Lombards as they welcome the best jazz performers in the industry. The venue opens its doors from Monday to Saturday at 7:30 PM and then again at 9:30 PM for its second show. Although the club doesn't serve food, it has a rich wine, beer, and cocktail menu, so be sure to eat dinner before or after the show.

## 5 38 RIV

38 Rue de Rivoli,
75004 Paris
01 48 87 56 30

This intimate and low-key jazz bar and lounge features local as well as touring artists in its cave-like venue where the acoustics highlight the artists' skills. Every night from Monday to Saturday, starting at 9 PM, this rare gem puts on themed nights showcasing Brazilian, baroque, jazz and funk music to keep you entertained.

## 6 L'INTERNATIONAL

5/7 Rue Moret,
75011 Paris

You're likely to find locals having a great time at L'International where their live music line-up changes every week. The cover ranges usually from 5 € to 12 € for entry but is well worth the show and a guaranteed good time! The music choice is a wide spectrum of anything from punk, to rock, to house, to new wave— check the line-up before going. They're open Mondays to Saturdays starting at 6 PM to 2 AM (some Saturdays until 5 AM depending on the line-up), with happy hour from 6 PM to 9 PM.

## 7 LA BELLEVILLOISE

19-21 Rue Boyer,
75020 Paris
01 46 36 07 07

This live music venue that boasts a cafe/restaurant in a grandiose and unique space is a self-proclaimed cultural fortress. With its humble beginnings as a co-op of green grocers and entrepreneurs in 1877, this historic venue has evolved into an art and cultural epicenter in the east of Paris where local musicians, artists, and professionals come together in a cultural center made for all citizens. When you step into La Bellevilloise, it is nothing short of your expectations— it's a diverse venue full of life. Check out their line-up for more insight on live music shows.

## 8 LA PETITE HALLE - LA VILLETTE

211 Av. Jean Jaurès,
75019 Paris
09 82 25 91 81

This hybrid live music venue and restaurant, with its inviting allure, welcomes artists, musicians and patrons alike to enjoy a nice time listening to music, eating their handmade brick oven pizzas, or sipping a coffee or beer on their garden terrace. This stunning lieu, located in La Villette area, north of Paris, runs along the Canal Saint Martin. You can end up spending hours here if you want to lose yourself in the city and have nothing scheduled in your calendar for the day.

## 9 BUS PALLADIUM

6 Rue Pierre Fontaine,
75009 Paris
01 45 26 80 35

This legendary bar, restaurant, and music venue got its start in the 60s with the dream that James Arch executed— the idea was to put in place a bus system for only 2 francs, transporting the youth after hours throughout the city and suburbs when public transportation didn't exist after normal business hours. Arch then had the idea of launching his own nightclub that was open late, welcomed all, and didn't have a dress code. As partying and nightlife became more accessible to Parisians, this venue has transformed into a popular venue for artists of all kinds to perform and visit from the likes of Dali to the Beatles.

## (10) LA BULLE NOIRE

120 Blvd Marguerite de Rochechouart,
75018 Paris
01 49 25 81 75

Local musicians to international acts play at this small, but intimate 1970s inspired bar and music venue, part of the grand theatre La Cigale. You'll feel like you're getting a private concert in this space filled with nostalgia.

The beverage prices are not outrageous, but expect to pay a cover fee in support of the artists and venue. Definitely check the line-up online ahead of time so you can plan out the best experience and don't run into any surprises.

## (11) L'OLYMPIA

28 Bd des Capucines,
75009 Paris
08 92 68 33 68

We cannot talk about live music in Paris without mentioning L'Olympia! This live music hall's history dating back to 1888 wasn't always a music venue attracting rock bands and international artists. With its humble beginnings at the end of the 19th century, L'Olympia was opened by the co-creators of the Moulin Rouge and was a venue welcoming the opera, ballet, and theatrical troupes with music performances. The venue reinvented itself as a cinema at the start of the 20th century when cinema was all the craze, then again in 1954, reopening as a live music concert hall with the notable French music producer, Bruno Coquatrix, as its executive director. Today, the music hall's wall of fame includes the likes of Édith Piaf, The Beatles, Jimmy Hendrix, and Taylor Swift— just to name a few. If you're lucky enough to see a performance here, you'll be stepping into a treasured gem of music history.

## 12 PARC DE LA VILLETTE

211 Av. Jean Jaurès,
75019 Paris
01 40 03 75 75

This art, music and cultural hub on the edge of Paris invites cultural patrons as well as artists and musicians to participate in all that the Park has to offer. On the south end of this park, you'll find Cité de la Musique, a music hall and performing arts center for classic music and art expos. The neighboring venue, the Philharmonie de Paris, is another large music hall welcoming large orchestras and music troupes. Additionally, Le Zenith Paris is a 6,000 seat live music venue featuring live music concerts and sporting events. Finally, Cabaret Sauvage boasts a nightclub as well as a live music venue located in the park.

Moreover, La Villette hosts performing art centers like the Pavillon Villette, and the theater Paris-Villette, a convention center Grande Halle de la Villette, and many restaurants, bars, cafes, cinemas and businesses.

# Clubbing & Table Service

The clubbing and dance scene may look different in Paris than other party capitals of Europe. In Paris, the night life scene, especially that of music and dance seem to be almost invisible. There are no dance clubs that are out in the open as they would be in cities like Berlin that have a conspicuous night life. No, Paris' club scene is usually underground, in the shadows, hidden away from the public view or disclosed in old buildings that are reinvented for night life.

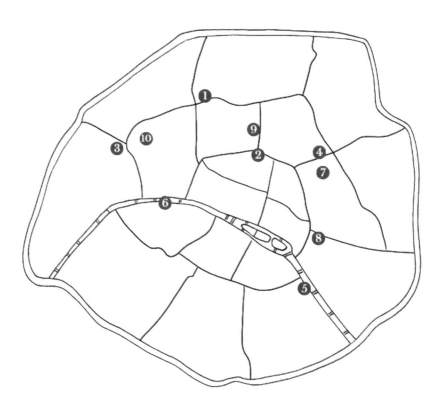

This is what makes Paris' party scene so fun. Once you arrive, you feel like you've unlocked access to undercover scenes that you wouldn't know exist unless you find them. Of course, going to these places with a local is preferable, but meeting people in the club is just as fun! You can appreciate a plethora of music genres and styles— local as well as internationally renowned DJs perform in Parisian clubs of all shapes and sizes. You may want to do a little digging around on Paris music blogs and night club sites to see who is performing and when to stop by.

Sit back and enjoy these picks of my favorite night clubs to check out in Paris. Have a drink for me and don't be afraid to shake it on the dance floor!

 ## LA MACHINE DU MOULIN ROUGE
90 Bd de Clichy,
75018 Paris
01 53 41 88 89

The underground nightclub of the Moulin Rouge welcomes you for live music, DJ sets, table service, and their famous **bar à bulles** (champagne room). This multifaceted venue offers something for everyone! You can enjoy drinks on their secluded rooftop and then rock out to music into the late night hours. So, the next time you're looking to visit, check out their website for an updated calendar of events.

## 2  REX CLUB
5 Bd Poissonnière, 75002 Paris

01 42 36 10 96

The Rex Club is ideally located on the Grand Boulevards and is known for its techno and electronic music scene and exceptional sound system. Usually, the crowd is diverse and the music fun to jam out to, especially with international DJs playing here. The Rex is your typical club with guys and girls mingling and the perfect spot to drink and dance 'til the sun comes up.

## 3  DUPLEX PARIS
2 bis Av. Foch, 75116 Paris

01 45 00 45 00

You can definitely order table service at Duplex while dancing your butt off in their **grand salon** to a high-energy DJ set. If you're celebrating a birthday on the last Saturday of the month, they offer free entry, cloak room, and a complimentary bottle of champagne for ladies!

## 4  LA JAVA
105 Rue du Faubourg du Temple, 75010 Paris

09 80 54 94 51

Each night, there's a different dance theme from gay nights, to 1920s mix and Balkan jams, to techno and 90s music for you to appreciate depending on your thrill. The interior is inspired by Art Nouveau, but the grungy basement adds to the messy/chic French charm.

## 5 WANDERLUST

32 Quai d'Austerlitz, 75013 Paris

06 14 96 77 64

Nestled on the Quai d'Austerlitz, facing the Seine River, is the funky and lively open terrace rooftop club Wanderlust. This modern club has a youthful vibe and serves up street food, beers and cocktails against a glistening city view. You can definitely go early and stay late while taking in the city and jamming out to hip and catchy international acoustics.

## 6 FAUST

Rive Gauche, Pont Alexandre III, 75007 Paris

01 44 18 60 60

Check out Faust in their unique location under Pont Alexandre III bridge along the Seine for a memorable experience. The club and bar is chic and stylish, so dress up for this one and don't be surprised to pay more for drinks here than you would some of the local bars. The exclusive locale makes for a somewhat snooty environment, but you are sure to have a blast if you go there with friends searching for a good time.

## 7  ALIMENTATION GÉNÉRALE

64 Rue Jean-Pierre Timbaud,
75011 Paris
09 81 86 42 50

This funky, hip bar and music venue offers great live music with a revolving set each week. Getting in is usually a breeze and is perfect with larger groups because the chill and minimalist scene encourages you to relax and have fun. The drinks are not overpriced for Paris and you can definitely stay late into the morning hours on the weekends. The cherry on top is that Parisians go here, so it's a very laid back scene, no dress code required. Check the website for the monthly music lineup.

## 8  PACHAMAMA

46-48 Rue du Faubourg Saint-Antoine,
75012 Paris
01 55 78 84 75

This four-level venue is a lounge bar and dance club all rolled into one. You can order table service if you want a more intimate setting for your party or journey from one floor to the next enjoying the different music and ambiences. They have decent cocktails and a sleek, gothic, edgy vibe with a balcony overlooking each floor.

## 9 LA MANO

10 Rue Papillon,
75009 Paris

You want a Latin vibe? La Mano is the place to be for Mexican-inspired cocktails created with Mezcal although they do have a wide selection of other drinks too. The music surprises you each night; it's never the same, so see their music lineup if you want a certain ambience. It's a great and quirky space to hang and dance with friends or with a special someone. My recommendation is you go there early and stay late!

## 10 BOUM BOUM NIGHT CLUB

37 Av. de Friedland,
75008 Paris
06 33 33 88 88

This swanky dance club is the perfect place to end your night with drinks and a lounge bar. Their rotating DJs know how to bring the music to light up the place for the soulful to strut their moves. You will want to dress to the nines to get a pass in because this place is known as the celebrities club; you may even spot one or two while you're inside (but keep your cool, of course!).

# Lounge Bars

So maybe clubs aren't your thing, but you still want to get out and take in Paris in a serene environment while lounging around, possibly with a great cocktail or beer in hand. I have the perfect list of lounge bars you'll want to check out and try for yourself.

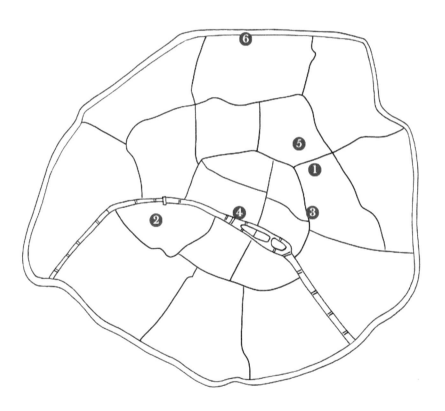

These spots are ideal for a calm night out in a fun setting, each place has something unique to offer whether through tropical vibes or by transporting you to yesteryear. Come for the ambience and the drinks; you may even get to enjoy some music from local or international artists if you're lucky.

 **LE TIKI LOUNGE**

26 bis Rue de la Font au Roi, 75011 Paris

01 55 28 57 72

Taking you across the Pacific to enjoy a Hawaiian atmosphere where lounging is in their name, Le Tiki Lounge invites you to recline in their exotic atmosphere with one of their specialty tropical-inspired cocktails. The patrons rave about the cocktails that are **sympa**, or nice, and recommend the must-try Mai Tai cocktail for the full experience. They also present a menu of non-alcoholic drinks that are just as tasty.

 **GATSBY**

64 Av. Bosquet, 75007 Paris

01 45 51 56 24

This cocktail lounge bar is a rare gem in a sea of restaurants and cafes and brings some excitement to the 7th arrondissement which would otherwise be a little humdrum. This bar, inspired by the roaring 20s where Mister Gatsby himself invites you for a pleasant evening, has specialty drinks and a casual environment to chill and relax.

### 3 CUBA COMPAGNIE CAFÉ

48 Bd Beaumarchais, 75011 Paris

01 48 06 07 11

If you want to getaway without leaving the city, another go-to is Cuba Compagnie Café where the fresh rum mojitos and fried plantains will transport you to Havana. This lounge bar and cafe is the ideal spot to relax on any given day of the summer. They provide comfy lounge chairs that will make you feel like you're at the beach rather than in the Bastille neighborhood of Paris. Pay a visit if you're craving some Latin vibes because they often feature Cuban musicians that lighten the mood and help you unwind, not to mention that they have cheap beers and cocktails during their happy hour from 4 PM to 8 PM.

### 4 LE FUMOIR

6 Rue de l'Amiral de Coligny, 75001 Paris

01 42 92 00 24

This restaurant, bar and Salon de thé, neighboring the Louvre, is everything rolled into one with a classy and sophisticated ambience. Besides serving up some impressive French meals without the huge costs, Le Fumoir serves up fabulous cocktails. As you can probably tell, my favorite time to visit Le Fumoir is in the late afternoon in time for an **apéro** and time to unwind from work in their library-esc lounge area. Le Fumoir, which means "the smoking room", no longer allows smoking indoors, but it's still a great hangout spot with a relaxing setting, especially if you are looking for English-speaking waiters.

## 5  LE COMPTOIR GÉNÉRALE

84 Quai de Jemmapes, 75010 Paris

01 44 88 24 48

No place exemplifies or captures *l'art de vivre* quite like Comptoir Générale. At this lounge bar, you're invited to "just be" and hang out with a nice cocktail in your hand, in a clean and eclectic environment inspired by the West Indies. The place is extensive so you can peruse until you find a comfortable semi-private room or settle on the flowery terrace filled with overgrown vegetation, adding to the midsummer night feel. The mood is curated by their personal playlists that play all day to provide the most relaxing setting. They offer brunch on the weekends and privatization of their rooms for larger groups.

## 6  LA RECYCLERIE

83 Bd Ornano, 75018 Paris

01 42 57 58 49

Another fun cafe/bar/cafeteria-style hangout that is a lovely place to enjoy an afternoon with friends drinking, eating and chatting. What makes La Recyclerie is their aim to provide patrons with a fun time in a beautiful setting while doing everything with a sustainability mindset. Their unique and versatile location on the edge of an old railroad provides a space for them to urbanize and create a green space for their visitors while maintaining a neighborhood compost on location. Their weekend brunch is made with fresh and local ingredients and worth a visit.

# Cabarets

Cabarets are a hybrid of two things: the French taverns of the late 15th century and the French music venues of the late 1800s.

Sprouting up in the late 1400s in France, cabarets distinguished themselves from taverns as places that served wine and warm food over tables with table clothes.

During the Belle Époque (1870s-1910s) period, cabarets evolved out of what were known as **café-chantant** or **café-concert**, or a singing cafe.

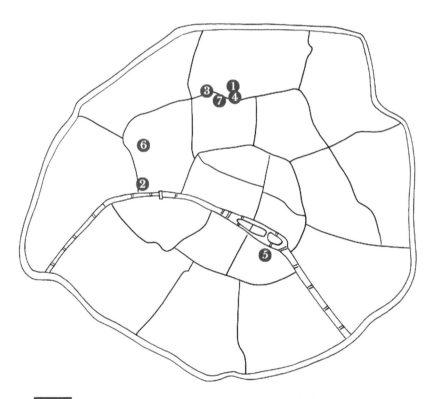

The **café-concert** was a type of cafe (that served food) where performers and musicians entertained the public by performing popular music of the time. The first modern cabaret that opened up in Montmartre in 1881 was Le Chat Noir and it attracted a mix of society's best, from writers and artists, to journalists and students, to the wealthy. Le Chat Noir started off as a lieu to entertain through musical performance and political commentary and humor then eventually transformed into something more. Fast-forward to 1889 when the Moulin Rouge opened with its famous red windmill façade and you get the birth of the French can-can dance, which forever epitomized the cabaret as a place of entertainment served alongside food and drink with their seductive dancing shows, often displaying nudity.

So, what are cabarets today? In my own words, I would describe them as a mix between a song and dance performance, a burlesque show and a striptease with an optional dinner and beverage service.

Today, in Paris, there are notable cabarets featuring nightly entertainment and risqué musical shows often involving some sort of nudity, or sexuality. They are almost always accompanied with a meal and refreshments. Here are my top recommendations for cabarets not to miss in Paris.

**1** **CHEZ MICHOU**

80 Rue des Martyrs, 75018 Paris

01 46 06 16 04

Chances are you haven't heard of the one and only Cabaret Michou! This enticing show that has been running since 1968 transforms the crafted artists into a myriad of showstoppers from Céline Dion to Lady Gaga.

The cabaret is an authentic experience unique to France and one of the best things to do in Paris for entertainment on a midsummer night. At Chez Michou, you can see the show with drinks only or make a night of it and have dinner plus a show.

## 2 THE CRAZY HORSE

12 Av. George V, 75008 Paris

01 47 23 32 32

If you are looking for a more classic approach, spice up a night in Paris with your girlfriends or your babe at one of the city's sexiest cabarets— The Crazy Horse. This contemporary take on cabaret is a terrific spectacle that has many songs in English for an Anglophone audience.

To be warned, there is nudity up top and you do get bare **fesses** (bums), but the dances are so sophisticated that you couldn't have them any other way. The ladies and men in the show are sexy, entertaining, and captivating from the time the champagne pops to the last glass.

## 3 MOULIN ROUGE

82 Bd de Clichy, 75018 Paris

01 53 09 82 82

What visit to Paris would be complete without a visit to the extravagant and glitzy Moulin Rouge. Reserve your tickets in advance to visit the **grand salle** where the spectacle of light, music, and talented ladies doing extraordinary moves takes place. Don't shy away from the nudity though as there is a bit, or a lot, depending on your sense of modesty.

You can enjoy dinner and the early show or opt for champagne and the later show starting at 87 €. They offer a Soirée VIP that is fit for a queen and includes a five-course meal and your choice of champagne or wine.

## 4 MADAME ARTHUR

75bis Rue des Martyrs, 75018 Paris

07 68 78 68 01

Eat, drink, laugh and cry with the flamboyant transvestite troupe, Madame Arthur, hailing as the first ever trans cabaret in Paris in 1946. You can reserve a table starting at 60 € for dinner and a show lasting 'til the early morning hours of 6 AM. Or opt for an early bird experience with entrance before 10 PM for **placement libre**. There is also open seating 'til 6 AM, to enjoy the cabaret, drinks, and their famous interactive quiz show.

## 5 PARADIS LATIN

28 Rue du Cardinal Lemoine, 75005 Paris

01 43 25 28 28

This is a cabaret with a Latin twist! They are famous for their show Bird of Paradise or as it's known in French: **L'Oiseau Paradis**. This cabaret flaunts the most range of shows performed. Like the others, you can enjoy dinner and **spectacle** or just drinks and a show starting at 80 €. If you're under 26 years old, you can see the show for only 45 €. Paradis Latin performs lunch shows for the daring types who want to spice up their afternoon, and no, I'm not talking about the food!

## 6  LE LIDO

116 Av. des Champs-Élysées, 75008 Paris
01 40 76 56 10

The Lido de Paris is nothing but extraordinary! If you want to be blown away, try this breathtaking show of glitter, glitz, and glamorous girls, fit from head to toe in feathers, beads and sparkle! The Lido delivers what it promises with a sensual show from its troupe, the Bluebell Girls. Everything is gold and exactly what you would expect— the presentation from the spectacle to the smallest detail is delicately thought out and an ode to the highest Parisian sophistication imaginable. If you're in Paris for a special occasion or with that someone special, I cannot recommend Le Lido enough!

## 7  LA NOUVELLE EVE

25 Rue Pierre Fontaine, 75009 Paris
01 48 74 69 25

La Nouvelle Eve is a hybrid music hall and cabaret that has entertained its public for over 120 years. It's a self-proclaimed hidden gem— and rightly so. Performing its show **Paris je t'aime** with its 26 leading ladies on the stage is beautifully raw and cerebral. The show remains elegant and intimate without all the flashiness of a million little lights offering a closeness that the bigger stages don't portray. The performers hone their craft, delivering not only a dance show but a performance focused on jazz music and live theatre. You're in for a treat from the moment you arrive to the last drop of bubbly.

# Interview with
# **Hannah S.,**
# a digital nomad and
# seasonal Paris visitor

Hannah

ustinite, casting associate, writer and book cover designer, Hannah S. has always been a Francophile at heart. When she was 12 years old, she took her first French language class. Her first trip to Paris was in 2015 to work on a short film, which we co-directed.

Hannah and I met in our last year of college, making films together. To my pleasant surprise, we quickly bonded over our mutual love for great stories, French culture and the French language. I didn't realize it at the time, but Hannah was a huge Francophile!

After a couple of years of living in Paris, I invited Hannah to Paris to co-direct the short film **Margot** with me, based on a script I had written. Ever since her first trip to Paris to work on this film, she has become a seasonal visitor, staying anywhere from 3-6 weeks each time.

She didn't want Paris to be the "one that got away", so she has been back every year since and her ideal vision is to split her time 50/50 between home and Paris.

Here's Hannah's love story with Paris and how it keeps bringing her back.

## Why did you move/go to Paris?

I've always been a Francophile, probably since I was 12 years old. I took my first introduction to the language, and I immediately fell in love. Growing up, I had entertained the idea of being a foreign exchange student...

I was lucky enough to know you, Céline, who lived in Paris and wanted to work with me on **Margot**, our short film, so that gave me the opportunity to go and do something that I loved in the city that I've always wanted to visit.

And it really helped to have a friend there because it made something that seemed impossible really possible.

Now, I've been five times since 2015. I've spent 6 total months of my life in Paris! I usually come about once a year in the spring, late summer, or fall.

## What was your first impression of Paris?

Surprised by how dirty it is. It's not pristine the way that you think it is. Real people live there; it's a very real place.

At the time, the trash men went on strike, which is apparently a very big part of French culture, so that was pretty funny. I guess I didn't realize how rebellious the people are.

I was also surprised by how transient it is. People there are in and out so much that I think that it was a little more challenging to connect than I hoped it would be.

You come into it with your expectations so high that you almost don't expect the realness of it. And in that way, the grittiness and frustrations of Paris can be a negative— but they're also the things that make it a complex, authentic place.

## What do you love about Paris?

There is nothing like a Parisian croissant for a single Euro! I love that the Eiffel Tower sparkles. I love the architecture; I love that everything is mostly cohesive; you feel like you're in a snow globe.

Also, the air there is just... Paris. Like, I know when I step out of a taxi and I'm in Paris. I don't know, it's just charming in all the ways you would imagine it would be.

All the clichés about it are true. And they're actually made richer by the fact that it's MORE real than anything else.

One of my first weeks in Paris, I saw this kid in a striped shirt with an armful of baguettes. And I was so thrilled!

Another thing that I love is that you can drink on the streets there. All the basic enjoyments in Paris are all super simple, like eating and drinking and being with people, and picnics and walking...

**What does living in France mean to you?**

I've only lived in one place pretty much my whole life, and going to Paris challenges me in a way that I'm not challenged in my everyday life. Paris represents a different lifestyle, a different living situation; it's a different language.

It forces me to be brave; it makes me live smaller, and it makes me get out of my comfort zone. It makes me chase after something that I really want, but I've also spent enough time there that at this point, it feels a little bit like home.

**What challenges did you face with moving to Paris?**

The language barrier and the conversion rate.

It can be really isolating and lonely, too. I don't know why, but if you talk to people who actually live there, they will tell you the exact same thing. Paris is hard and there isn't a clear explanation for why. Everything you do is going to be challenged somehow, getting from point A to point B is a trek.

I'm from Texas and everything is bigger in Texas. Spaces are a lot tighter in Paris. You can feel a bit claustrophobic sometimes and you have to make a big effort to make your experience worth it. At least in my experience, you do.

But on the positive side, people were not as snippy as I thought. I haven't really had a hard time with people in Paris at all. I think if you're eager and positive and kind, people are not going to be frustrated with you or roll their eyes that you're in their city.

## What is a lesson you have learned from living in Paris?

I've learned that you have to go after what you want. You have to fight through the fear and sometimes do things alone.

I got tired of not experiencing the things that I was too afraid of.

To experience the full benefit of Paris, you have to figure out a way to get out of your comfort zone and explore and just be content not knowing or doing it perfectly. Paris forces you to go with the flow.

## What has been your visa situation while living in France?

I've always had a tourist visa because I always visited for 2 months or less at a time. My ideal vision would be to split my time. I don't want Paris to be the one that got away, but it's scary for me. Leaving my life in Austin is a big ask. I do want to move to Paris eventually. I would love to commit to Paris a little bit more permanently.

## What is your biggest frustration with Paris?

Because I haven't moved there full time, I haven't had to deal too much with the crazy bureaucracy, but everything is ten times harder than it has to be.

Nothing happens quickly in France, which is why people are good with going with the flow, but that's also why they're really impatient.

Things take longer there and it's good to manage your expectations.

## What's your favorite thing to do in Paris?

Going down to the boulangerie and getting croissants. Or sitting in a park or coffee shop, working for a few hours, having appetizers and drinks with friends then wandering in the city and seeing what it has to offer.

**What would you tell someone who is like you and wants to move to Paris?**

Just do it.

Look into visas. Think about all the practicalities. Think about how you're going to spend your time and make Paris your own.

If you don't know those things, it can be really easy to walk into a place that is frustrating and lonely.

Dreams are put on your heart for a reason, and doors can open for you to follow them. If you see that happen, go after it.

**How can Céline Concierge help you in the future?**

If I moved there, relocation services, for sure!

Accommodations, pet relocation, basic steps, and tips and tricks like how to set up a bank account and which visas to apply for— all the things you need to do to get set up in a foreign country.

Céline, you have so many good ideas for things to do, so having someone who has experience is helpful for pointing you in the right direction. Because you've already done those things and have personal experience, I trust that you know how to navigate French bureaucracy.

**Would you recommend Céline Concierge services?**

Recommend for sure! I trust your expertise; I would turn to your resources and blog posts for direction.

**Do you have a favorite book, film, or song about Paris?**

I loved listening to corny French music growing up like Jenifer, Alizée, and Zazie.

After a three year hiatus, Hannah is excited to plan her next six-week trip to Paris in March 2022.

# SHOPPING

# Shopping in Paris

It's no surprise that with the treasure trove of styles, tastes, and imaginations that exist within Paris, there is definitely a wide selection of shopping to be had to match whatever you're on the hunt for. From vintage to bargain finds, to high-end luxury to boho concept boutiques and traditional department store shopping, if you dream it up, you're sure to find it in Paris. If the city does anything right, it's the fashion and shopping sense that you'll discover in the labyrinth of shops, stores, and boutiques across the city. Below are the main types of shopping you can expect in Paris with neighborhoods and famous streets where, you too, can delve into the Parisian style.

## DIFFERENT TYPES OF SHOPPING YOU'LL FIND IN PARIS:

### Luxury and Designer

The Golden Triangle of shopping in Paris' 8th Arrondissement: Champs-Élysées | Avenue George V | Avenue Montaigne

### Vintage Shopping:

Montmartre | South Pigalle

### Department Stores

Throughout Paris

### Concept Stores

the Marais | Canal St. Martin | Pigalle area | Montmartre

### Jewelry

Place Vendôme | Throughout Paris

### Brocantes / Antiques

Throughout Paris

## A BRIEF LEXICON OF TERMS TO KNOW

**le coût** | the cost

**coûter** | cost

**acheter** | purchase, buy

**vendre** | sell

**marché** | market

**supermarché** | supermarket

**magasin** | store

**brocante** | flea market or second-hand trade

**marché aux puces** | flea market

**Combien cela coûte-t-il ?** | How much does this cost?

**Je veux l'acheter, s'il vous plaît.** | I want to buy it, please.

# Best Shopping Streets for Luxury and Designer

Starting off our virtual voyage across Paris' shopping scene, we'll pass through the **Triangle D'or,** or Paris's Golden Triangle: Champs-Élysées, Avenue George V, and Avenue Montaigne. Then we'll journey through some of the lesser-known areas for shopping in Paris like Rue Montmartre where you can discover concept stores and vintage shopping.

Come along with me to explore all the shopping that Paris has to offer.

## CHAMPS-ÉLYSÉE

From eating delicious food at the many **cafés Parisiens**, popping into the cinéma or visiting a tantalizing cabaret, to shopping your heart out, the Champs-Élysées is undoubtedly the most famous and recognizable boulevard in the world.

The famous avenue connects Place de la Concorde and the grand Arc de Triomphe that are the beacons of the glorious boulevard and captures a sense of grandeur and opulence that epitomises the neighborhood where many designer shops line the boulevard.

You will find the popular French drugstore/bookstore, Publicis Drugstore, the grandiose window displays of Louis Vuitton, Cartier, Bulgari, and Maje, as well as the notable landmarks nearby: Le Grand Palais and Le Petit Palais.

## AVENUE GEORGE V

The lovely Four Seasons Hotel and the stunning American Cathedral are home to the avenue surrounded by the many designer storefronts that will be inviting you to shop here such as Kenzo, Hermès, Bvlgari, and Balenciaga.

## AVENUE MONTAIGNE

Finally, the last leg of the Golden Triangle, Avenue Montaigne, entices you with Céline, Gendi, Chanel, Prada, Dior, among many other prestigious names.

You'll love walking by the Hôtel Plaza Athénée with its charming window displays of overgrown flowers as well as the elegant Théâtre des Champs-Élysées.

Other renowned luxury shopping streets you should visit are the following:

## PLACE VENDÔME & OPÉRA NEIGHBORHOODS

### Rue Saint Honoré | Rue de la Paix | Boulevard Capucines | Boulevard Haussmann

The Champs-Élysées' little sister, Rue du Faubourg Saint-Honoré, offers less traffic and more tightly knit shops side by side in an intimate and walkable area. You'll discover the likes of Apostrophe, Alexander McQueen, Jimmy Choo, Missoni, Valentino and many others here.

Leading you up the picturesque area of Place Vendôme, you'll find upscale jewelry shops like Chaumet, Boucheron, Van Cleef & Arpels, and Rolex. Go further north, past the classic Opéra Garnier, to the famed perfume shop Fragonard and finally the extravagant department shops Printemps and Galeries Lafayette.

## SAINT-GERMAIN-DES-PRÉS NEIGHBORHOOD

### Rue des Saints-Pères | Rue du Four | Rue du Bac | Rue Grenelle

This neighborhood opens up a Pandora's box of shopping possibilities from its designer shops, to antiques stores to art and beauty; if you find yourself in this neighborhood, brace yourself and your wallet at the endless possibility of things to purchase.

You'll find the likes of Paul Smith Women's, the Parisian-style women's apparel shops like agnès b., Ines de la Fressange, and Ba&sh.

## LE MARAIS

### Rue des Francs Bourgeois | Rue Vieille Du Temple | Rue St. Croix de la Bretonnerie | Boulevard Beaumarchais

In the Marais, you'll recognize some designer stores as well as some trendy French boutiques. But the shopping doesn't end at the clothing stores, the Marias has many home goods stores like Merci and Le BHV Marais worth perusing, too.

### Rue Montmartre | Rue Étienne Marcel | Rue Réaumur

Want to change up the shopping adventure to something a little more edgy and unique? You can't miss the many concept boutiques, vintage shops, and home good stores along Rue Montmartre and Rue Réaumur. Starting south on Rue Montmartre and walking north, you'll find leather goods stores like Nat & Nin, Repetto, as well as shops like COS and & Other Stories. Stray slightly east to find the original French Anthropology store: the Sézane Apartment, full of French clothing, home, and lifestyle goods.

# Vintage Shopping in Paris

In the proximity of Rue Saint Denis, you'll find the highest concentration of eclectic vintage shops like **Kiliwatch**, **Épisode**, and **La Chiffonnerie** where you can dig up one-of-a-kind finds. Beyond this, you can discover pockets of vintage boutiques scattered throughout Paris where you can unearth various treasures, be it a Dolce & Gabbana wool coat, or a vintage Hermès scarf at a fraction of its original price.

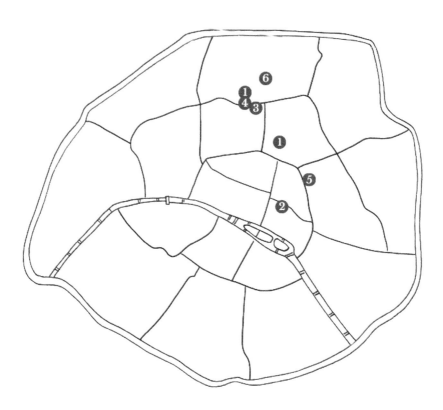

One thing's for sure, no matter which of these shops you pop into, you're going to find a utopia of buried gems. Continue reading for my picks of the best vintage shops to hit up if you're in the mood for vintage shopping and treasure hunting.

## 1 CHINE MACHINE

**Location 1**

100 Rue des Martyrs, 75018 Paris

01 80 50 27 66

**Location 2**

10 Rue des Petites Écuries, 75010 Paris

01 77 17 03 62

Chine Machine is vintage at its best. This two-story shop is sitting on a corner of the famous Rue Des Martyrs. When you step in, it's like stepping into a wonderland of possibilities. I once purchased a never worn pair of Rogan designer heels (worth 350 €) for only 30 €. You can find anything from 10 € vintage Hermès scarves, to 60s style pumps and flares, to designer coats. This place is a must visit for clothes and fashion lovers.

## 2 VINTAGE DÉSIR

32 Rue des Rosiers, 75004 Paris

01 40 27 04 98

Located on the charming Rue des Rosiers in the Marais neighborhood, Vintage Désir is a tiny shop offering up rare accessory finds, hats, and clothes. If you have the patience to leaf through and peruse, you are sure to find something special. Even if the shop managers seem indifferent, it has never stopped me from going in and coming out with a bag full of goodies at a bargain.

### 3 TEMPOLINO

5 Rue Gérando,
75009 Paris
09 54 79 47 67

A visit to Tempolino is like stepping into Alice in Wonderland's vintage shop, if she owned one. The colorful and quirky vibes are inviting, and it breathes an air of potential, awaiting the perfect object, hat, or scarf to take home with you. The small boutique is lovely and clean; the shop owner doesn't try to sell too much in the limited space but keeps the visual noise down, so you can actually hear when that special piece calls your name.

### 4 BY FLOWERS

86 Rue des Martyrs,
75018 Paris

If your pace is more of a sprint than a walk, then you may enjoy the challenge of digging for fashion treasure at By Flowers. The tiny space is filled with as many objects as can fit and the layout is presented so you have to work for your finds. If you can get past the overwhelming nature of the shop arrangement, you are likely to find expensive fur coats, jackets, shoes and boots at a discounted rate.

## 5 VINTAGE CLOTHING PARIS

10 Rue de Crussol,
75011 Paris
01 48 07 16 40

The look and feel of Vintage Clothing Paris is a fresh take on vintage fashion. When you walk into the shop, you feel like you're walking into Madonna's closet from the 80s— everything is cool, chic, and colorful. The minimalist feel of the shop makes everything feel extra refined and expensive without having to pay the cost of luxury. You will be pleasantly surprised to find plenty of designer items at a fraction of the original cost.

## 6 IGLAÏNE VINTAGE

14 Rue Nicolet,
75018 Paris
06 11 69 75 08

For upscale vintage, look no further than Iglaïne Vintage. You can expect to go here and walk out looking like a million bucks without paying the high cost of designer brands. The prices do tend to run on the higher end compared to other vintage shops, but the items they sell are in mint condition, so it feels like you're jumping decades back to have the fashion of the late 20th century. Who says you have to strive for new fashion when vintage styles are here to stay, especially in Paris!?

# Grands Magasins de Paris

P aris' **grands magasins,** or luxury department stores, can be compared to American staples like Macy's and Nordstrom but with a French twist, of course. These quintessential shopping spots are key to Parisian society and come alive during the Christmas holidays with extravagant window displays and an unforgettable shopping experience for the local and visitor alike.

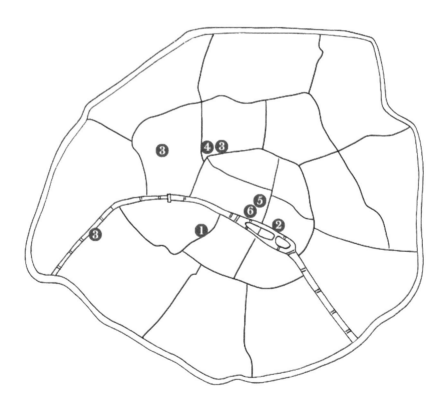

France experiences **les soldes**, or the sales, twice a year with the summer sales (**soldes d'été**) and winter sales (**soldes d'hiver**) whose dates are officially set by the French government[1]. The winter sales happen about 2 weeks after Christmas and the summer sales are at the end of June through the end of July.

## 1 LE BON MARCHÉ

24 Rue de Sèvres,
75007 Paris
01 44 39 80 00

Located on the **Rive Gauche**, or left bank of Paris, this Parisian favorite is a landmark of luxury shopping in one place. Its two-fold name, which means "the good deal" and "the good market" was acquired by the LVMH Group in 1984 and remains a crown jewel for Parisians and out-of-towners alike. La Grand Épicerie de Paris, or treasure trove of fine foods, is Whole Foods meets fine French gastronomy and is definitely worth a visit in the adjoining building. In the department store, you can find the likes of Sézane, Céline, and Chanel, just some of the iconic luxury French brands, as well as home decor stores like Caravane and its Book and Stationary shop.

---

[1]  https://www.economie.gouv.fr/particuliers/dates-soldes#

## 2 BHV

52 Rue de Rivoli, 75004 Paris
09 77 40 14 00

What makes the Bazar de Hôtel de Ville (or BHV for short) unique is its underground hardware store. It's literally a treasure trove of all things big and small. The upper levels contain prestigious French brands; you can shop for anything from a purse, to a coat, to a couch.

They also have a home decor department where you can create anything from custom curtains to paint. This bazaar is a fun way to spend an afternoon window shopping or actual shopping if you're ready to take that big, or little, purchase home with you.

## 3 GALERIES LAFAYETTE

### Location 1

40 Bd Haussmann,
75009 Paris
01 42 82 34 56

### Location 2

60 Av. des Champs-
Élysées, 75008 Paris
01 83 65 61 00

### Location 3

7 Rue Linois, 75015 Paris
01 83 18 08 00

The Galeries Lafayette is an upscale fashion department store focused on selling French brands and products. Its flagship store in the 9th arr. of Paris is located near Opéra Garnier, on the Boulevard Haussmann. The **magasin** is especially popular during Paris Fashion Week, hosting events throughout the week. During the holidays, the store transforms into Santa's workshop, showing off a giant Christmas tree as well as festive Christmas window displays. Don't miss out on a visit here during the holiday season!

## 4 PRINTEMPS

64 Bd Haussmann,
75009 Paris
01 42 82 50 00

Located next to Galéries Lafayette is Printemps, meaning springtime in French, L'Espace Mariage du Printemps is particularly geared to those hearing wedding bells. It is a place to help plan and execute your wedding needs. This paradise of wedding dresses calls the soon-to-be bride to try on and find her dream wedding dress (by appointment only). You have the notable boutiques of Maria Luisa Mariage and Rosa Clarà as well as tailor-made services for wedding planning, beauty, and travel for the future couple.

## 5 WESTFIELD FORUM DES HALLES

101 Porte Berger,
75001 Paris
01 44 76 87 08

This five-level shopping district and urban center features an underground cinema, shopping mall, gymnasium, and aquatic center among cafes, bars, and restaurants. The Forum was renovated over several years and completed in 2016 with the reopening and inauguration of **la Canopée**, or the Canopy— a green structural edifice that looms over **le forum** and her patrons. Underground of this shopping centre, you'll find the hub of the Parisian metro and train lines, Chatelêt-Les Halles, with six metro lines intersecting here, as well as numerous buses and three RER lines (grand train lines) including the notable RER line B (blue line) which connects to both airports.

## 6 SAMARITAINE

9 Rue de la Monnaie,
75001 Paris
01 88 88 60 00

Finally on our list, the newly renovated, Samaritaine is both the oldest and newest shopping center of Paris. It's in the historical Art Deco building that was deemed a historical French monument by the French Ministry of Culture and is located on the right bank just on the edge of Pont Neuf. It closed in 2005, apparently due to its building not meeting safety codes. But now, the new brainchild of LVMH has reopened (June 2021) after a major facelift that has taken many years to complete, only adding to the anticipated reopening. Along with the shopping, Samaritaine offers a boutique hotel that is equipped with a penthouse suite and its own private swimming pool.

# Specialty Home Good Stores

Starting at the south point of Rue Montmartre, near Les Halles Department Store, you'll find coveted pop-up stores and plenty of kitchen supplies stores like Bruit dans la Cuisine, Mora, Déco Relief, and A.Simon.

Sprinkled throughout the city are a great array of specialty home good stores (with multiple addresses) where you can find anything from bath tiles, to doorknobs, to curtains, and lighting stores. Below, I will highlight only the main stores that you, as a traveler, may be interested in checking out. Because who said it was a crime to dream up your future Parisian home— even if that's a fantasy?

### Empreintes

At Empreintes, you'll discover unique, hand-crafted goods from French designers. From home decoration like candlesticks and sculptures, to furnishings for your home, you can find anything under the sun that is a rare handcrafted treasure at this store.

### Merci Concept Store

Merci sells the ultimate French lifestyle dream, with items that range from clothing to home goods like dish ware, candles, and artwork. Their high-end pieces are minimalistic and simple, but chic. Expats love this shop because each item says "French", while bringing a certain level of design.

## Fleux

Sprinkled on the Rue Sainte-Croix de la Bretonnerie in the Marais; you will be delighted to find four individual Fleux boutiques featuring an assortment of home and fashion goods. Fleux displays everything from candles, to beauty products, to rugs and mirrors. This trendy boutique invites you to stroll the aisles of the shop for any item you desire to enrich your life with a bit more French flare.

## AMPM

AMPM is yet another lovely home furnishing store and go-to for the French and visitors alike. The overall aesthetic is all about clean lines and textures: wood, linens, and wicker. You can get anything from pottery, to lampshades, to dining tables here.

## Leroy Merlin, Bricorama, Castorama

At these three do-it-yourself and hardware stores, you can get anything for your home remodel or redecoration projects. They offer simple solutions to almost any home problem and are equivalent to an American Lowe's or Home Depot. They also have a large gardening section in all of their stores.

## Truffaut

Speaking of gardening, Truffaut is a large nursery offering up every tool, seed, soil, plants and flowers for your next gardening project. The staff is usually quite friendly and willing to offer up advice on what tools to use, as well as planting and gardening tips for the beginner as much as for the seasoned gardener. Besides the wide gardening and outdoor selection, they sell plenty of home supplies and goods that could inspire any home makeover. They have several locations in and around Paris that you'll love to peruse if you're a plant lover.

## BHV Marais

As I mentioned in the Grands Magasins chapter just before, BHV is a huge multi-level department store. But what many people (even some locals) don't know is that it has an underground hardware store, or **quincaillerie** (one of the hardest words to pronounce in French). It's your one-stop-shop for a personal, as well as a home makeover. With their myriad of stores within the store, you can purchase designer clothes, handbags, and perfumes but also wall paint, furniture, and window treatments.

## La Grande Épicerie de Paris

No visit to the left bank's Le Bon Marché is complete without as little as a peek into LGEP. The store's name that translates as "Paris' grand grocery store" is just that— an emporium of specialty food and drink choices. Get any item that can squeeze into your kitchen here, from wine for your wine cave, fine chocolates, fish, meat and poultry, to the finest international spices.

## La Trésorerie

Selling homeware and hardware goods, La Trésorerie can be considered an everything-for-the-home store. Its open shelving helps create a clean presentation while showing off every single item, small or large. You can discover items like bed linens, gardening materials, and mirrors as well as home furniture.

### Maison Trudon

As the self-proclaimed oldest candlemaker in Paris, Maison Trudon shows off its waxy creations that are nothing less than **haute gamme**, or luxury grade, in four unique locations in the city. The establishment that has ties to French royalty dating back to Louis XV, and specializes in the art of scented candles as well as perfumes. Definitely check it out if you love nice smells and fragrances.

### Søstrene Grene

Hailing from Denmark, Søstrene Grene, is the home goods store where you can find almost anything for your home, or anything in arts and crafts for a great bargain. Although I've never figured out how to pronounce the name, it doesn't matter because you can find any knick knacks to complete your Parisian apartment like baskets of all shaped and sizes, candles in any color of the rainbow, and framed artwork for your blank walls. Even if you're not living in Paris, pop into the shop where you can find items to help with any DIY project or tokens that could help you along your travels like a pretty journal or cute stationary for sending letters back home.

### HEMA

Another store, with a Swedish twist, claiming influence in France is HEMA. If you're familiar with Target in the States, I would say it's like a mini-Target with all sorts of fun and inexpensive home items, stationary, kids toys and kitchen supplies. Even though I still go here, I loved going to HEMA **especially** when I was a poor freelancer because you get almost anything you could need for your home or kitchen for very reasonable prices. It has been my go-to when I need party supplies to throw a spontaneous celebration or birthday party— they have quite the choice of party favors.

## Rougier & Plé

If you're looking for paints, specialized paper, or craft goods items, you'll be happy to stumble upon this arts & crafts store that houses hundreds of items for the creative arts. It's a great shop for anything like ribbons, scrapbooking supplies, paint and paint brushes.

## Magasin Sennelier

You can't step into Sennelier without gaining inspiration. You don't even need to be an artist to find yourself swooped into the artist's mindset while here. Sennelier specializes in art supplies such as canvases, paint brushes and paints. This colorful and rustic store will bring out the artistry in anybody who steps inside, making you wonder about the artists of antiquity that used to wander the aisles. Check out their two locations on the left bank when you're in an artistic mood.

# Favorite Food & Beverage Stores and What You Can Get at Them

Unlike supermarkets like Target and Walmart, which sell almost anything under the sun, grocery stores in France usually only sell food. This is one of the main differences between grocery stores or supermarkets between France and America. Secondly, locals, no matter if you're in Paris or the rest of France, love and covet the idea of getting their specialty items from the specialty stores that sell them and not all at once at the main supermarket.

For example, if I was doing the shopping for a typical dinner, as a Parisian, I would go to a main grocery store like Monoprix for some items like rice or pasta, sauces, ingredients for the sides, snack-like items for the **apéritif**, and maybe even wine. Then, if I wanted to go all out and make it a three course or even five course meal— **apéritif** (drink and light pre-dinner snack to get the appetite going), **l'entrée** (starter), plat (meat or fish main), **fromage** (cheese plate), then **le dessert** (dessert) — I would stop into **la boucherie** (butcher) to pick out my meat first because that will determine the wine, then to a **caviste** for a few bottles of red wine recommended by the **sommelier** (wine expert). Next, I would go to **la fromagerie** for a few of their classic choice cheeses based on my meat and wine picks, and finally to **la boulangerie** for my **baguettes** and maybe **une tarte** (a tart) for dessert.

I mention all of this to emphasize my point that the French are experts in creating specialty stores that specialize in one particular product or good instead of ten or thousands. The French would rather have the best cheese from the cheese monger than to purchase it from the grocery store, even if that means going out of their way to do so.

In France, and in Paris in particular, you can find specialty shops for anything from doorknobs to seafood canned goods. This list is not at all exhaustive but will give you a taste of some unique items you can get in France that make shopping all the more fun and quirky when visiting.

## Monoprix | Carrefour | Franprix

People usually shop at one of these three French grocery chains depending on what's closest to their home. There are, of course, others, but these are the three main ones.

The best way to describe Monoprix is that it's like a French Target. Besides the usual grocery items you can get here, Monoprix carries mid-range, but nice apparel, as well as household furnishings. Every French home I've ever been in has some goods from here spread throughout the home— anything from tableware to decorations.

Carrefour and Franprix are two other very common household names. Carrefour's prices, I would argue, are more competitive than Franprix's, although Franprix tends to have more upscale products most of the time. You can find anything you need in terms of produce at these three supermarkets, too.

## La Vie Claire | Bio c' Bon | Biocoop | Naturalia

These four **magasins bio**, or organic produce shops, sell food staples, beauty, and cleaning products that are natural, organic, and safe for your body as well as the environment. You can find these four shops throughout Paris and France for all your consumables if you shop organic.

Nicolas (pronounced Ni-co-la), recognizable from its dark burgundy and bright yellow logo, is a famous wine retailer who champions the **art de vivre** of purchasing and drinking wine. Besides the abundant selection of wine, Nicolas sells champagne, spirits, and liqueurs. Their friendly service welcomes you to ask questions and take away the best knowledge from their trained **sommeliers** when choosing wines for food pairing or special occasions.

Of course, there are plenty of small and independent **cavists** or **cave à vins** who specialize in wine from a certain country or region in France that are also worth stopping into to purchase your bottles.

---

### TIP:

There is a little-known secret among the French and expats living in France that you can get a great bottle of wine for under 20 €. In other words, don't be fooled, you don't need to spend 50 € for a tasty bottle of wine, when a 10 € bottle will do the trick. So, the next time you walk into a **cavist**, or wine shop, tell them your budget and they are sure to have something nice for whatever budget you have in mind.

---

Also, be sure to check out the All Things Wine chapter for more about French wine.

## Conserverie la Belle-Iloise

A rare gem among all the French stores is Conserverie La Belle-Iloise, which specializes in canned produce from the sea. If you love sardines, tuna, or the like, you are in for a treat at la Belle-Iloise. They produce and distribute all kinds of seafood conserves that you can not only enjoy for a meal, but also entertain with. Their wide selection of canned goodies compliment any cocktail hour you're hosting. These little canned gems make unique gifts for someone who loves seafood.

# French Beauty Stores

Whether you love to spoil yourself with fancy beauty products or like to keep it **au naturale**, you're gonna want to know of a handful of the most popular beauty boutiques out there. In a culture that is all about embracing the natural beauty, and enhancing those features instead of covering them up, the French still adore their share of make-up, creams, lotions, toners, serums, and fragrances. Don't miss out on these stores if you happen to be on the lookout for all things beauty.

### Officine Universelle Buly

Since 1803, Officine Universelle Buly has been making the world smell better with their sumptuous perfumes, oils, and diffusers. Just a stop in one of their three luxe Paris apothecary shops is a sensory experience that's worthy of a botanical garden in your nose and heart-shaped eyes. Their stunning packaging is part of the appeal, too. Their products make great gifts or original souvenirs from France.

### Mademoiselle Bio

A trendy cosmetic store selling natural and organic, Mademoiselle Bio, promotes a positive beauty image and health and wellness. **Bio**, which is short for **biologique**, translates as organic and is exactly what they carry— only organic and natural products. They have over a dozen boutiques and beauty spas in Paris where they offer more than just their knowledge on the products—they also provide facials, massages, and epilation in house.

## CityPharma Pharmacy

You can find the most popular pharmacy in Paris on the corner of Rue du Four and Rue Bonaparte. This tri-level pharmacy is not only a place you can purchase medicine for whatever ails you, but also a plethora of beauty products ranging from shampoos to facial creams to organic make up. I recommend stopping in if you're looking for advice on a specific brand or beauty product because they have over 30 dermo-specialists waiting patiently to answer any questions– not to mention they have the best prices in town!

## Marionnaud

Marionnaud is your one-stop-shop for make-up, perfume, and beauty treatments à la française. The "Sephora of France", Marionnaud is not only a boutique, but a beauty institute offering spa-style care for face, body, and hair. The shop features a large selection of local as well as international perfumes and make-up brands.

## L'Occitane en Provence

L'Occitane is another household name among the French and is a retailer of body, face, and hair products that feature fragrances and traditions of Provence, a region in the South of France. In addition to the lovely smells that will transport you to Provence, the packaging is lovely and classic. I personally love their moisturizing handcreams and body lotions. Their products are a little slice of France to take back home with you!

### Fragonard Perfumeur

Famous for being one of the oldest perfume makers in the Côte d'Azur, Fragonard gained popularity in the early 1900s and established a shop in Paris in 1936. Now, Fragonard has around 20 shops in France, and its reputation is known as one of the best perfumeries in the world, bringing classic **eau de parfums** that have stuck around since the store's inception. They even opened up the Musée du Parfum, a free museum about perfume in the 9th arrondissement of Paris.

# Antiques, Brocantes, Flea Markets and Shops

Old art and antiques are still very much a part of the French culture. Proof of this is seen in their many weekend brocantes, or second-hand flea markets, and antique shops sprinkled throughout the city. The weekend flea markets[2] go on throughout the city on varying weekends.

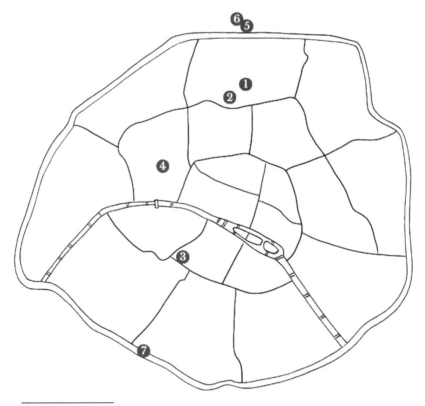

2  https://vide-greniers.org/75-Paris/semaine?_otid=navbar-period

Otherwise, stop by one of the regulars from the list below so that you can uncover hidden treasure in the trove of goodies. Even if you're traveling, a stop to one of these markets makes for fun window shopping.

Also peruse the **Best Outdoor Markets** chapter of this book for more of my top market recommendations, including Paris' oldest food market and the vibrant flower and bird market. Here are seven main markets and shops you should know of for art, antiques, and stamps.

 ## DE L'AUTRE CÔTÉ DE LA BUTTE

5 Rue Muller,
75018 Paris
01 42 62 26 06

If you're on the lookout for anything quirky, from Michèle Lamy vintage sunglasses, to puppets, bronze statues and fossils, don't look anywhere other than De l'Autre Coté de la Butte. This shop, which is a film set dresser's dream, is located in the 18th arrondissement east of Sacré Cœur and contains plenty of knick-knacks to keep you entertained for an afternoon—you may even end up taking an object or two home with you.

## 2 L'OBJET QUI PARLE
86 Rue des Martyrs,
75018 Paris

This cabinet of curiosities is as amusing as it is perplexing. You will stumble upon daily-use items like unique kitchenware pieces to rare gems and artifacts as well as **l'objet qui parle**, or the object that speaks to you. This shop knows all about that special item that speaks to you as their whole motto is helping connect those objects to their future owners.

## 3 BROCANTE HÉTÉROCLITE
111 Rue de Vaugirard,
75006 Paris

This tiny shop situated on Rue de Vaugirard is a treasure trove full of vintage finds, antiques, furniture and accessories for any and all occasions. If you're ever near Montparnasse, this little store is worth a stop to discover what old objects will find a new home **chez toi**.

## 4 MARCHÉ AUX TIMBRES | STAMP MARKET
Av. de Marigny,
75008 Paris

On Thursdays, Saturdays and Sundays, you'll find the stamp market that takes place on the cross road of Avenue Gabriel and Avenue de Marigny, 75008 Paris. This market is notably special because of the enthusiastic vendors who sell here and love to talk to visitors about the intricacies of stamps and the art form.

##  MARCHÉ AUX PUCES DE SAINT OUEN | MARCHÉ VERNAISON - ANTIQUE AND FLEA MARKET

99 Rue des Rosiers,
93400 Saint-Ouen

Welcome to the Parisian Flea Market where you will enter a vast wonderland filled with 200 merchants and over 1 million objects to discover! It's the largest antiques and second-hand marketplace in the world, conveniently located just outside Paris city limits in Saint-Ouen. It's under a 10-minute walk from metro stop Porte de Clignancourt to reach the market. You can spend a whole day here as a **flâneur** (wanderer), shopper, or antique buyer. You can even enjoy a meal and drinks in one of their many bars and restaurants nestled in the market. You'll love walking through the Marché Vernaison if you love exploring and mingling with the locals.

## 6 MARCHÉ PAUL BERT SERPETTE

110 Rue des Rosiers,
93400 Saint-Ouen
01 40 11 54 14

An extension of the Marché aux Puces de Saint Ouen is the antique, art and jewelry hub, Marché Paul Bert Serpette. Be dazzled and inspired by the sophisticated articles you're sure to discover here like a new tableau for your dining room or a vintage ring.

## 7 PARIS PUCES DE VANVES

Av. Marc Sangnier,
'75014 Paris

Get a taste of local life by strolling and perusing the sidewalks of the Vanves Flea Market. Here, you'll find cheap second-hand items for sale where it feels like you've walked into a city-wide yard sale. This down-to-earth market takes place every weekend, rain or shine, for the locals, by the locals.

For an extensive list of various markets in Paris and in its surrounding area, check out Parisinfo.com.

# Best Flower Shops

Flowers may not be the first thing that springs to mind when you think of Paris, but they are intrinsically present in France's history, culture, and geography. The most famous has to be France's national flower, the **fleur de lys**. You have probably noticed this stylized lily on flags, shields and logos. A symbol of royalty, the **fleur de lys** is said to be the king of flowers, with the rose as its queen.

France's love of all things floral is present all across the country. If you get a chance to travel, make sure to check out the lavender fields of Provence, the cherry blossoms in spring across Paris, Gourdon's famous rosemary bushes, the sunflowers in the South West and the roses in Var and Finistère, to name a few! Even the mountainous areas have their native flowers. And as for Paris, there are many places to buy flowers in all their forms.

Here are some of my recommendations for the best flower shops in Paris to pick up a bouquet.

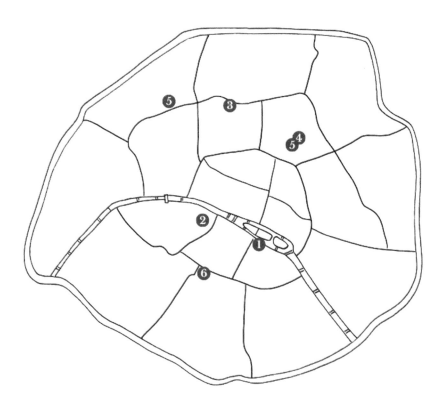

# 1 LA MAISON FLOWER

14, Rue de l'Hôtel-Colbert,
75005 Paris
01 44 50 00 20

You feel like you're stepping into a baroque fairytale when you set into this lush and vibrant shop in the 5th arr. that's overflowing with foliage, flowers, and blooms from every corner of the cozy shop.

This **artisan de luxe** won't disappoint as they have fresh blooms from the flower market regularly throughout the week. I've been working with La Maison Flower on behalf of clients of mine who love their stunning, elaborate flower arrangements and gardens. Julien and his team are the ones to call if you're looking for over-the-top, fanciful, and high-end flower arrangements. They also have a garden service to create and maintain garden terraces in the city.

To order, you can pay a visit to their shop, call in, or order online. Get in touch with them for your next special event, birthday, or wedding!

# 2 LE 69 BAC

69 Rue du Bac,
75007 Paris
01 43 35 41 97

Leading through an open passage from 69 Rue du Bac is a trail of flowers and blooming plants that lead to the most charming florist in Paris. Finding the passage is half the fun of getting here! The tiny but abundant shop is nestled in a small corridor with seasonal favorites all year round.

The women who run the shop can put together a lovely bouquet on the spot or can prepare something for a special occasion, if called in ahead of time. Besides the vibrant flower selection, they sell beautiful plants you'll love to take home with you.

 ### DEBEAULIEU

30 Rue Henry Monnier,
75009 Paris
01 45 26 78 68

You could be forgiven for thinking that Pierre Banchereau's all-white boutique shows a lack of creativity. Nothing is further from the truth! This white canvas is, in fact, the perfect backdrop for some of Paris' most innovative bouquets.

Louis Vuitton's official florist prides himself in never making the same arrangement twice. He is renowned for pushing the traditional limits of his craft and creating "unstructured" bouquets, using subtle mixes of colors and shapes, using original flowers, and even bringing back blooms that have fallen out of fashion.

His favorite influences are Dutch styles and decorative pieces from the sixties and seventies. If you need flowers for an extra special occasion, Debeaulieu is definitely worth checking out!

## 4 IKEBANART

49 Rue Lucien Sampaix,
75010 Paris
09 81 79 79 86

If you're looking for something out of the ordinary, try Ikebanart. This little boutique specializes in Japanese floral art and suspended gardens. Remember to mind your head as you walk in!

The airborne succulents, leafy greens and bonsai trees grow directly out of their little green planets that are suspended from the ceiling. Pretty cool! They also offer a range of flowers and potted plants, with some original options such as mini cacti in teacups.

## 5 GREEN FACTORY

**Location 1**

17 Rue Lucien
Sampaix, 75010 Paris
01 74 64 56 15

**Location 2**

98 Rue des Dames,
75017 Paris
01 74 64 56 15

This list wouldn't be complete if I didn't mention Green Factory. The walls of this small boutique are lined with industrial-style shelving, housing hundreds of terrariums. Coming in all shapes and sizes, these miniature ecosystems are entirely self-sufficient. Who doesn't want to have their own miniature forest in their living room?

Aside from making an awesome and original gift, either for a friend or just for yourself, terrariums are perfect for pet lovers as they remain closed. Fluffy will no longer be tempted to dig up your favorite plants!

## 6 GEORGES FRANCOIS

36-38 Rue Delambre,
75014 Paris
01 43 20 52 34

Last but not least, this teeny tiny florist right around the corner from the Montparnasse station is one of my personal faves. I never knew you could fit so many flowers into such a small space! Plus, they spill out onto the sidewalk, making the street smell heavenly as you walk by.

The owner is always ready to help you choose just the right flowers for the occasion, and they even organize private "Floral Art" classes upon request.

## SOME WEBSITES TO GET FLOWERS DELIVERED IN PARIS:

Aquarelle
www.aquarelle.com

Bergamotte
www.bergamotte.fr

Interflora
www.interflora.fr

Monceau Fleurs
www.monceaufleurs.com

Monsieur Marguerite
www.monsieurmarguerite.com

# Best Bookstores & English-Speaking Bookstores

**P**aris has a rich history of literature, books, and bookstores. In a country that still sells physical copies of periodicals, newspapers, magazines, and **bouquins**, or books, at the **presse** kiosks, you can see that the French highly value reading and often prefer to read hard cover books over electronic copies. Pointing to this fact, France boasts 3,500 bookstores nation-wide.

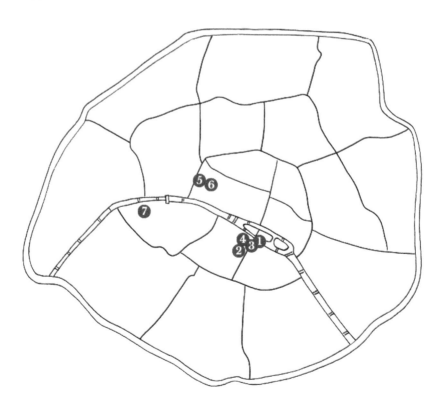

When it comes to bookstores, they have laws set in place to protect the small bookstores in order to keep the large chains like Amazon from squeezing them out of business. For example, in 1981 a French law was passed that required editors to set a unique selling price, with discounts limited to 5% percent, in order to protect small merchants. Again in 2013, France passed another law that prohibits Amazon and similar retailers from selling books at a 5% discount bundled with free shipping. These bills were put in place, not only to protect their independent booksellers from online competition, but as a tribute to the French bookstore as a national treasure.

If you're a literary fan, Paris has the iconic green **bouqunistes** stands, selling second-hand books along the Seine. It also has historical bookshops like Shakespeare & Company that are a must-visit for travelers. If you're itching to pick up a book in English, below are my recommendations for the best bookstores to find your next read!

 **SHAKESPEARE & COMPANY**

37 Rue de la Bûcherie, 7

5005 Paris

01 43 25 40 93

It's probably the most recognizable bookshop in the world to expatriates and travelers alike. Shakespeare & Company has English-language books as well as a strong community of expats who hang out amongst its nooks. Come for the books but stay for the coffee at the coffee shop next door to the bookshop. Its doors stay open until 10 PM if you're looking for a late night read. The staff is friendly and very informed on the selection of books and genres, so if you have any specific questions, don't hesitate to reach out to them.

## 2 THE RED WHEELBARROW BOOKSTORE
9 Rue de Médicis,
75006 Paris
01 42 01 81 47

Nestled on the Rue de Médicis, opposite the lovely Luxembourg Garden, you'll find the discreet Red Wheelbarrow Bookstore, a **librairie Anglophone**, or Anglophone bookstore. The bookstore, where you're likely to find contemporary as well as English and French classics in both languages, holds events with authors and poets for the literary community every month. The shop owners welcome you seven days a week where you can ask for book recommendations or just stop in for a chat about their latest arrivals. If you happen to be in when Penelope, one of the owners is in, she can chat with you and lend any recommendations.

## 3 THE ABBEY BOOKSHOP
29 Rue de la Parcheminerie,
75005 Paris
01 46 33 16 24

Canadian owner, Brian Spence, opened up this bookshop in 1989 in the Latin Quarter on what was once called the Rue des Escrivains, or "street of the scribers" (currently Rue de la Parcheminerie). The bookshop features a nice collection of new and used anglophone and francophone books. You can get lost in the charming cave-like shop, leafing through the storehouse of reads available. It's a nice spot to park yourself for an afternoon of discovery.

## ④ THE SAN FRANCISCO BOOK COMPANY

17 Rue Monsieur le Prince,
75006 Paris
01 43 29 15 70

You'll feel like you've stepped through Narnia in this arsenal of mostly used English-language books. The vast assortment of books stockpiled in the boundless shop near métro Odéon will keep you there for hours if you don't mind the time slipping by— that is, if you have nowhere to be. The friendly staff can point you in the right direction if you have a book in mind, or likewise recommend a title if you're browsing. It's a great local shop to unearth something wonderful.

## ⑤ WHSMITH

248 Rue de Rivoli,
75001 Paris
01 53 45 84 40

If you can't find an English-language book at the other local bookstores, WHSmith will probably carry it. Known as one of the oldest and largest English bookshops in Paris, the shop proudly carries 70,000 titles. You can pay a visit to the shop, purchase your books, then head over to their beautiful English tearoom on the first floor, overlooking the Tuileries Garden.

## 6 LIBRAIRIE GALIGNANI

224 Rue de Rivoli,
75001 Paris
01 42 60 76 07

The Library Galignani is a mainly French bookstore with a very large English department dedicated to a selection of British and American books. These range from but are not limited to fiction, non-fiction, children's books, as well as political, science, and university publications. Galignani is like the Barnes & Nobles of France, most notably known for its extensive assortment of reads in French and in English.

## 7 AMERICAN LIBRARY IN PARIS

10 Rue du Général Camou,
75007 Paris
01 53 59 12 60

Ok, so it's not technically a bookstore, but the American Library in Paris has a wonderful selection of English-language books to borrow— over 100,000 to be exact. If you plan to stay in Paris for an extended period, I suggest that you look into signing up for a library membership if you're a true bookworm. Not only can you go here to check out books from their physical library and e-book collection, but it's also a sweet spot to study, print and scan documents, and plug into free wifi if your home internet is down. They offer day passes as well as short-term memberships from four months to one year starting at 9 € for students and 12 € for adults per month.

# Interview with
# **Eliza Sweeny**,
# art and drama therapist from Melbourne, Australia

Eliza

**E**liza moved to Paris for acting school in 2009 and ended up making Paris her home, building a career, and starting a family.

Eliza was an actress-scenographer and now works as an art and drama therapist. She is originally from Melbourne, Australia. When she was 16, Eliza did a study exchange program in Montreal, Canada which sparked her love for living in a different city and being in a different culture than her own.

She first visited Paris a few times when she was living in London, but never really fell in love with it; it was never her dream to move to Paris. But she applied for acting school there, was accepted, and moved to Paris in 2009 and has never looked back.

Eliza and I go to the same church and are connected not only through our faith, but as well as through the challenges of being an expat in Paris in our thirties.

I chatted with Eliza over a socially distanced Zoom call back in 2020. She and her family had escaped the Paris lockdown and were enjoying more space at her family home in Deauville at the time of the interview.

She explained how even though she was grateful for more time spent with her family, she was having to share shifts with her husband to care for their 1 year old daughter at home while finding the gaps to continue working remotely. All this while adapting her client work online via Zoom.

This is her adventurous journey of building a life in France over a decade ago.

## Why did you move to Paris?

I moved to Paris in 2009 and had just turned 23. I got accepted to the Jacques Lecoq acting school. It's a school that is based on the poetry of the body, mime, and clowning etc. And this is what I wanted to study because I wanted to connect to my body as a performing artist.

When I arrived, I basically left my whole life behind in Australia— my boyfriend at the time, my family. I arrived in Paris and I barely spoke any French and I knew nobody.

I planned to be in Paris for one year, but it has now been 13 years.

## What was your first impression of Paris?

This is one of the clearest memories of my life. I landed in Paris, got into a taxi and I gave the address, in Montmartre, of the apartment I was renting with some girls. And I remembered driving down the highway and arriving at the north exit of the highway, near Saint-Ouen.

And as we came over a bridge and off the highway, there I saw Sacré Coeur and I just started crying because I felt so happy to be in France and I felt like it's where I should be. I had this sensation of "I'm home", just from the taxi ride!

## What do you love about Paris?

I love the authenticity of the French. It's funny, I said I was never drawn to living in Paris, but all my high school friends remember me by how much I loved French. I think I was always somehow drawn here.

I was very drawn to the revolutionary spirit. I appreciate the French revolution and how the people really claimed back their rights. Human rights are fundamentally important to me. And I find that spirit very present in the French people today (even if that means lots of protests that can be a hassle at times).

I appreciate that as an artist you can live, and live well... I think France opens up so many opportunities for people to be independent workers and to be artists. As a student, as an artist and as a small business owner, you can really live your life to the full extent.

I also love the beauty of the city, with architecture that dates back older than my actual birth country.

## What challenges did you face with moving to Paris?

Bureaucracy!

In order to get an apartment contract, you need a bank account; in order to get a bank account, you need a phone account, and in order to get a phone account, you need to have an apartment.

I also found isolation was quite difficult; I found it hard to break into friendship circles with the French— and I still do. I now have some very close French friends though I do find the Parisian women especially very difficult to make friends with.

Another challenge was financial. I just wasn't earning much money and as an artist, it was difficult. But I think that if you're ready to live simply, (minimalist living was a necessity not an 'in-vogue' lifestyle at that point) and have simple things, then you won't suffer.

**Did you know French? If yes, where did you learn the language? If not, how did you learn?**

I knew the basics. Then I threw myself into acting classes that were only in French. Every opportunity I got, I would just speak French, avoiding the English speakers.

After 2 years, I was bilingual. The best way to learn is to try and make mistakes and not be too proud to try.

**What is a lesson you have learned from living in Paris?**

Patience.

You wait in lines, you wait on the phone, things take forever! It's not today, it's in three weeks; you have to be very patient with the French.

I've learned to be more direct and honest with my feelings. Now, I'm much more confident to say something when things don't sit right. I also think that being bilingual, you don't always have time to nuance things, so you just get to the point. I'm glad I've developed the skill of being more direct.

**What is your biggest frustration with Paris?**

Stress. Living in Paris is like living in a pressure cooker.

**What is your biggest love about Paris?**

My husband and daughter, who are French, but Paris, I would have to say architecture, art, theatre, culture and food.

**What kind of visas/resident permits did you have to be able to stay in France?**

I went from a student visa for the first two years then I converted it to a working holiday visa, which is for one year, which allowed me to work full time.

After that, I went back to Australia and I worked really hard to develop a dossier for the profession libérale titre de séjour. It's a very difficult card to get; you have to prove that you have a lot of business that's going to be generated— that you have clients already interested in working with you.

I got this visa so I could get the official auto-entrepreneur status. It took about six months to get the dossier together. So, I stayed on that until I met my now-husband and now I'm on the vie privée et familiale card and have just applied to be French myself, something I will be proud to be.

**What's your favorite thing to do in Paris?**

I love picnics on the canals or in the parks in Autumn— some good red wine, smelly cheese, fresh bread with friends.

I think that's something I love about Paris. I mean, you can do this in any city, but it just feels special in Paris.

**What would you tell someone who is like you and wants to move to Paris?**

Do it!

I really feel like you can be a family with kids going to a local school and you'll find a great community here. You can be a business person who's looking for great restaurants and you'll find that.

What's great about Paris is that there's really something for everybody.

You can open up a door to whoever you are into Paris.

**What would you tell your younger self if you could speak to that person today?**

I would have said, pray, about everything.

I would have also said, don't waste your time going on dates with so many bad French men... haha.

**Would you recommend Céline Concierge services?**

You're a trustworthy person who will work hard for the client and will deliver quality work. I already have recommended you to our clients from the school I have co-founded, Lindenwood International School.

I think your services are important because you seem to offer everything that someone could need; it's not just the flights, it's cultural, integration and administrative.

Your strength is that you can open a door into Paris for anybody; whoever they are, you have something to offer them.

**Do you have a favorite book, film, or song about Paris?**

I love the film **Le Dîner des Cons**! And for music, it's cheesy but I do love the **Amélie** soundtrack.

*Eliza still lives in Paris with her family.*

*In 2022 she opened* **Lindenwood International School**, *an international, bilingual school for children ages two to 15, focused on encouraging the child's independence and curiosity where students can experiment with ideas.*

*She is also doing her doctorate. You can find out more about her work at* **Creative Health Space** *and* **Milpera.**

# LIFESTYLE

There's no better way to understand the French lifestyle than to explore **l'art de vivre des français**, or the art of living of the French people. The art of living encompasses not only a way of living, but also a way of being and of thinking.

Short of coming here and living your day-to-day life as the French do, appreciating their artists will help you immerse yourself, even if you're an ocean away. Listening to French music, cooking French food, using French products, watching French films, and reading French books are all ways to get yourself adjusted to the culture. Who knows, you may even end up falling deeply in love with **les français**, as I did when I studied French cinema in college.

Here, I'll discuss the best ways for you to use all of these tools, and which to explore first.

# 10 Secret French Lifestyle Rules Revealed

The French are iconic for living differently than the rest of the world, and there's a certain **je ne sais quoi** about the people, their culture, and their lifestyle. Known as classy people with one of the most romantic languages, their signature lifestyle that we find so fascinating boasts the best designer brands, wines, cheeses, perfumes and architecture in the world, not to mention art and food.

As an American expat living in Paris, there have been certain habits and customs I've had to set aside in order to welcome new ones that I discovered in my adopted country. Throughout my 8+ years of living in Paris, I have observed, absorbed, and embraced certain aspects of the French lifestyle that have helped me to integrate and even thrive in France.

These lessons are coming from my real and true experience of living with the French, immersed as an expat, that no traveler can attest to. You can also adapt these 10 secret rules into your life to rock a French lifestyle anywhere.

## 1 How to say *NON*

No one else knows how to say "No" quite like the French do. They embody a culture of setting boundaries that I appreciate now, which I didn't always admire. Saying "No" is hard. I grew up in a "Yes, man" culture, where the customer is always right, not to mention the culture of YOLO (You Only Live Once) or FOMO (Fear of Missing Out) that my generation is defined by.

When I first came to Paris, this "no" attitude was such a turn off. A taxi driver turned me down for a ride because he was eating lunch. A cafe owner refused me service because he accepted cash only. I couldn't secure housing because as a freelancer I was a "risky" prospective tenant. These experiences made the French feel like the cold and arrogant clichés I wanted so hard not to believe were true.

But I slowly learned that saying no is actually a healthy part of life and helps avoid being taken advantage of. Saying no is the French way of playing it safe. I stole this secret rule of the French lifestyle and rocked it in my life, which brought me more balance. I embraced their culture of saying "no" to unnecessarily long work days or going out on most weekdays (a girl's gotta rest, too). Buying the latest clothes or iPhone are no longer a priority. I am content with my life because it isn't carried away by the whims of the "yes culture" I used to exemplify.

## 2 The Art of Discretion

The French live and breathe discretion— the complete opposite of their American counterparts who want to be seen and heard by the world. Before I was a proper French resident, I visited Paris several times and did so in the least discreet way possible, attracting attention from all directions— ostentatious flirting with boys, public intoxication, and dancing on the streets of Paris in the rain, just to name a few.

In contrast, the French have this confident shyness about their allure. It leaves you wondering what the key is to these people. Their secrecy is what is so attractive because they say enough to be present but don't overshare. Respectively, they are always the most interesting ones in the room. I've adapted the secret of discretion into my own rhythm of life, too. I've learned to shut my mouth and observe the world around me. You can learn a lot more from others when you aren't the center of attention. Even my fashion reflects the French lifestyle by dressing modestly, simple and slightly anonymous, not to give too much of myself away.

## ③ Cinema Obsession

Next to their love for books, art, and the theater is their love for films. France claims the birthplace of cinema along with pioneering in cinema production in the 50s and 60s with the film movement known as the French New Wave. The French left a global footprint on the film scene that is still felt today. French filmmakers of the time left a lasting impression on my soul, inspiring me to be a filmmaker. But it wasn't until I moved to Paris that I discovered that going to the cinema is a coveted national pastime.

Paris claims the most movie screens per inhabitant at 1 per every 6,000 residents. The French boast the cinema carte illimité or unlimited cinema card that gets you exactly that— unlimited access to movies at the theater every day. For a little over 20 € a month, you can have your very own (I recommend it if you live in France)!

Having access to films is one thing but going to the cinema is another— in an age when Netflix and downloading is so entrenched in our culture, they make it a valued experience to leave the house, buy the popcorn and sit through a blockbuster or art house film. The French taught me that cinema going is a pastime that is alive and ingrained in the French lifestyle.

## ④ The Curious Sweet Tooth

French people normally enjoy a small dessert to top off their lunch or dinner. Better yet, they have the whole dessert for **le petit déjeuner** in the form of **un croissant au beurre** or **chausson au pomme**. They love their sweet treats but do so in moderation—never three in one day.

Growing up, my mom was conservative when it came to what sweets we were exposed to as kids and rarely made dessert. So naturally, I didn't develop a sweet tooth as a kid. However, when I moved to Paris and had patisseries and boulangeries available to satisfy that buried sweet tooth, oh, boy did I learn that I indeed have a huge sweet tooth. I jokingly once told my mom that I moved to Paris just for the croissants and she scoffed saying that it wasn't a reason you move to another county. I laughed and said you do when the croissants are this delicious!

## 5 How to Look Chic with Little Effort (and red lipstick)

"Less is more" is a way of thinking that the French apply to their culture and style. Parisians aren't out to prove anything. But with this very attitude, they end up proving they are chic with little to no effort at all. Contrary to their American friends who love makeup, the French tend to focus on the **au natural** and would rather be caught dead with no makeup than with too much of it.

Nothing is sexier than a bold red lipstick and a downplayed casual look. My favorite classic beauty combo (that's not so secret) I pull together to rock my French-ness is a striped tee, slim cut denim jeans, my hair in a bun or shaken out (depends on my mood), and black flats finished off with a touch of mascara and **rouge à levre**. This look is perfect for Paris— embodying simple, sleek, sass with a touch of class.

## 6 Patience is key

The French indirectly taught me this rule. If you weren't aware, most things are slow here. France is notorious for bureaucracy and systems that don't function as smoothly as in other parts of the world. Although the secret is patience, the French are still learning this one, too. Patience is a prerequisite for living, working and making your life in France.

From the wait time to get your coffee sitting at a terrace, to learning the French language, to waiting for your papers to push through the French bureaucracy, patience is needed— if not demanded— for one to live in this beautiful country.

I've spent countless hours at the Prefecture over the nearly 8 years I've been in France, waiting to get visas and work permits. If you move to France, you may be blessed to find the perfect apartment, loving partner, and ideal job. But chances are, it will take time, and trial and error to get there. One thing that living in France proves is that it's the art of patience and perseverance to build your life and livelihood here.

From my personal experience, the most thriving French people (and expats) are the most patient ones, too. Part of the French experience is letting life unfold and embracing it instead of trying to control or plan out every detail.

## 7 Les Petits Plaisirs

The French fancy their **petits plaisirs**—from a two-hour lunch, a 5-minute cigarette break, the bottle of wine shared between lovers, to sitting on the terrace of a cafe and catching up with a friend for hours on end. From **les soldes** (twice yearly commercial sales), to their **jours fériés** (bank holidays) — the list of everyday pleasures is endless! They simply love to enjoy all aspects of life. It's those little moments that count for them and make life worth living.

Since moving across the pond, I've welcomed— no, I've taken advantage of— the French lifestyle of indulging in the little things. From the enjoyment of sitting at a cafe reading a book mid-day, to enjoying a glass of wine at dinner, to snacking on the hot out-of-the-oven baguette, the French mindset is naturally focused on the little things. I challenge you to take a pause in your workday and go for a walk, buy yourself flowers from the florist every week, or take a bath before bed to live a little bit more like the French do.

## 8 Moderation & minimalism

Apart from **la cigarette,** I would say most French people don't tend to overindulge in food, entertainment, or commercialism, as their American counterparts do. The French lifestyle reflects moderation and minimalism. The French tend to buy less consumer or household goods, but when they do, it's of higher quality. Many own one television set in a household and limit their TV watching time. They enjoy more food courses at restaurants, ranging from **l'apéritif** to dessert, in consequence, enjoying smaller portions of better quality food. Apply this French lifestyle rule of moderation and minimalism to your life by embracing quality over quantity.

## 9 *Les vacances*

The French adore **les vacances** like none other. A French salary employee in France has 30 potential paid days off in a year (not including bank holidays!). That's a lot of time off! But the French are still one of the most productive people in the world in terms of work productivity even though they work an average of 12 hours less during the week than Americans. How do we measure their productivity? One of the telling signs is that France is the seventh largest economy in the world.

Paid vacation time has been one of the most exciting aspects of the French lifestyle that I've adopted. It's introduced me to an aspect of self-care I didn't even know existed and is 100% necessary for the average working adult. Plus, more holiday means time for gardening, reading, visiting friends and family, and exploring the world. Ever wondered why the places you've visited seem to have a higher concentration of French travelers than other nationalities? It's because of all those vacation days the law requires them to take. Vacation time is part of their lifestyle and a vital contributor to their happiness! Even if you don't have as many paid days off, maximize on your vacation days. Take long weekends to recharge or plan smaller trips throughout the year to visit new places. This is one alternative to using all your vacation time at Christmas and New Year's.

## 10 Life is more than work

The best-revealed secret I discovered about the French lifestyle is that life is so much more than work. Yes, it certainly is important, but it's not all that life is about. The French have mastered the craft of work with play, the **mélange** of business with a little pleasure. They build their lives on the essential and special moments of the day, not making their whole lives career-centered.

I've grown to embrace my career, but not obsess over it. If the French lifestyle has left me with anything, it's that your work should run parallel to your life, not be the engine running the show. I've interacted with dozens of career-focused French people but even they know when to pause and have fun outside of their jobs. The French typify balanced lives and truly know how to embrace and cherish the little treasures of everyday life.

You too can embrace and fearlessly apply these French lifestyle rules to your life wherever you are! And don't stop there—continue your study of French lifestyle by picking up a copy of one of the books on my Recommended Reading List Before You Go To France chapter.

# Recommended French Cooking Books

Here's a list of easy-to-follow cook books as well as a couple for those cooks who want to hone their craft in French cuisine. Whether you're a beginner or master chef, dig into one or two of these books. They also make excellent gifts for your francophile friends and family!

### 🛡 How to Cook French Cuisine by Julie Soucail

From **madeleines** to **bœuf bourguignon**, here are 50 traditional French recipes with easy to understand and execute instructions that you can do at home without a hitch. I recommend this cookbook if you're starting out cooking up French cuisine.

### 🛡 Mastering the Art of French Cooking (2 Volume Set) by Julia Child

Any fans of Julia Child know what you're getting yourself into with this two volume set cookbook. Combined, these two volumes are both for the novice chef looking for a challenge as well as a seasoned chef looking to take their game to the next level.

### 🛡 Let's Eat French by François-Régis Gaudry

This in-depth guide on French cooking, its history, and over 300 recipes is your go-to French cookbook if you want to get into the technical aspect of the art form. I recommend this book if you're serious about French cuisine or are in cooking school to make it a career.

### Tasting Paris: 100 Recipes to Eat Like a Local: A Cookbook by Clotilde Duscoulier

This cookbook is both for the traveler and lover of Paris. You'll find the old classics as well as a spin on some delectable French favorites. No matter which ones you choose to cook, they'll all transport you to the terrace of your favorite Parisian restaurant.

### The French Market Cookbook: Vegetarian Recipes from My Parisian Kitchen by Clarkson Potter

Here's a vegetarian-focused cookbook that will help you appreciate fruits and vegetables in a seasonal and sustainable way. The author helps the reader to create recipes that focus on traditional French recipes while incorporating more fresh ingredients for vegetarians and health-conscious chefs alike.

### French Pastry 101: Learn the Art of Classic Baking with 60 Beginner-Friendly Recipes by Betty Hung

This cookbook is a must if you're serious about the art of French pastries. This book will help you refine and hone your skills in **crème brûlées**, **éclairs**, **madeleines**, and many more classic French desserts.

# Favorite French Products

Do you want the insider's scoop on all things French lifestyle? Well, you're going to want to start off by studying the kinds of goods and products the French love to buy! Here are my top picks of French products from food and beverage to household items you are sure to spot in the average household. You can purchase many of these in the local supermarket on your next trip to France as well as online (for the non-perishables).

 **ALIMENTATION**
(food goods you may find in any Parisian's pantry)

### Fromage Chaussée aux Moines
Soft cow cheese with a thick rind

### Fromage Caprice des Dieux
Extra soft cheese with a soft, edible rind

### Beurre demi-sel
Salted butter, popular from the Brittany region

### Carambar Candy
A chewy caramel candy

### Calissons
Soft yellow almond wafer coated in a white frosting from Aix-en-Provence

### Bergamotes
A tart and translucent hard candy with bergamot flavor from Nancy

### LU Petit Beurre
Shortbread biscuits

### Le Chocolat des Français
French chocolate brand

## Bonne Maman Confiture
A popular French jam

## Foie gras de canard
The duck liver delicacy

## Fleur de Sel
Salt that is collected from sea water and used to season and garnish food

## Mariage Frères tea
French gourmet tea company

## Dammann Frères tea
French gourmet tea company

## La Parisienne Beer
Craft beer company brewed locally near Paris

## Bret's Flavored Chips
Chip company, seasoned in popular French flavors

## Amora Mayo
Popular mayonnaise brand from Dijon

## Maille Mustard
Gourmet French mustard brand

## Grey Poupon Dijon Mustard
Mustard brand originating in Dijon, France

## Anchois de Collioure
Anchovies from the south of France

## La Belle-iloise
French conserves shop, famous for its canned food products

## Garrigue honey
Honey that comes from the south of France in a Mediterranean climate

## Cidre de Normandie
Cider that is popular and made in the Normandy region

## Ricard
Summer liquor made from anise in the south of France that is diluted with ice and water

## Red Wine & White Wine (of course)

## Baguettes fresh from any bakery

## FRENCH HOME PRODUCTS

### Le Creuset "Cocotte"
The colorful cast-iron cookware/casseroles

### Duralex Cups
Durable French glassware, popular in bars and restaurants

### Savon de Marseille
Fragrant soap made from vegetable oils

### Opinel #8 Pocket Knife
Popular, foldable pocket knife that is easy to store

### Diptyque Perfume and Candles
Luxury Parisian fragrance brand favored for its strongly scented candles

### Sophie La Girafe
Well-known children's giraffe toy

 ## FRENCH LUXURY GOODS

### Christian Louboutin Escarpins en cuir So Kate 120
Elegant black stilettos with the iconic red backing

### Hermès Bags, Scarves, and Leather Goods
Luxury designer brand popular for its handbags and vibrant orange shopping bags

### Dom Pérignon Champagne
Premium Champagne

### Veuve Clicquot Champagne
Premium Champagne

### Louis Vuitton Luggage
Iconic chocolate brown luggage with the LV motif

## FRENCH BEAUTY PRODUCTS

### Le Petit Marseillais Soap and Shampoos
Fragrant soaps sold in all the supermarkets

### Any lavender products

### Yves Saint Laurent Perfume
Recognizable scent whose bottle showcases the famous three letters YSL

### Chanel No 5
Sleek bottle and scent are from Chanel

### Chanel Nail polish
Durable and lasting nail polish

### Mixa Bébé
Skincare line known for its gentle products and scents

### Signal Toothpaste
Toothpaste line with many flavors

### Nuxe Beauty Oils & Beauty Products
Premium skincare and cosmetics line

### La Roche-Posay Sunscreens & Skin Care Products
Premium skincare and cosmetics line

### Biafine
A cream to treat burns

### Doliprane
The French answer to aspirin

### Klorane
Popular hair care line

### Yves Rocher Beauty & Cosmetics Products
Beauty and skincare line made from only vegetable ingredients

### Typology
France's natural skincare line, comparable to The Ordinary in the States

# Recommended Reading List Before You Go France

I'm guessing you're somewhat of a book worm if you've made it this far in the e-book! Either way, your love for France will probably be enough to peak your interest in this curated list of my favorite and recommended books to pick up before, during, and after your travels.

**Bonne lecture !**

**FRENCH LIFESTYLE:**

How to Be Parisian Wherever You Are: Love, Style, and Bad Habits
by Caroline de Maigret, Sophie Mas, Anne Berest, Audrey Diwan

Things Parisians Like
by Caroline de Maigret

Older, but Better, but Older
by Caroline de Maigret

How to Become a Parisian in One Hour?
by Olivier Giraud

 **HISTORICAL NON-FICTION:**

Les Parisiennes: How the Women of Paris Lived, Loved, and Died Under Nazi Occupation
by Anne Sebba

The 7 Ages of Paris
by Alistair Horne

Is Paris Burning?
by Larry Collins & Dominique Lapierre

A Bite-Sized History of France: Gastronomic Tales of Revolution, War, and Enlightenment
by Stéphane Hénaut & Jeni Mitchell

The Seine: The River that Made Paris
by Elaine Sciolino

 **HISTORICAL FICTION:**

All The Light We Cannot See
by Anthony Doerr

The Longest Day
by Cornelius Ryan

##  HUMOR/TRAVEL LITERATURE:

Paris On Air
by Oliver Gee

Stuff Parisians Like:
Discovering the Quoi in
the Je Ne Sais Quoi
by Olivier Magny

WTF?!: What the French
by Olivier Magny

The Only Street in Paris
by Elaine Sciolino

La Seduction: How the
French Play the Game of
Life
by Elaine Sciolino

One year in the Merde
by Stephen Clarke

The Bonjour Effect: The
Secret Codes of French
Conversation Revealed
by Jean-Benoît Nadeau and Julie
Barlow

The New Paris: The People,
Places & Ideas Fueling a
Movement
by Lindsey Tramuta

The New Parisienne: The
Women & Ideas Shaping
Paris
by Lindsey Tramuta

Sixty Million Frenchmen
Can't Be Wrong
by Jean-Benoît Nadeau

##  AUTOBIOGRAPHICAL/MEMOIR:

A Moveable Feast
by Ernest Hemingway

The Autobiography of
Alice B. Toklas
by Gertrude Stein

I'll Never Be French (no
Matter what I Do): Living in
a Small Village in Brittany
by Mark Greenside

##  TRAVEL GUIDE:

Don't be a Tourist in Paris        by Vanessa Gall

# French Songs for Inspiration & Music to Get You in the French Mindset

H ere's a list of popular contemporary and historical 150 French songs to get you in the French mood. If you have Spotify, you can listen, follow, and download the playlist.

## MOOD FRANÇAIS

| | |
|---|---|
| **365 Jours** | Oxmo Puccino |
| **Alexandrie Alexandra** | Claude François |
| **Alors on Danse** | Stromae |
| **Amoureux de Paname** | Renaud |
| **Amsterdam** | Jacques Brel |
| **Andalouse** | Kenji Girac |
| **Au bout de mes rêves** | Jean-Jacques Goldman |
| **Avenir** | Louane, Jean-Philippe Massicot, Tristan Salvati |
| **Bal De Bamako** | Toumani Diabaté, Sidiki Diabaté, Fatoumata Diawara, Oxmo Puccino |
| **Bang Bang** | Sheila |
| **Bella** | GIMS |
| **Belle demoiselle** | Christophe Maé |
| **beau-papa** | Vianney |

| | |
|---|---|
| **Bonnie And Clyde** | Brigitte Bardot, Serge Gainsbourg |
| **Ça va ça vient** | Vitaa, Slimane |
| **Cendrillon** | Téléphone |
| **Ces mots simples** | Vanessa Paradis |
| **Ce soir** | Kumisolo |
| **Ce Soir Je M'en Vais** | Jacqueline Taieb |
| **Ce soir je m'en vais - Dombrance remix (edit)** | Slove, Dombrance, Maud Geffray |
| **C'est si bon** | Yves Montand |
| **Cette année-là** | Claude François |
| **Chanson populaire (Ça s'en va et ça revient)** | Claude François |
| **Christine** | Christine and the Queens |
| **Comme dab** | Vitaa |
| **Comme des enfants** | Cœur De Pirate |
| **Comme d'habitude** | Claude François |
| **Comment te dire adieu** | François Hardy |
| **Comptine d'un autre été, l'après-midi** | Yann Tiersen |
| **Cyclop** | Exsonvaldes, Helena Miquel |
| **De l'or** | Vitaa, Slimane |
| **Demain, c'est loin** | Iam |
| **Dès que le vent soufflera** | Renaud |
| **Dis-Moi Encore Que Tu M'Aimes** | Gaëtan Roussel |
| **Douce France** | Charles Trenet |
| **Elle a les yeux revolver** | Marc Lavoine |

| | |
|---|---|
| **Elle me dit** | MIKA |
| **Emmenez-moi** | Charles Aznavour |
| **Equilibre** | Hocus Pocus, Oxmo Puccino |
| **Ex-fan des sixties** | Jane Birkin |
| **Femme libérée** | Cookie Dingler |
| **For Me Formidable** | Charles Aznavour |
| **Formidable** | Stromae |
| **Foule sentimentale** | Alain Souchon |
| **Hexagone** | Renaud |
| **Hier encore** | Charles Aznavour |
| **Hymne à l'amour** | Édith Piaf |
| **Il est cinq heures, Paris s'éveille** | Jacques Dutronc |
| **Il jouait du piano debout** | France Gall |
| **Il y a** | Vanessa Paradis |
| **J'ai demandé à la lune** | Indochine |
| **J'ai Deux Amours** | Madeleine Peyroux |
| **J'aime les filles** | Jacques Dutronc |
| **J'aimerais** | Charles Aznavour |
| **J'aimerais trop (feat. SAP)** | Keen'V, SAP |
| **J'attendrai - Tornerai** | Rina Ketty |
| **J'attends** | Hocus Pocus |
| **Je danse le Mia** | Iam |
| **Je l'aime à mourir** | Francis Cabrel |
| **Je m'appelle Jane** | Jane Birkin, Mickey 3d |
| **Je m'en vais** | Vianney |

| | |
|---|---|
| **J'en ai marre !** | Alizée |
| **Je suis venu te dire que je m'en vais** | Serge Gainsbourg |
| **Je t'aime moi non plus** | Serge Gainsbourg & Jane Birkin |
| **Je te promets** | Johnny Hallyday |
| **Je veux** | Zaz |
| **Joe le taxi** | Vanessa Paradis |
| **J'te l'dis quand même** | Patrick Bruel |
| **Juste quelqu'un de bien** | Enzo Enzo |
| **La ballade des gens heureux** | Gerard Lenorman |
| **Là-bas** | Jean-Jacques Goldman, Sirima |
| **La belle et le bad boy** | MC Solaar |
| **La bohème** | Charles Aznavour |
| **La foule** | Édith Piaf |
| **Laisse béton** | Renaud |
| **La Java bleue** | Fréhel |
| **La javanaise** | Serge Gainsbourg |
| **La madrague** | Brigitte Bardot |
| **La même** | GIMS, Vianney |
| **La mer** | Charles Trenet |
| **La Seine** | Vanessa Paradis, -M- |
| **La valse à mille temps** | Jacques Brel |
| **La Valse d'Amélie - Version piano** | Yann Tiersen |
| **L'aventurier** | Indochine |

| | |
|---|---|
| **La vie en rose** | Édith Piaf |
| **La vie est belle** | Indochine |
| **Le dîner** | Bénabar |
| **L'empire du côté obscur** | Iam |
| **Le reste** | Clara Luciani |
| **Les Champs-Elysées** | Joe Dassin |
| **Les Copains D'abord** | George Brassens |
| **Les filles d'aujourd'hui** | Joyce Jonathan, Vianney |
| **Les rues de Paris** | Nicolas Godin |
| **Le Sud** | Nino Ferrer |
| **Le temps de l'amour** | François Hardy |
| **Le temps des fleurs** | Dalida |
| **Le temps est bon** | Isabelle Pierre |
| **Le tourbillon** | George Delerue |
| **Le tourbillon de la vie** | Vanessa Paradis, Jenne Moreau |
| **Le vent nous portera** | Noir Désir |
| **L'Île au lendemain (feat. Clara Luciani)** | Julien Doré, Clara Luciani |
| **Lunatique** | Stereo Total |
| **Maintenant ou jamais** | Catastrophe |
| **Manhattan-Kaboul** | Renaud, Axelle Red |
| **Ma philosophie** | Amel Bent |
| **Message personnel** | François Hardy |
| **Milord** | Édith Piaf |
| **Mistral gagnant** | Cœur De Pirate |
| **Mistral gagnant** | Renaud |

| | |
|---|---|
| **Moi je joue** | Brigitte Bardot |
| **Moi... Lolita** | Alizée |
| **Mon amie la rose** | François Hardy |
| **Mon homme** | Mistinguett |
| **Nathalie** | Gilbert Bécaud |
| **Ne me quitte pas** | Jacques Brel |
| **Nés sous la même étoile** | Iam |
| **Non, je ne regrette rien** | Édith Piaf |
| **Nuit de folie** | Début De Soirée |
| **Padam padam** | Édith Piaf |
| **Papaoutai** | Stromae |
| **Paradis Perdus** | Christine and the Queens |
| **Paris sera toujours Paris** | Zaz |
| **Parlez-moi d'amour** | Lucienne Boyer |
| **Paroles paroles** | Dalida, Alain Delon |
| **Poupée de cire poupée de son** | France Gall |
| **Pour que tu m'aimes encore** | Céline Dion |
| **Pour un infidèle** | Cœur De Pirate, Julien Doré |
| **Printemps Éternel** | Flo Delavega |
| **Quelqu'un m'a dit** | Carla Bruni |
| **Quitte A T'Aimer** | Hocus Pocus, Cesária Evora, Magik Malik |
| **Résiste** | France Gall |
| **Sacré Charlemagne** | France Gall |
| **Saint Claude** | Christine and the Queens |

| | |
|---|---|
| **Solaar pleure** | MC Solaar |
| **Sous le ciel de Paris** | Édith Piaf |
| **Sous le ciel de Paris** | Yves Montand |
| **Sympathique** | Pink Martini |
| **Tant besoin de toi** | Marc Antoine |
| **Tiago** | Kenji Girac |
| **Toi et moi** | Guillaume Grand |
| **Toucher l'horizon** | Oxmo Puccino |
| **Tous les cris les S.O.S** | Daniel Balavoine |
| **Tous les garçons et les filles** | François Hardy |
| **Tous les mêmes** | Stromae |
| **Tout le bonheur du monde** | Sinsémilia |
| **Trois nuit par semaine** | Indochine |
| **Tu me manques (pourtant tu es là)** | Gaëtan Roussel, Vanessa Paradis |
| **Vesoul** | Jacques Brel |
| **Zou bisou bisou** | Gillian Hills |
| **Une belle histoire** | Michel Fugain & Le Big Bazar |

# Recommended Films to Watch Before You Go to France

This list is not at all exhaustive, but I want to suggest some films and TV series to watch that are either set in France, about France and its citizens, or French produced that will inspire you to travel to **l'Hexagone**.

## COMEDY

**Zazie Dans le Metro** | Zazie in the metro (1960) Louis Malle

**Paris When It Sizzles** (1964) Richard Quine

**How to Steal a Million** (1966) William Wyler

**Céline et Julie vont en bateau : Phantom Ladies Over Paris** | Céline and Julie Go Boating (1974) Jacques Rivette

**La Vie est un Long Fleuve Tranquille** | Life is a Long Quite River (1988) Étienne Chatiliez

**Le Fabuleux Destin d'Amélie Poulain** | Amélie (2001) Jean-Pierre Jeunet

**Paris Je T'aime | Paris, I love you** (2006) Various directors,
compilation of shorts

**2 Days in Paris** (2007) Julie Delpy

**L'Arnacœur** | Heartbreaker (2010) Pascal Chaumeil

**Midnight in Paris** (2011) Woody Allen

**Je Ne Suis Pas un Homme Facile** | I Am Not an Easy Man (2018) Éléonore Pourriat

## MUSICAL

**An American in Paris** (1951) Vincente Minnelli
**Funny Face** (1957) Stanley Donen
**Gigi** (1958) Vincente Minnelli
**Les Demoiselles de Rochefort** | The Young Girls of Rochefort (1967) Jacques Demy
**Moulin Rouge!** (2001) Baz Luhrmann
**The Phantom of the Opera** (2004) Joel Schumacher
**Les Misérables** (2012) Tom Hooper

## ANIMATED / CHILDREN'S FILMS

**The Hunchback of Notre Dame** (1996) Gary Trousdale, Kirk Wise
**Les Triplettes de Belleville** |The Triplets of Belleville (2003) Sylvain Chomet
**Ratatouille** (2007) Brad Bird, Jan Pinkava
**Hugo** (2011) Martin Scorsese

## DRAMA

**Les Quatre Cents Coups** | The 400 Blow (1959) François Truffaut
**À Bout de Souffle**| Breathless (1960) Jean-Luc Godard
**Jules et Jim** | Jules and Jim (1962) François Truffaut
**La Piscine | The Swimming Pool** (1969) Jacque Deray
**Last Tango in Paris** (1972) Bernardo Bertolucci
**Au Revoir les Enfants** | Goodbye, Children (1988) Louis Malle
**Le Grand Bleu** | The Big Blue (1988) Luc Besson
**The Accidental Tourist** (1988) Lawrence Kasdan

**Trois Couleurs (trilogie) : Bleu, Blanc, Rouge** | Three Colors Trilogy: Blue, White, Red (1993-1994) Krzysztof Kieslowski

**La Haine** (1995) Mathieu Kassovitz

**La Fille sur le Pont** | The Girl on the Bridge (1999) Patrice Leconte

**The Dreamers** (2003) Bernardo Bertolucci

**Before Sunset** (2004) Richard Linklater

**Paris** (2008) Cédric Klapisch

**Mignonnes** | Cuties (2020) Maïmouna Doucouré

## ACTION / THRILLER

**Charade** (1963) Stanley Donen

**La Femme Nikita** | Nikita (1990) Luc Besson

**The Da Vinci Code** (2006) Ron Howard

**From Paris with Love** (2010) Pierre Morel

## ART HOUSE

**Une Femme est une Femme** | A Woman is a Woman (1961)
Jean-Luc Godard

**Contempt** | Le Mépris (1963) Jean-Luc Godard

**Play Time** (1967) Jacque Tati

**Belle du Jour** (1968) Luis Buñuel

**Irréversible** (2002) Gaspar Noé

## BIOGRAPHICAL / HISTORICAL

**Marie Antoinette** (2006) Sofia Coppola

**La Môme** | La Vie en Rose (2007) Olivier Dahan

**Julie & Julia** (2009) Nora Ephron

**Yves Saint Laurent** (2014) Jalil Lespert

**J'Accuse...!** | An Officer and a Spy (2019) Roman Polanski

## SHORTS

**Un Chien Andalou** | An Andalusian Dog (1929) Luis Buñuel

**Le Ballon Rouge** | The Red Ballon (1956) Albert Lamorisse

**Hotel Chevalier** | Hôtel Chevalier (2007) Wes Anderson

## TV SERIES

**Dix Pour Cent** | Call My Agent! (2015-2020) Fanny Herrero

**Marseille** (2016-2018) Dan Franck

**Alice à Paris** | Alice in Paris (2016-) Alysse Hallali, Thibaud Martin

**Plan Cœur** | The Hookup Plan (2018-) Chris Lang, Noémie Saglio

**Family Business** (2019-) Igor Gotesman

**Emily in Paris** (2020-) Darren Star

**Lupin** | (2021-) George Kay

**L'Agence : L'immobilier de luxe en famille | The Agency** | The Parisian Agency: Exclusive Properties (2021-)

# Instagram Accounts to Follow For Your Daily Dose of Paris

If you're anything like me and are obsessed with looking at pretty pics of Paris, then sit tight for your list of must-follow Instagram accounts to get your daily dose of French inspiration. You can learn a lot from some of these accounts as they offer insider secrets and local recommendations on the city; others are just fun to look at and peruse through while you plan your next trip to Paris.

**Profites bien !**

## THEWAYSBEYOND. PARIS

@thewaysbeyond

They are the creators of unique cultural learning expeditions in Paris and beyond. Their Instagram is a wealth of places to visit.

## PARIS FOR DREAMERS

@parisfordreamers

A great lover of Paris and author of multiple books on the city of light, Katrina has some great advice on how to get the most out of your trip.

## SPEAK FRENCH FOR REAL

@speakfrenchforreal

Célia is a French teacher at the Sorbonne and she is here to help you learn to speak French with ease, grace, and joy.

## THIS FRENCH LIFE

@thisfrench.life

Shannon's travel blog tells you all about her life here in France and gives you some interesting facts along the way.

## ART & ABANDON

@artandabandon

If interior design is your thing, you'll love this blog filled with space design photography.

## RUE RODIER

@ruerodier

Follow the glamorous adventures of Marissa, a Brit living in Paris and experiencing all that is chic!

## ALEXANDER STUDIOS PARIS

@alexanderstudiosparis

If you're looking to buy in Paris or France, you're gonna want to follow real estate agent, Alexander Martin, as he shows you the ins and outs of Paris real estate.

## KANAKOKUNO

@kanakokuno

Enjoy the whimsical drawings from the illustrator that you may recognize from the My Little Paris blog.

## MY LITTLE PARIS

@mylittleparis

A bilingual blog that will help you pick up more French whilst also seeing Paris' hottest new spots.

## MESSY NESSY CHIC

@messynessychic

This blogger is the queen of candid, Parisian videos and also the author of the **DON'T BE A TOURIST** books.

## SÉZANE

@sezane

A clothing brand that was made in Paris and embodies all that is French style. Follow for Parisian fashion ideas!

## ROUJE PARIS

@rouje

Another Parisian fashion brand showcasing the looks of the Filles en Rouje (girls in Rouje). So many cute options to choose from!

## SOI PARIS

@soiparis

With boutiques in Paris and St Tropez, this sustainable fashion brand was founded by two French sisters with excellent taste in clothes.

## THE PARISIENNE

@theparisienne

Follow the creator of the Parisienne blog and discover all the best things to do and see in Paris.

## PORTRAITS OF PARIS

@portraitsofparis

Beautiful people in a beautiful city! This Paris Photographer & Videographer showcases her wedding and portrait photos.

## ALEYNA MOELLER

@aleynamoeller

Aleyna's the illustrator of this e-book and she shows off cute snapshots of the life of an illustrator, designer, and traveler living in Paris.

## PARISIAN POSTCARDS

@parisianpostcards

Join Lina, new mom, designer, and talented illustrator on her Parisian adventures. Check out her latest designs, including shoes and purses, while she fabulously goes around the city.

## THE EARFUL TOWER
@theearfultower

Here's an award-winning podcast about Paris with interviews, travel tips and secrets galore from Oliver Gee! Oliver lives in Paris with his wife Lina from @parisianpostcards (above). They are two expats in the city collaborating on children's books while they take in Paris as a family!

## PANAME PODCAST
@panamepodcast

If you're a fan of the everyday extraordinary, you'll love this blog of the overlooked history of Paris.

## PARIS DINE
@paris.dine

This is a food photography blog featuring the best brunch, coffee, fine dining, and nightlife Paris has to offer.

## LIGNE NOIRE
@lignenoire.art

He's a Paris-based artist named Matthieu who draws exceptionally detailed line drawings of our beloved city.

## LYDIE PICTUREZZ
@lydie_picturezz

Lydie literally captures the best Paris photos I have ever seen. Perfection!

### DOORWAYS OF PARIS

@doorwaysofparis

I'm not sure how many doorways there are in Paris, but here are some of the most interesting.

### FRANK ADRIAN BARRON

@cakeboyparis

He's an American cake maker in Paris. Follow Frank for a sneak peek into his life in the capital, as well as to see his mouth-watering creations!

### JOANNA LEMANSKA

@misscoolpics

Joanna takes lovely photos of Parisian life. Follow her to be transported to the city.

### VUTHÉARA KHAM

@vutheara

VuThéara is yet another photographer capturing that Paris magic through the lens of his camera.

### ANNA LEBEDEVA

@paris.with.me

You'll want to follow Anna, blogger and content creator, for day-in-the-life snapshots of a Russian girl living in Paris and discovering its treasures.

And last but not least, don't forget about lil old me—

### CÉLINE CONCIERGE

@celine.concierge

your expat turned Paris expert for images of the French capital, usually accompanied by tips and recommended things to do and see!

# *LES PETITES CHOSES*
## (THE LITTLE THINGS)

In this section, you'll find some more practical travel tips and ins and outs you should brush up on before visiting the land of wine.

Additionally, you'll find useful travel resources including the Travel Planning Timeline, Travel Budget Template, and All Things Parisian Bucket List for your enjoyment.

# Safety and Emergency Numbers

**DIAL 112**    for all emergencies in Europe (the equivalent of 911 in the US)

**DIAL 114**    emergency number for deaf and hard of hearing

**DIAL 15**    in an emergency, it calls first aid responders or what is known in French as the SAMU

**DIAL 17**    Police / Gendarmerie (military police)

**DIAL 18**    Fire Department

# Non-Emergency Doctors Consultation

If you're visiting Paris and need to get to medical care for emergency or non-emergency assistance, you have several options.

**DOCTOLIB**　　　This site is widely used across France to book appointments with generalists and specialists. I recommend it if you have a carte vitale (French Medical Card) and can be reimbursed through social security.

**LEMEDECIN.FR**　　　Use this site for virtual doctors' consultations; you'll be able to see the consulting doctor via a video call. I recommend it for non-emergencies and when you can easily describe your symptoms.

**SOS MÉDECIN**　　　A certified doctor can come to your home to provide care and treat any issues without you leaving your home. If your medical emergency constitutes going to the hospital, the doctor will say so.

If for some reason you cannot get yourself out of your house and you need a doctor, I recommend you call SOS Médecin. An in-person consultation costs from 25 € (during regular business hours) to 76,50 € (after hours, on weekends, or holidays). These rates include the consultation solely and other medical costs and treatment are charged separately. In general, the cost isn't outrageous for a house call— especially if you're used to high-priced medical care in your home country.

# Hospitals In Paris

I f you can get yourself out of the house, in a cab, and to one of these hospitals, I recommend these:

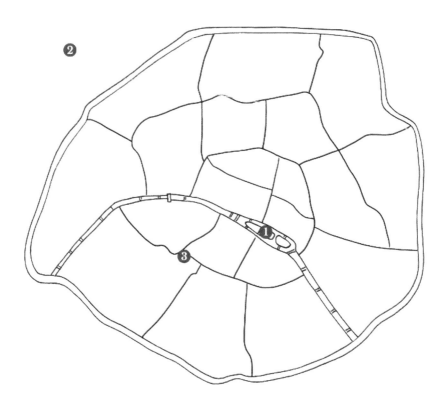

### 1 HÔTEL-DIEU HOSPITAL
1 Parvis Notre-Dame - Pl. Jean-Paul II, 75004 Paris
01 42 34 82 34

This hospital has a 24/7 ER and is centrally located on l'Île de la Cité, the bigger of the two islands on the Seine.

### 2 THE AMERICAN HOSPITAL OF PARIS
63 Bd Victor Hugo, 92200 Neuilly-sur-Seine
01 46 41 25 25

Located on the northwest side of Paris in Neuilly sur Seine (92), The American Hospital has a reputation for taking in American expats and travelers. They have services in several languages besides French/English and provide care 24/7. Additionally, they have a 24/7 medical surgical unity.

### 3 HÔPITAL NECKER-ENFANTS MALADES
149 Rue de Sèvres, 75015 Paris
01 44 49 40 00

This is a children's hospital located on the left bank, not far from the Montparnasse tower. Their emergency pediatric unit welcomes children 24/7.

Here's a list of English-Speaking hospitals[1] and healthcare professionals recommended by the US Embassy and an extensive list of hospitals in Paris[2] and its surrounding area.

---

[1] https://fr.usembassy.gov/english-speaking-medical-professionals-and-hospitals-in-paris/
[2] www.aphp.fr

# Useful Apps to Download
# When in France

Here is a list of recommended transport and travel apps that you may find useful when traveling to Paris and throughout Europe.

### BONJOUR RATP APP
### (PARIS METRO APP)
▶ **Available in Paris**

Download this app for accurate metro, intercity, and commuter rail systems (RER and Transilien), tramway, bus, night bus maps, itineraries, timetables, and updates.

### CITY MAPPER
▶ **Available in Paris and certain cities**

I have friends who swear by this app! It's an all-around good transportation app, no matter if you're traveling by bus, bike, or metro. The ease and functionality of the app with its live timing feature is definitely worth downloading. The best part is that it sends you alerts when it's time to get off at your stop— this can be super useful when you're new to a city!

## MAPS.ME
▸ **Available everywhere**

My editor Claire recommended this app to me and prefers it over Google Maps. After testing it out myself, I found that it was very user-friendly. It allows you to pin your favorite spots while making searches for anything from restaurants to places of entertainment easy and streamlined. It has downloadable offline maps with almost everything on them, including the ability to color-code pins to see places you want to visit, places you've been, and any category you want!

## OUI.SNCF APP
▸ **Available in France / Europe**

From this useful app, you can look up, book, and purchase regional, national, and Europe-wide train and bus tickets. If you have already-purchased tickets, the app is useful to view your itinerary as well as to display ticket and billing information for quick and easy, paperless access.

### OUIGO
▸ **Available in France / Europe**

Use this in parallel with the SNCF app to find economy, budget, and student fares. You can book and purchase cheap travel tickets, but be aware of the occasional inconveniences like departure/arrival stations that may be out of the city center due to the economy fares.

### GOOGLE MAPS OFFLINE
▸ **Available everywhere**

This app has the potential to work solely through GPS, no wifi required.

You can also download a specific city by opening **Google Maps**

▸ Type in "Paris" in the search
▸ In the white tab, near the bottom of the screen, scroll left through the buttons until you see the "Download" button
▸ Zoom out to capture a range of the city
▸ Click "Download" (downloads can only happen when connected to wifi or mobile network)

Voilà, now you can use and search Google Map and track yourself on the little blue dot without wifi access.

**FLOWBIRD**

► **Available in France and certain countries**

FlowBird is your best friend if you're traveling by car and need to find and pay for parking in Paris.

**TRAINLINE**

► **Available in Europe**

With Trainline, you can easily search for and purchase train and bus tickets for travel within Europe.

**EUROSTAR TRAINS**

► **Available in Europe**

Download this app if you plan to travel between the UK and mainland Europe via the Eurostar.

**WAZE**

► **Available most everywhere**

If you're taking advantage of a car or traveling by motorcycle or moped, download Waze on your phone to map out itineraries and turn-by-turn navigation suitable for your mode of transportation. It also features real-time updates from fellow drivers and travelers.

### GÉOVÉLO
▶ **Available in France**

This GPS mapper for bike routes is suitable for the biker and eco-friendly traveler. It provides much safer, updated, and more accurate routes for the cyclists than Google Maps.

### VÉLIB
▶ **Available in Paris and its suburbs**

Vélib is a for hire city bike app in Paris. You can download this app to purchase and unlock public city bikes for one time, occasional, or monthly subscription use.

For an exhaustive list of recommended travel websites and resources, visit the Travel Resources chapter.

# Simple Paris Travel Tips /
## *Les Petites Astuces*

**B**elow are some quick, on the fly, but very important travel tips every traveler must know before visiting Paris.

## *L'ARGENT*

▸ Notify your bank and think about signing up for a travel credit card when traveling abroad.

▸ Travel with a bit of petty cash in your wallet, but not too much. Most places in Paris and in France take most credit cards; some establishments don't accept AMEX.

▸ While visiting Paris, carry no more than 100 € on your person. And leave your passport and important belongings at your accommodation— pickpockets are a thing here, unfortunately!

## TIPPING AND GRATUITY

▸ In France, like in much of Europe, tipping isn't really present in the lifestyle as much as in other countries like the US. A guideline to follow is that tipping is never necessary or expected. However, if the service was exceptional and you would like to show that you appreciated it, feel free to leave a tip! You can follow the guideline of 10-20% for the service provided.

▸ Places where your tips will be appreciated are with the following: bar and wait staff, hairdressers, massage parlors, drivers and private chauffeurs, couriers and food delivers, private tour guides, musicians and artists, or any other place you feel like the service deserves a special monetary reward.

## SOLICITORS/SCAMMERS

▶ You will get solicited at least once while you're in Paris— it's just that kind of city. Whether it's the homeless, pickpockets, or scammers, you never really know— so better just to refuse, especially if they are speaking French and you don't understand. If you're too nice, they will probably take advantage of that, so it's better to be on your guard.

▶ There's a kind of scam where people will pass by on the RER trains and give you a small slip of paper saying that they are either disabled, deaf, or in need of money. Don't accept their slip of paper and don't give these people money.

▶ Never sign anything on the street. There is one type of scam that people will do where they will try to get you to sign a petition and while you're distracted, pickpocket you— so don't sign anything and don't give them the time of day!

## *LES ADRESSES*

▶ Most all Parisian buildings are accessible by a code. If you are on your way to a private address, you will usually be given an access code or interphone to buzz into the building. If for some reason you don't get this, ask your contact for the code, building number or letter, and floor (remember the ground floor in France begins with 0, then 1, 2, etc.).

▶ **Bis** and **Ter** on an address means second, alternative, or another.

- You may see 7 then 7 bis on the same street. It means that these are two separate addresses, not to be mistaken for the other. It's very important to add the word **bis** and **ter** on an address if it includes one.

## L'EAU ET L'ALIMENTATION

- Think about bringing your own refillable water bottle or canteen when out and about.

- When requesting free water at a restaurant, ask for **une carafe d'eau**, or a pitcher of (tap) water. This is **always** free unless you order **l'eau gazeuse**, or sparkling water, in which case they charge.

- And yes, it is ok to drink the tap water in France!

- Even though the water is drinkable here, in Paris, it does contain a lot of **calcaire,** or limestone, which makes it hard water that leaves water marks on surfaces. These can usually be removed and cleaned with diluted vinegar and water.

## LES TOILETTES

- Public restrooms do exist in Paris; in fact, there are supposedly around 750 free **toilettes** available for the restroom needs of locals and tourists. The city has installed outdoor public restrooms called **sanisettes**, and there are apparently 435 of them for your use.

- Besides these free public WCs (from the British— Water Closet) the city of Paris provides, there are additional public restrooms that are (sometimes) accessible for a fee.

- A last note about restrooms: always go before leaving your hotel/ accommodation and before leaving the restaurant, cafe, etc. You won't regret it when you're walking on the street or stuck on the metro. It's just better to be prepared!

## LA COMMUNICATION

- Phone plans and communication: If you need a SIM card while visiting France, you can get prepaid cards with these four major phone companies in France: Bouygues, FREE Mobile, Orange, and SFR.

# Savoir Faire: Quirks About Paris You Must Know Before Visiting

In this chapter, I want to introduce you to some quirky things that the French do differently than us English speakers, in case you didn't know. Many of these little know-hows I've picked up by immersing myself in the culture and living side-by-side the French.

You may already know about some of these things, but maybe I can teach you something you didn't know!

## Phone Numbers Are Said 2 digits At A Time

A funny quirk about the French is when communicating phone numbers, they usually say the digits by twos. For the cell number: 06 65 08 84 18, it would sound like zero-six, sixty-five, zero-eight, eighty-four, eighteen. Or in French as: **zéro-six, soixante-cinq, zéro-huit, quatre-vingt-quatre, dix-huit**.

## Last Names Are in All CAPS

Another eccentricity about the French is that they have this habit of capitalizing last names when they are written. For example, a French person's last name will be capitalized on their email signature such as:

Anne-Sophie DE LA CROIX

Jean-Pierre MARTIN

This is very prominent in French culture and it's kind of annoying sometimes, to me personally.

Another note about names is that I've discovered that French people sometimes have two or three middle names. This isn't something you would notice until you've seen a few French ID cards. Their names would be something like:

Thibault François Pierre GAILLARD

Guillaume Thomas Antoine MOREAU

## A Thing About Driving

In France, they love their roundabouts and **la priorité à droite**. Whether you're driving a car or on a bike, anywhere in France, cars have what is called **la priorité à droite**, or the right-of-way of the driver on the right-hand side. If you don't see any driving signs that direct you, then it usually means the rule of **la priorité à droite** applies, so be careful!

## 0 + 1

When visiting France and any other European country, know that the ground floor is floor zero, or **Rez-de-chaussée** (RDC) in French. They don't count the ground floor as a "floor". The floor above the ground floor is subsequently the 1st floor and so on.

French (and most of Europe) would say the 5th floor while it is the 4th floor to Americans.

## 24-Hour Time

Again, in the whole of Europe, it is common to refer to the time by a 24-hour clock, or military time as it's known in the US. We do not use AM or PM, but rather we would write 6 PM as 18h00 or 18:00. When it is said, you can either say "six in the evening" or by using the local language: "*Il est six heures du soir*" (it's six in the evening), or "**Il est dix-huit heures**" (**it's eighteen hundred**). So don't be surprised when you see your train ticket time as: 9h00 for 9 AM, and 21h00 for 9 PM.

## Celsius And Metric Systems

France, like the rest of the world, uses Celsius to measure the temperature as well as the metric system for all other distances and measurements.

For me, as an American, these systems can seem confusing at first, but when you start using them, you understand they are more direct. Let's take Celsius; zero degrees is the freezing point, and 100 degrees is the boiling point. Therefore, everything else in between is either cold or warm depending on where they fall on the spectrum.

When I am converting measurements, an easy way for me to measure a kilo is to remember that it's a little over two pounds (2.2 lbs.). And for distance, one kilometer is almost half a mile (0.6 mi).

## VAT

Most services and products in France are taxable with what is called a value-added-tax, or VAT. A price displayed on merchandise already includes the VAT or TVA, as it's known in France. For most goods and services, the standard taxable amount is 20%, while food is taxed usually at 10% or 5.5%. There also exists a 2.5% tax on certain cultural events, newspapers and periodicals. Occasionally, no VAT will be applied which is the case with stamps and postal shipping.

Contrary to what we are used to in the States where tax is added upon checkout, in France, when you see the price of goods or products, the tax or VAT is already included into the price. This was a confusing concept for my French boyfriend when he came to the US and saw that the price you paid was different than what the original price tag reflected.

## Everything Is Smaller in France

Contrary to Texas, where "everything is bigger in Texas", I can affirm that everything is smaller in France— from their cars, to the roads, to the elevators, to apartments, to the chairs. Almost every aspect of daily life is smaller than the American norm.

The large portion of McDonald's french fries is equivalent to the medium size in the US, for example.

Especially in Paris, take note that the cafes and restaurants squeeze as many seats into their restaurants as humanly possible to optimize their space. This often means that the chairs and tables are small and compact and usually packed into small spaces. Even their WCs, or toilet rooms, are tiny with barely enough room for your knees.

## Stairs and Elevators

Speaking of small spaces, don't automatically expect your hotel or accommodation to provide an elevator. Do remember that most of Europe is very old— old buildings, roads, and infrastructure. Many new buildings will normally have elevators, but this is still a new thing for France and much of Europe.

If you are so blessed to have an elevator in the building where you're staying, they are usually small, for one to two people max.

Hot Tip: I discourage sending luggage up in an elevator unaccompanied. I have heard horror stories of friends and clients doing this only to be devastated when the doors get blocked and have had to call a technician to open up the doors manually. This can be very costly, and the person responsible for blocking the elevator will have to foot the bill. So always accompany the luggage that fits in the elevator (if it fits with you inside), and take the stairs with your large luggage. Always ask for help with heavy loads.

On that note, stairs are also very prevalent in France and throughout Europe. You need them to take the metro, to enter buildings and to reach the floor where you're going and staying.

So, when you're traveling, bring comfortable walking shoes, be mentally and physically prepared to walk more than you're probably used to, and pack light!

## TIP:

I discourage sending luggage up in an elevator unaccompanied. I have heard horror stories of friends and clients doing this only to be devastated when the doors get blocked and have had to call a technician to open up the doors manually. This can be very costly, and the person responsible for blocking the elevator will have to foot the bill. So always accompany the luggage that fits in the elevator (if it fits with you inside), and take the stairs with your large luggage. Always ask for help with heavy loads.

## Summer heat

In the summer, don't expect to have readily available AC anywhere. Although throughout the years, it has become a trend for businesses, hotels and restaurants to equip their spaces with AC, or **climatisation**, this is a rare luxury that many public places still don't possess.

## Grocery Stores and Shopping

Unlike in other Westernized civilizations, France doesn't afford the pleasure of mega shopping stores like Walmart or Target, where everything is a one-stop-shop. Rather, in France and much of the rest of Europe, you will see shops and businesses that are specialized. We do have grocery stores where you can get most of your groceries, but one of the charms of France is that you can go to open-air markets and street shops that specialize in one product, good, or service. You can enjoy the experience of shopping when you purchase your chicken and meat from the butcher, or cheese from the cheesemonger, while additionally stopping by the bakery for your fresh bread and the florist for your freshly cut flowers.

Read more about shopping in the chapter Favorite French Stores and What You Can Get at Them for more details about grocery stores.

# An Abridged History of France and French Culture

You cannot look at the history and identity of France without looking first at the history of its European neighbors, mainly England, Germany and Belgium, which all play a very important role in shaping France as we know it today.

Broadly speaking, France, over the centuries started out as a land of nomadic and Celtic people living in what was known as the Gaul region.

In the 1st century B.C., Julius Caesar and the Roman Empire brought the Latin language— the ancestor of modern-day French— to the region, helping to define and shape the language and culture.

Modern-day France, came to be in 1792, with the end of the reign of kings and queens, also known as the First Republic.

The influence that France still has today is a consequence of the power it had throughout the centuries via colonization and involvement in spreading democratic principles over monarchical or authoritarian rule that gained momentum at the turn of the 19th century.

Today, France is the second largest economy in the European Union, after Germany, and exerts soft power mainly through the French language, **style de vie** (lifestyle), culture, democratic values, and tourism. Did you know that France is the most visited country in the world? And it prestigiously produces and exports some of the world's rarest luxury items, some of which include fine goods such as champagne and fois gras, as well as designer fashion, and exceptional art and jewelry.

Continue reading for more tidbits into the French culture, lifestyle, and history.

## Liberté, Égalité, Fraternité

The French **devise**, or motto, is "**liberté, égalité, fraternité**", or liberty, equality, fraternity.

The national motto originated during the French revolution but wasn't a definite part of French culture until much later. It wasn't officially adopted as the national motto until 1848 with the February Revolution where disputes were taking place over the national flag. Subsequently, the tricolor flag and tripartite motto were both adopted shortly after the publication of the French's human civil rights document, The Declaration of the Rights of Man and of the Citizen.

As you can see, the theme of civil liberties and the universal rights of man helped shape the motto which signifies a civil contract between the members of society and helps uphold the responsibilities of said society for the proper functioning as a whole.

Liberty for me signifies the human's ability to choose for oneself and express themselves without being interfered by government or their fellow citizen as long as they are within the law and not harming their neighbor.

Equality is the notion that all humans are created equally and have the same rights as their neighbors. No one is above the law, and all are seen as the same through the eyes of the government.

Fraternity in the French context implies that all citizens have a duty to care and look out for their fellow citizen. This comes into play when the French protest and "stand in solidarity" with each other for change. You can also get a sense of this ideal when disaster strikes the nation and people unify to support each other in difficult times.

# Drapeau Tricolore (Tricolor Flag)

The French tricolor flag of blue, white and red was adopted in 1853 as the official flag of France. The tricolor flag was inspired by the cockade of France, the tricolor symbol used in the French revolution. On October 24, 1790, the tricolor, **bleu, blanc, rouge** drapeau was approved by the Constitutional Assembly.

# La Marseillaise

This song became the battle cry of the French revolution, hence its adoption as the national anthem when it was sung by residents of Marseille in Paris. The lyrics manifest the invasion of foreign armies and elicit French patriotism. As a consequence, it was officially adopted on July 14, 1795 as the French national anthem.

## FRENCH LYRICS:

Allons enfants de la Patrie
Le jour de gloire est arrivé !
Contre nous de la tyrannie
L'étendard sanglant est levé
L'étendard sanglant est levé
Entendez-vous dans les campagnes
Mugir ces féroces soldats ?
Ils viennent jusque dans vos bras
Égorger nos fils, nos compagnes !

Aux armes, citoyens
Formez vos bataillons
Marchons, marchons !
Qu'un sang impur
Abreuve nos sillons !

## ENGLISH TRANSLATION:

Arise, children of the Fatherland
Our day of glory has arrived
Against us the bloody flag of tyranny
is raised; the bloody flag is raised.
Do you hear, in the countryside
The roar of those ferocious soldiers?
They're coming right into your arms
To cut the throats of your sons, your comrades!

To arms, citizens!
Form your battalions
Let's march, let's march
That their impure blood
Should water our fields.

# Who is Marianne?

Marianne is a symbol of and personification of the French Republic that came about during the time of the French Revolution. She is a beautiful, busty French version of the Statue of Liberty and has many similarities. She personifies the caretaker of French citizens and represents their motto of liberty, equality, and fraternity. When portrayed, she's usually showing a breast or two, enveloped in the tricolor French flag and draped clothing in a passionate stance, or pose, ready for battle. Her name was conceived from the two most common French women's names: Marie and Anne.

Photos and statues of Marianne can be seen throughout culture such as on coins, stamps, magazines, and paintings, and is traditionally given homage via statues placed in city halls and official courts of law.

The most prominent statue in Paris you can locate her is at Place de la République. A gigantesque statue of Marianne overlooks the plaza and is oftentimes a notable locale for citizens to protest around.

Most recently, the Paris 2024 Olympic and Paralympic logo official emblem represents Marianne. A woman's face is juxtaposed with the flame in the icon, bringing new life to the national symbol.

# A Brief History of France

As you're probably aware, France is a republic. This means that, like in the US and many other democratic countries, the people hold power along with their elected representatives. France has gone through many different government forms, but the country is currently in its fifth form of a republic, established in 1958.

Since France's early history, kings ruled the region. Clovis, who ruled from 481 to 511, was the first King of the Franks, who were the regional people in the area. Throughout the 1st to late 18th centuries, France continued as a kingdom.

It wasn't until the late 1700s that the French started to rebel and rise up due to a plethora of national issues. These included bankruptcy due to fighting too many wars, a succession of bad harvests, gross socio-economic inequalities, inefficient taxation systems, and inadequate transportation systems. All this and more led the French people to start a revolutionary movement.

And a revolution they would have! French citizens stormed the prison of Bastille on July 14, 1789; the French revolution was the dawn of France as we recognize it in modern society.

Here is a breakdown of some key dates in French history:

# French History Timeline

## SINCE AT LEAST 600 B.C. << ◇

France started out as a land of Gallic tribes who were a group of Celtic people living in what was known as the Gaul region.

## ◇ >> 58 B.C to 50 B.C

The Gauls fought against the invading Roman Republic in a series of battles called the Gallic wars. Even though both militaries were equally as strong, due to the Gallic tribes' discord amongst themselves, the Romans gained a stronghold over them and in 52 B.C they declared complete victory over the land and peoples.

## 1st CENTURY B.C TO MID 5th CENTURY << ◇

Through the Roman Empire, Julius Caesar helped bring the Latin language, the ancestor of modern-day French, to the region, helping to define and shape the language and culture. The Roman Empire controlled the Gaul region for five centuries.

## ◇ >> 1st TO LATE 18th CENTURIES

France continued as a kingdom, until around the late 1700s.complete victory over the land and peoples.

## 4th CENTURY A.D. <<  ◇

Barbaric peoples, most
notably the Franks, were
allowed to settle in the
Roman Empire in the
northeastern border of the
Gaul region in a weakening
Roman Empire.

◇ >> **481 - 511**

Clovis I was the first King
of the Franks, who were the
regional people in the area.

## 768 - 800 <<  ◇

Charlemagne, or **Charles
le grand**, became King of
the Franks in 768. He later
also ruled as the Emperor of
the Romans, who lived in
the territory of current day
central Europe from 800.
Charlemagne was considered
great because he helped
unit the majority of western
and central Europe under
his Carolingian Empire.
Since the fall of the Western
Roman Empire over 300
years before his rule, he was
the first recognized emperor
to reign over western
Europe. He was known as
the "Father of Europe" and
also for inventing formalized
education.

◇ >> **1643 until his
death in 1715**

Louis XIV, known as Louis
the Great or the Sun King
(le Roi Soleil) ruled as the
king of France from 1643 until his death in 1715. Under
Louis' reign, France was the
leading European power
with an increasing population and a professional army.

## 1756 - 1763 <<

The Seven Years' War, a global conflict between rivals Great Britain and France and their North American colonies, takes place. The Seven Years' War combined with aiding the Americans with their revolution bankrupted France. Bad harvests, inefficient taxation systems, and inadequate transportation systems precipitated France's own revolution.

## >> 1789

French citizens stormed the prison of Bastille on July 14, 1789, preceding the French Revolution.

## 1792 <<

The First Republic was formed shortly after the storming of the Bastille Prison when the people said au revoir to monarchies (for the time being). King Louis XVI and Queen Marie Antoinette were executed in 1793 by the infamous guillotine.

## >> 1795

The Marseillaise was officially adopted on July 14, 1795, as the French national anthem.

## 1804 - 1815 <<

Napoléon Bonaparte was Emperor of the French. He rose to power during the French Revolution and led the country in a series of military coalitions in Europe known as the Napoleonic Wars.

**>> 1814 - 1848**

The last three Kings of France sat on the throne: Louis XVIII, Charles X, and Louis Philippe I. But, as these rulers were not willing to adapt to the evolving French society, the perilous kingdom fell apart and ultimately ended the reign of kings in France for good.

**1848 <<**

The French motto "**Liberté, Égalité, Fraternité**" was officially adopted as the national motto in 1848 with the February Revolution where disputes were taking place over the national flag.

**>> 1848 - 1870**

Napoleon III (1848-1852) became the first President of France in 1848, establishing the French Second Republic. In 1851, Napoleon III staged a coup d'état and declared himself Emperor of France, reverting to a monarchy. He was the last monarch to reign over France.

**1848 <<**

The French Tricolor flag of blue, white, and red was adopted in 1848 as the official flag of France.

**>> 1870 - 1940**

After Napoléon III's death and the disintegration of the Second French Empire, the French Third Republic was formed.

**1875 <<**

The Constitution of Laws of 1875 were defined which established the laws of the French Third Republic.

## ◇ >> 1914 - 1918
World War I took place between European powers.

## 1939 - 1945 << ◇
France declared war on Germany in 1939, after its invasion of Poland, Luxembourg, and the Netherlands. World War II takes place across Europe.

## ◇ >> 1946 - 1958
After World War II, France rebuilt its republican government, forming the Fourth Republic and adopting the constitution of the Fourth Republic.

## 1958 TO THE PRESENT << ◇
In 1958, France held a referendum that dissolved the Fourth Republic following instability mainly from decolonization issues and the Algerian War of Independence of 1958. Shortly afterwards, the country founded the present-day Fifth Republic.

France went through a tumultuous history of evolving republics over the centuries that coincided with many major world events, such as WWI, WWII, and the Algerian War.

France was involved in World War I from 1914–1918 against Germany and its allies, during the era of the Third republic. A mere eighteen years later, France, having been occupied by Germany, went to war against the Axis Powers from 1936–1945.

After France's liberation, reconstruction began in the country and throughout Europe. Women were granted the right to vote in 1944.

In 1946, the Fourth Republic replaced the Third. And only twelve years later, after the Algerian War where Algeria won independence from France, the Fifth Republic replaced the Fourth in a referendum. This was established by Charles de Gaulle, who was appointed President of France from 1959–1969 by the Council of Ministers.

## The 5th Republic and Modern-Day France

The Fifth Republic, which still exists today, has a dual-executive system that splits power between the Prime Minister as the head of Government and the President, who represents the Head of State.

Since the beginning of the Fifth Republic, there have been eight elected Presidents with two acting Presidents.

At the time of writing this book, the current President is Emmanuel Macron, and his Prime Minister is Jean Castex.

Some of the major characterizing events in France's modern-day history have been terror attacks the country has endured due to a rise in extreme Islamist groups and religious tensions.

The first of such attacks was on January 7th, 2015 when Islamist extremists attacked the Charlie Hebdo satirical newspaper offices in Paris.

That same year, on November 13th 2015, a series of attacks took place in Paris and around its suburb, Saint-Denis. The sequence of events took place at a football stadium where suicide bombers struck outside of the Stade de France. The next assault happened that evening around Paris' 10th arrondissement with attackers and a suicide bomber targeting crowded cafes. The third group of attackers carried out a mass shooting at the Bataclan theatre during a rock concert. During this attack, 130 people were killed and over 400 injured.

Sadly, the following year (2016) in Nice, France, another strike was carried out by a man driving a truck into a crowd of onlookers during the July 14th Bastille Day fireworks. 86 people died from this assault and over 450 people were injured.

Despite the tumultuous past few years, the country has managed to rebound from these terrorist attacks and even grow stronger. I think Paris' city motto, which is displayed on the coat of arms in Latin as **Fluctuat nec mergitur**, is a true depiction of France as a whole: "It is tossed [by the waves], but does not sink".

To read a more in-depth account on French history, I recommend this title: A Brief History of France by Cecil Jenkins (in English).

And if you want to challenge your French, I recommend the illustrated: Histoire de France De La Gaule À Nos Jours by Armand Colin (in French).

## OFFICIAL LANGUAGE SPOKEN

Unlike the US, which doesn't have an official registered language, France's official language is— you guessed it— French!

# Helpful Words and Phrases to Know When Visiting France

**fn** means feminine noun

**mn** means masculine noun

**pl** means plural

**exp vb** means expressive verb

## LOCATION PHRASES:

**Une rue** fn | a street

**La banlieue** fn | the suburbs

**Escalier** mn | stairs, staircase

**Étage** mn | Floor, story

**Bâtiment** mn | building, property

**Cour** fn | courtyard

**Porte** fn | door

**Sonnette** fn | doorbell

**Interphone** mn | interphone, buzzer

## SUMMER PHRASES:

**été** mn | summer

**les vacances** fn, pl | vacation, holidays

**les soldes mn, pl** | sales

**faire les soldes** exp vb | take part in the sales/ go shopping during the sales period

*un flâneur / une flâneuse* | a person who wanders, gets lost, a person who strolls

## FOOD AND DRINK PHRASES:

**une planche** fn | meat and/or cheese board

**une bière** fn | a beer

**une pinte de bière** fn | a pint of beer

**vin** mn | wine

**un verre de vin** mn | a glass of wine

**un café** mn | an espresso/coffee

**un allongé / américano** mn | long coffee, Americano coffee

# France Timeline of Events

The French's life philosophy is synonymous with **la joie de vivre**, the joy of life and an "exultation of spirit". They love to enjoy the little things and that often involves taking time off to do so.

Yet, France is unique and odd when it comes to the way that the country takes time off. France does this 1) in the form of what are called **les jours fériers**, or bank holidays, that are often tied to celebrated (Catholic) saint's days and 2) by commemorating historical events often linked to the end of wars, and 3) events linked to art and culture. To the French's satisfaction, the month of May famously has the most bank holidays out of the year— four to be exact!

For a country that prides itself on being secular, or **Laïc** as the French say, they sure do love to take advantage of Catholic holidays to take time off. (Ok, France, maybe you're not so **Laïc** in the public sphere as you claim to be!)

## SOME FRENCH TERMS TO KNOW:

**La laïcité** | secularism, separation of church and state

**Les jours fériés** | public holidays, bank holidays

**Les vacances** | vacation, holidays

**Saints** | Saints

**Journée de** | the day of

**Faire le pont** | take a long weekend

## NOTE:

According to the French government: **Secularism guarantees freedom of conscience.** From this, derives the freedom to manifest one's beliefs or convictions within the limits of respect for public order. **Secularism implies the neutrality of the State** and imposes the equality of all before the law without distinction of religion or belief.

In short, this is a separation of church and State that is similar to what we know in the US, but I would go even further to say that outwardly expressing and talking about your religion/faith in France is looked down upon.

## NOTE:

**Faire le pont**, or taking a long weekend, is widely accepted in France. The employer may grant "a bridge", or long weekend, to employees in between one or two days off and a public holiday. In other words, if a public holiday lands on a Thursday, the employee may request the Friday off to **faire le pont** and take advantage of a long weekend. Hours lost as a result of time off can be made up, with the employees having to work the lost hours on another day.

Take a look at this fun overview by Paul Taylor[3] and his take on the jours fériés[4] in France.

Continue reading if you want to know what the main holidays are in France. The eleven that have asterisks (*) next to them are considered public (or bank) holidays. You can expect to see businesses and schools closed these days.

## JANUARY

### 1 January - Jour de l'an | New Year's Day*

We don't only celebrate the New Year on the 1st. For the entire month of January, it's acceptable to wish friends, family and colleagues "**Bonne Année !**" or "Happy New Year!"

### 6 January - *Épiphanie* | Epiphany

What better way to celebrate a New Year full of hope and light than with a delicious Kings' Cake **à la française** with une galette des rois? Every January, all month long, the French bake and eat these simple, yet delectable flaky almond pastries to celebrate **L'Epiphanie**, or the Epiphany of the three wise kings. The tradition is, the person who bites into the **fèvre**, or tiny figurine that's hidden in the cake, becomes the King or Queen of the day.

### 21 au 25 janvier 2022 - *Salon Maison & Objet* | Home and Object Exposition (spring edition)

### Mid-January (dates vary) - Men's Paris Fashion Week (spring collection)

### Mid-January - *Soldes d'hiver* | Winter Sales

Every year, following tradition, on the 2nd Wednesday of January, **les soldes d'hiver** (winter sales) begin. This is an

---

[3]  www.paultaylorcomedy.com
[4]  www.youtube.com/watch?v=0-6sMov09Tk&t=11s

opportune time to find great clearance deals at all the stores with their after-Christmas winter sales. These twice annual sales take place one in the winter (hiver) and once in the summer for **les soldes d'été** (see June below).

## FEBRUARY

### 2 February - *Chandeleur* | Candlemas

Aka the Feast of the Presentation of Jesus Christ. The history of this holiday ties in to pagan celebrations and Christian ones. Today, in France, Belgium and part of Switzerland, we traditionally celebrate this day as **crêpe** day. The **crêpe** is a hopeful symbol of the sun and a welcome of spring after cold dark days of winter.

### 14 February - *Saint Valentin* | Saint Valentine's Day

France acknowledges saints' days, and Saint Valentine isn't unlike the others. They don't take time off for this day but recognize it in the public sphere as we would in the US as a day to celebrate love in all its forms.

### Late February, early March (dates vary) - Women's Paris Fashion Week (spring collection)

### Beginning to Mid-February - *Vacances d'hiver* | School Winter Vacation

If you have kids in school, you are more than aware of **les vacances scolaires**, or school vacation. Depending on what zone in France you are living in, you are likely to take time off and/or plan a winter vacation trip for your family during this period.

### 22 - 29 February - *Salon de l'agriculture* | Paris International Agricultural Show

France's yearly international agriculture and trade show

## MARCH

**1 March 2022 - *Mardi Gras* | Mardi Gras or Fat Tuesday**
(Sometimes mid-February to early March (dates vary))

The celebration of the Carnival Season, the day before Ash Wednesday, and the last day of "fat eating" or "indulging" before the fasting period of Lent.

**27 March - *Journée nationale du fromage* | National Cheese Day**

**Month of March to end of April - Spring Cherry Blossoms**

## APRIL

**1 April - *Poisson d'avril* | April Fool's Day**

**17 April 2022 - *Pâque* | Easter** (Early to mid-April - dates vary)

**18 April 2022 - *Lundi de Pâques* | Easter Monday***

Easter is a Christian holiday, celebrating the resurrection of Jesus Christ from the dead after his crucifixion.

**Mid to late April - *Vacances de printemps* | School Spring Vacation**

**15th April - *Journée mondiale de l'art* | World Art Day**

**18th April - *Journée internationale des monuments* | International Day for Monuments and Sites**

**29th April - *Journée internationale de la danse* | International Day of Dance**

## MAY

1 May - *Fête du Travail* | Labor Day*

8 May - *Victoire 1945* | Victory Day*

13 May - *Ascension* | Ascension Day*

15 May - *La Nuit des musées* | The Night of Museums

17 May - 6 June 2021 - Roland-Garros | French Open

22 May – Jun 6, 2022 - Roland-Garros | French Open

23 May (Sunday) - Penecôte | Pentecost

24 May - Lundi de Pentecôte | Pentecost Monday* / also considered La journée de solidarité | Day of Solidarity**

 **NOTE:**

** This day of solidarity is an additional public holiday of unpaid work for employees to stand in solidarity with the elderly and handicap. The 7 hours of unpaid work that the employee works, and that is required by law, is equally matched by the employer to support a national fund for the elderly and handicapped. This day is controversial but was written into law in 2004. Some employers allow their employees to work from home or take the day off all together.

**Mid-May - Museum week** (online event)

> This is a worldwide festival for cultural institutions on social media with 12 French museums participating.

**Mid-May - Festival de Cannes | Cannes Film Festival**

> It's an annual, international film festival held in Cannes, France.

**Mid-May - La Fête de la Nature | The Festival of Nature**

**28 May - Fête des voisins | Neighbor's Day**

**Last Sunday in May (usually) - *Fête des mères* | Mother's Day**

## JUNE

**12 - 13 June - 24 heures du Mans | 24 Hours of Le Mans**

> Endurance motor speed racing

**18 June - International Picnic Day**

**19 - 25 June 2023 - Salon International de l'aéronautique et de l'espace, or the Paris Air Show**

> Occurs on odd numbered years.

**21 June - Fête de la musique | International Live Music Festival**

> On this day, we also celebrate the summer solstice with La Fête de la musique, aka International Live Music Festival.

**Mid-June** (dates vary)**- Men's Paris Fashion Week** (fall collection)

**End of June through July** (dates vary) **- Le Tour de France | Tour de France**

> Is an annual men's bicycle race primarily held in France with its finale taking place in Paris.

**Mid-June through mid-July - Soldes d'été | Summer Sales**

**Third Sunday in June -** *Fête des pères* **| Father's Day**

## JULY

**14 July - Fête nationale | National Holiday** (aka Bastille Day in English, although the French **do not** call it this)*

## AUGUST

**Les Vacances**

> From mid-July through the end of August, Parisians take time off for **les vacances**, or summer vacation. Expect to see an exodus of Parisians to the South of France, much of the city deserted and lots of shops and businesses to close for the summer break.

**15 August - Assomption de Marie | Assumption of Mary***

**27 - 29 August - Rock En Seine**

> Three-day live music festival on the Seine River

## SEPTEMBER

**First week of September - La Rentrée | Back to school/ work**

> The first week of September, everyone goes back to school and work for the fall semester.

**Late September to early October** (dates vary) - **Women's Paris Fashion Week** (fall collection)

**9 - 18 September - Paris Design Week**

**9 au 13 septembre 2021 - Salon Maison & Objet | Home**

and **Object Exposition** (fall edition)

**Second Sunday of the Month - Fête du Pâté Lorraine | Festival of Lorraine (region) Pâté**

> The famous **Pâté Lorraine** is a ground pork loaf mixed with spices, enveloped in a flaky crust that is the cause of celebration every 2nd Sunday of September, primarily in the region of Lorraine but also around Paris, too.

**Weekend of the 18 - 19 September - Journées européennes du patrimoine | European Heritage Days**

> These days commemorate European Heritage, education and culture. Museums, monuments, events and workshops are held throughout the city and are open to the public for free.

**Week of the 20th September** (dates vary) **- Journée sans voiture | World Car Free day**

> Paris and other cities in France participate in a car-free day to allow bicyclists and pedestrians to enjoy the city without cars!

## OCTOBER

**Month long - Octobre Rose | Pink October**

> Breast cancer awareness month

**2 October** (date varies) **- Nuit Blanche**

> City wide art and culture festival that goes on late through the night hence "**Nuit blanche**", meaning a sleepless night.

**3 - 12 October 2020 - La Fête de la Science | Science Festival**

**First week of October** (dates vary)**- Paris Beer Festival**

**Week of 17 October - 2 November** (dates vary depending on regions) **- Vacances de Toussaint (All Saints' Day) | Fall School Vacation**

31 October - Halloween

## NOVEMBER

1 November - Toussaint | All Saints' Day*

18 November - Armistice 1918 | Armistice Day*

18 November 2021 - Beaujolais Nouveau

Celebrated on the 3rd Thursday of the month, the **Beaujolais Nouveau** is the day that wine producers of the Beaujolais region present their bottled Beaujolais harvested that same year. It is a young wine, but the only one honored by the French as well as many Americans as its roots go deep. This is a country-wide celebration and one not to miss! If you're in France at the end of November, order a glass of the Beaujolais Nouveau next time you're at a cafe or restaurant.

17 November 2022 - Beaujolais Nouveau

Marchés de noël | Christmas Markets

All over Paris and France, open air markets start to pop up from mid-November to the 5th of January to kick off the Christmas season. In Paris, you can visit the markets at Trocadero and Boulevard Saint Germain. If you want bigger and grander markets, I recommend taking a day or weekend trip to the region of Alsace where they are known for their Christmas markets, notably Strasbourg and smaller towns like Obernai, Colmar, and Riquewihr and Ribeauville for a particularly Alsatian medieval charm.

## DECEMBER

4 - 5 December - Téléthon | Telethon

Annually, the first weekend of December, organized by the French Association against Myopathic Diseases to raise money, research and awareness for the disease. It takes place over the weekend in a televised marathon event with the help of France Télévision where artists and celebrities pledge donations for the cause.

## 6 December - Saint Nicolas | Saint Nicolas Day

This day commemorates the legendary Saint Nicolas himself and is another festive day that kicks off the Christmas season. It is usually celebrated between close friends and family as a day to get together and drink mulled wine and eat Christmas treats.

## 19 December 2020 - 4 January 2021 - Vacances de noël | Christmas Vacation

## 25 December - Jour de Noël | Christmas Day*

## 31 December - Le Réveillon or Saint Sylvestre | New Year's Eve

Saint Sylvestre is the saint's day that marks New Year's Eve. **Réveillon de la Saint-Sylvestre** or **Le réveillon (Eve)** is what the French call New Year's Eve. **Le réveillon** means the awakening and is the eve of the New Year. All of France is happy to welcome a new year like much of the world on the eve of January 1st with the proclamation "**Bonne Année !**" or "Happy New Year!".

# Conclusion and Merci

As you now understand, Paris, and France as a whole, is a complex place— one that is beautiful and rich, full of history, culture, and so many good things to eat and to see: wine, cheese, art, films, etc...

Beyond what you may already know of Paris, there is and will always be so much to discover. I hope this Ultimate Paris Survival Guide has given you a jumping off point along with much **savoir faire** to help you on your journey to experience Paris like you already live there. In addition, I hope it will help you avoiding the mistakes I've made, as well as others before you. Dive into the magnificent French capital without the stress or fear of traveling to a new place, and be all the more equipped to dive in with fervour and an open heart!

It has been the biggest honor and pleasure to be able to write and share my Paris with you— from my own experiences, to pointing out my favorite places, things to do and visit, to advising you on the best spots that you should check out on your Parisian adventures.

**Féliciations** ! You're now ready to take on Paris for yourself. Not only will you have the expertise to navigate the city, but you'll be on the path to thriving, not just surviving on your next trip! And who knows, maybe like me, you'll fall so deeply in love with this unique place that you'll want to move here, too.

Whether you're a seasonal traveler, lifetime Francophile, or an expat, I hope that the information and stories I've shared in this book will inspire your inner Parisian. I have enjoyed this journey with you, but don't let this book limit your understanding or experience of the French people, the language, their culture, and their country; now it's up to you to go explore and discover the wonder that is Paris and France!

I will be here, **bien sûr**, if you still need some assistance and I would be thrilled to help you along the way.

**Merci**, thank you, from the bottom of my heart and soul for being my reader and a huge part of The Ultimate Paris Survival Guide.

# Let's Discover Paris Together

Coming to Paris? Enlist my assistance for your next trip to France. Whether that's navigating the city for your first dream trip, planning a special occasion with a loved one, creating a tailor-made itinerary, or even relocating, I can help with all aspects of your trip by providing various lifestyle services.

See my Services5 page on my site for more details and let's chat to begin your perfect Parisian getaway! I currently provide all of the following services, but if you need something unique and exclusive, don't hesitate to contact me[6].

## I PROVIDE THE FOLLOWING SERVICES:

### Travel Services

Trip Planning
Experience Curation

### Local Services

Property Management
Relocation Services
Personal Assistance

Plus, with the purchase of this book, I want to offer you an exclusive offer of **10%** off all future services with Céline Concierge. When you **contact me**, mention that you purchased this book, and I would be happy to apply this discount toward your services.

---

[5] www.celineconcierge.com/services/
[6] www.celineconcierge.com/contact-us/

# Let's Connect

Before we say **au revoir**, let's connect.

I certainly don't want our conversation to end here. Sign up for my Paris Newsletter for Travel Tips, Paris Updates, and French Lifestyle.

And, I'm regularly on the following channels:

- Instagram **@celine.concierge**
- Twitter: **@celineconcierge**
- **Facebook**
- **Pinterest**
- **LinkedIn**

And as always, check out my blog for more valuable travel resources and insights about life in Paris as an expat.

# Thank You

Liliana Flores (Mom)
Juan Flores (Dad)
All of my family
(too many to name ;)
Selim Tavukçuoğlu
Hannah Smith
Jim Le
Eric Davis
John Arndt
Hope Curran
Eliza Sweeney
Daniel Tostado
Marissa Wu
Grace Moutier
Aleyna Moeller
Elesha Casimir
Claire Staley
Megan Sanders
Rachel Immaraj
Andrea Martinez

Emma Martinez
Jackie Valencia
Matthew Buckingham
Clara McBrayer
Noël Cambessèdes
Vanessa Cambessèdes
Thiébaut Kientz
Guillaume Kientz
Danielle Drake
Rachel Buillet
Erin Cafferty
Olivier Fourcade
Anne Muraro
Laurence Dupuy
Nikki Wang
Carolyn McFarlane
Fred Dalais
Vanessa Dalais
Église La Cité
Audrey Henry

And finally to all of the Céline Concierge clients
who trust me with their Paris plans everyday!

# Acknowledgments

Grace Moutier | Researcher and Content Contributor
Aleyna Moeller | Illustration and Book Cover Design
Elesha Casimir | Support and Marketing
Claire Staley | Developmental Editor
Megan Sanders | Proofreading Editor
Davor Nikolić | Book Layout Design

# About the Author

Selene

Native Austinite, Selene Flores, is the CEO of Céline Concierge, where she dedicates her time to helping fellow Francophiles get the most out of their time in Paris. In 2013, Selene took a leap of faith and moved 5,000 miles across the ocean, with little knowledge of the French language and a vision for her life that was too big to resist. Now a full-time **Parisienne**, Selene is committed to helping others realize that their own dreams of Paris are equally as possible, whether through a long-awaited trip to the City of Light, or a long-term stay like her own.

She lives with her bearded Frenchman and their skittish kitty, Hélios.

# About the Illustrator

Aleyna

Aleyna Moeller is an artist from the US who lived in the UK before happily relocating to Paris in 2020. She loves to escape to different parts of France and Europe, preferably by bike and like every Parisian loves to enjoy cafes with friends or picnics along the Seine. When she's not illustrating, she's chasing sunsets at golden hour or riding off to other cities to explore and chase the beauty of the world.

# BONUSES

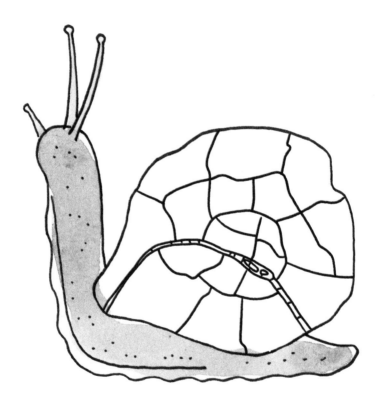

## What Visa You Need to Move to France

## Travel Budget & Tracking Tool

## French-Style Chicken Pot Pie Recipe

# Travel
# Planning
# Timeline

# Steps for
# Downloading
# Google Maps
# Offline

# Useful
# Travel Glossary
# Terms

# All Things Parisian Bucket List

## EXPERIENCE PARIS LIKE A LOCAL:
## THE ALL THINGS PARISIAN BUCKET LIST

This is my take on Paris as a local if you're exploring Paris in 2022!

You can, and should visit the famous monuments and landmarks, but this bucket list isn't filled with those things. You can get all of that information from your handy guide book.

No - this bucket list is filled with unforgettable, fun, and off-the-beaten-path experiences you're gonna want to do to live and feel like a local.

Join me to celebrate the **art de vivre** the way Parisians experience Paris.

Take pleasure in the luxury lifestyle that you are all about! Contact Céline Concierge for a personally curated itinerary for your perfect Paris getaway, today!

THE ULTIMATE PARIS SURVIVAL GUIDE

## LANDMARKS, MONUMENTS & SITES

- [ ] Sacré Cœur
- [ ] Champagne Toast on the Summit of the Eiffel Tower
- [ ] Père Lachaise
- [ ] Notre Dame
- [ ] Panthéon
- [ ] Arc de Triomphe

## MUSEUMS

- [ ] Picasso Museum
- [ ] Musée de la Vie Romantique
- [ ] Musée de l'Orangerie
- [ ] Jeu de Paume
- [ ] Maison Européenne de la Photographie

## COVERED PASSAGES

- [ ] Galerie Vivienne
- [ ] Passage des Panoramas
- [ ] Passage Brady
- [ ] Passage du Grand Cerf

## PARKS & GARDENS

- [ ] Parc Monceau
- [ ] Parc des Buttes-Chaumont
- [ ] Jardin des plantes
- [ ] Place des Vosges

## TEA HOUSES

- [ ] La Grande Mosquée de Paris
- [ ] Le Loir dans La Théière
- [ ] Les Deux Abeilles
- [ ] Mamie Gâteaux

## COFFEE SHOPS

- [ ] Colorova
- [ ] Cuppa Coffee
- [ ] Arabica Beaupassage
- [ ] Café Loustic
- [ ] La Compagnie de Café

## FRENCH RESTAURANTS

- ☐ Le Comptoir du Relais
- ☐ Allard
- ☐ Chez George
- ☐ Le Refuge Des Fondue
- ☐ La Buvette

## INSTAGRAM-WORTHY SPOTS

- ☐ 228 Rue de l'Université
- ☐ 7 Rue de l'Abreuvoir
- ☐ Colonnes de Buren
- ☐ Avenue de Camoens
- ☐ Pont Alexandre III

## BEST STREETS FOR A STROLL

- ☐ Rue des Martys
- ☐ Rue des Rosiers
- ☐ Rue des Thermopyles
- ☐ Rue Crémieux
- ☐ Rue Mouffetard

## NIGHTLIFE

- ☐ Bar Hopping on the Rue de Lappe
- ☐ Show at Crazy Horse
- ☐ Dinner Cruise on the Seine
- ☐ Dancing at L'Alimentation Générale
- ☐ Private Speakeasy Tour
- ☐ La Perle

## SHOPPING

- ☐ Samaritaine
- ☐ BHV
- ☐ Anything on Rue de Marseille & Rue Beaurepaire
- ☐ Anything on Ave. Montaigne
- ☐ Galleries Lafayette
- ☐ Le Bon Marché

## BEST MARKETS

- ☐ Marché des Enfants Rouge
- ☐ Marché Anvers
- ☐ Marché Monge
- ☐ Bird & Flower Market

## EXCLUSIVE EXPERIENCES

- ☐ Boat Ride on the Seine
- ☐ Secret Passages Tour of Versailles
- ☐ Secret Phantom of the Opera Tour
- ☐ Illuminations Paris City Night Drive
- ☐ Covered Passages Food Tour
- ☐ The Marais as a local

## NEIGHBORHOODS TO LOSE YOURSELF IN

- ☐ Latin Quarter
- ☐ Oberkampf
- ☐ Marais
- ☐ Pigalle
- ☐ Montmartre

## LOCAL HANGOUTS

- ☐ Take a stroll on La Petite Ceinture
- ☐ Drinks at the Rosa Bonheur
- ☐ Afternoon spent at the Village de Saint Paul
- ☐ Evening spent at the Bercy Village
- ☐ Bowling de Paris at Beaugrenelle Commercial Center

BV - #0108 - 060125 - C560 - 210/148/32 - PB - 9781804671511 - Gloss Lamination